# Jesus, the Gospels, and Cinematic Imagination

## A Handbook to Jesus on DVD

Jeffrey L. Staley and Richard Walsh

Westminster John Knox Press
LOUISVILLE • LONDON

*Book design by Sharon Adams*
*Cover design by Eric Walljasper, Minneapolis, MN*

*First edition*
Published by Westminster John Knox Press
Louisville, Kentucky

07 08 09 10 11 12 13 14 15 16 — 10 9 8 7 6 5 4 3 2 1

**Library of Congress Cataloging-in-Publication Data**

Staley, Jeffrey Lloyd.
  Jesus, the Gospels, and cinematic imagination : a handbook to Jesus on DVD / Jeffrey L. Staley and Richard Walsh. — 1st ed.
    p. cm.
  ISBN 978-0-664-23031-9 (alk. paper)
  1. Jesus Christ—In motion pictures.  2. DVD-Video discs—Catalogs.  I. Walsh, Richard G.  II. Title.
  PN1995.9.J4S73 2007
  791.43'651—dc22

                                                                        2007004984

# Contents

Preface      v

1   Watching Jesus Films      1

2   *The Life and Passion of Jesus Christ*, 1905      6

3   *From the Manger to the Cross*, 1912      11

4   *Intolerance*, 1916      17

5   *The King of Kings*, 1927      23

6   *King of Kings*, 1961      33

7   *The Gospel According to Saint Matthew*, 1965      43

8   *The Greatest Story Ever Told*, 1965      51

9   *Jesus Christ Superstar*, 1973      63

10   *Godspell*, 1973      69

11   *Jesus of Nazareth*, 1977      75

12   *The Jesus Film*, 1979      90

13   *Monty Python's Life of Brian*, 1979      101

14   *The Last Temptation of Christ*, 1988      109

15   *Jesus of Montreal*, 1989      118

16   *Jesus*, 1999      125

17   *The Miracle Maker: The Story of Jesus*, 1999      136

18   *The Gospel of John*, 2003      144

19   *The Passion of the Christ*, 2004      153

20   Teaching Jesus Films      161

A Gospels Harmony of Jesus Films on DVD      175

Notes      189

*For our students*

*and in memory of Wilhelm Wuellner, PhD, 1927–2004,*
*who early in the VCR era recognized the value of using*
*Jesus movies in the classroom*

# Preface

The idea for this book developed in our classrooms. Like other college professors, we have grown more and more interested in Jesus films over the years, both in our research and in our teaching. Like many other professors working with Jesus traditions, our primary focus has been on historical, literary, and ideological approaches to the canonical and noncanonical Gospels. And like other professors, we have used Jesus films primarily as add-ons to classroom presentations in order to illustrate Gospel pericopes (short text segments) and/or particular interpretations of the Gospels, the Greco-Roman world, Jesus, and Christianity. We have also used Jesus films as research-paper topics, and (more often than not) we show at least one entire Jesus film to a class to provide a broader context within the Jesus-film tradition for discussing film pericopes.

Jesus films, however, are quite difficult to use in the classroom (and in research) because no easy tool exists for cross-referencing them with the Gospels. And the Gospels, after all, are still the most important source for studying Jesus. Generally, we, like other professors, have had to watch entire films in order to find the perfect clip for a class and then note the time that the clip appeared in the film. Like most professors, we have not had the time—nor have we wanted to take the time—to watch many Jesus films in their entirety. So we have been stuck using the same film clips over and over again, without really knowing what other similar scenes might be available for classroom use. Our book now resolves this problem by providing an easy-to-use list of Gospel parallels that tells students and teachers the precise hour/minute/second on a given DVD that the Gospel story or scene occurs.

We believe that DVD technology has radically changed the way scholars, teachers, and students can use Jesus films. Like the earlier innovation of chapter numbers and verse numbers for the books of the Bible, digitalization of Jesus movies makes it possible for all viewers to find easily the exact same place in a film by numeric code (hour/minute/second). This was not always possible with VHS cassettes. Since different VHS machines wind cassettes at slightly different speeds, viewers can never be sure that the numeric codes will be precisely the same from one machine to another. And even when the scene does occur at the same hour/minute/second, each time the film is used to access a different scene, viewers must rewind the tape to the beginning and reset the counter before looking for the new scene. Fortunately, digitalization has solved these and other VHS viewing problems.

DVD technology has enhanced the usability of Jesus movies in other ways as well. For example, the DVD version of Cecil B. DeMille's *The King of Kings* is now available in a two-and-a-half-hour version (1927), as well as in the more normally used, general-release two-hour version (1928). Our chapter on DeMille's film is thus the first to analyze the longer version for New Testament–reading audiences. The DVD version of Pier Paolo Pasolini's *The Gospel of St. Matthew* is a widescreen remastering of that film. If "what you see is what you get," then what viewers get in the DVD version of Pasolini's film is *almost* an entirely different film from the VHS version. The same holds true for most other Jesus films originally released for widescreen. The DVDs of these films are almost all widescreen editions, as originally produced for theater viewing, and generally have not been reduced for square television screens.

Finally, most of the DVD-released Jesus films have "DVD Extras" that greatly enhance their usability and interpretive possibilities for teaching and research. Directors' and actors/actresses' commentaries, along with printed brochures and deleted scenes, help to raise new questions about the Jesus-film tradition. Our book describes the extras included with each DVD, drawing attention to those places in the extras that are especially useful to Jesus-film scholarship. Thus, to our warped way of thinking, blind Bartimaeus's first-century shout "Jesus, son of David" (Mark 10:47) has become an inadvertent, twenty-first-century prophetic revelation: Jesus is now truly a technological "son of DVD."

Our book, however, is still primarily a guide and a handbook. It does not cover all Jesus films, and it does not pretend to be an exhaustive list of Gospel parallels in Jesus films. The notable DVD omissions from our survey are Edward and Morris's television remake of *Jesus Christ Superstar* (2000) and van den Bergh's *The Gospel of Matthew* (Visual Bible, 2002). We have omitted these two DVDs simply because their inclusion would have added significantly to the length of our book without adding anything substantive to our discussion. Like Saville's film *The Gospel of John*, *The Gospel of Matthew* is a visual, word-for-word rendering of a Gospel, and thus viewers can easily find any particular film scene they are interested in analyzing by simply following the chapters and verses in the book of Matthew. Further, we believe that the discussion of one such "literal film" within the Jesus-film tradition is sufficient to indicate the possibilities and nature of that approach. On the other hand, Edward and Morris's remake of *Jesus Christ Superstar* does recontextualize and contemporize again for a new generation Webber and Rice's 1970s rock opera. But it does not deviate from the original lyrics or musical score, and thus it is another "literal" rendering of a text.

Additionally, other important Jesus films are omitted from our discussion. For example, we do not discuss Michael Campus's *The Passover Plot* (1976); Ben Lewin's *The Favor, the Watch, and the Very Big Fish* (1992); or Catherine Hardwicke's *The Nativity Story* (2006). These films along with others have been left out of our book for obvious reasons. Our book concentrates on Jesus films available on DVD, and these are not yet on DVD.[1] However, these films and others are worth consulting for those committed to Jesus-film scholarship.[2]

Finally, we do not discuss the many Sunday-school Gospel-story films—mostly animated—that have been produced over the years. This is simply because there are too many of them. *The Story of Jesus for Children* (1999) is a reworking of parts of Sykes and Krisch's *The Jesus Film* and is included in the "Limited Collectors Edition" DVD. So we do briefly mention it in our discussion of Sykes and Krisch's film. We have also included in our book a chapter on Derek Hayes's *The Miracle Maker* (1999), arguably the best example of a Jesus film in the Children's Bible genre.

Our list of Jesus-film parallels is a list of *Gospels* parallels. We do not list Hebrew Bible (Old Testament) parallels. It would be wonderful to have a complete parallels list of Hebrew Bible references—especially for the analysis of Judaism, supersessionism, and anti-Semitism in Jesus films. But we will be kind and generous and leave that undertaking for another scholar or two.

For easy access, our Jesus-film parallels list uses a *Gospels-harmony* structure for locating scenes. The Gospels-harmony structure is well known to New Testament scholars, and is one that follows the basic order of Jesus' life from the Gospel prefaces/prologues, to the announcement of John the Baptist's birth, through to the death and resurrection of Jesus. Our harmony differs from the traditional format, however, in that we divide the public ministry of Jesus into three subject headings: miracles, teaching, and controversy. Within each of these subsections is an alphabetical listing of Gospel scenes.

Then, under each list of Gospel scenes is an alphabetical list (by director's last name) of the films that have that particular Gospel scene, followed by the hour/minute/second where the scene occurs in the film. This harmony, which is the generative heart of our work, begins on page 175, after the individual chapters on Jesus films.

Early on in our project we realized that a DVD harmony of Gospel pericopes would not really be helpful without some interpretative context. After all, Jesus films are imaginative narratives in their own right, and each one represents a particular place and time in modern, Western (largely American) culture. Accordingly, the first part of our book devotes a chapter to each of the eighteen Jesus films available on DVD, in the chronological order of the film's release date. Each chapter follows the same format: a short plot summary of the film; a list of key characters and memorable visual moments; a brief statement about the film's key Scriptures; a discussion of the film's genre and its cultural and historical context; a discussion of other films by the film's director, placing the Jesus film within the context of the director's broader repertoire; and finally, a listing of DVD extras and DVD chapters (with hour/minute/second).

Our book opens with a chapter titled "Watching Jesus Films," which offers a number of general questions that can be used with any Jesus film. We hope those questions will help teachers, church study groups, and students not familiar with Jesus films to begin their own interpretative work with these films. The main part of our book ends with a chapter titled "Teaching Jesus Films" that offers practical suggestions—beyond the questions of the first chapter—for other pedagogical uses of Jesus films.

If readers wish to supplement our discussion of Jesus films with discussion-starting questions, an annotated bibliography, or a glossary of important terms, these may be found at http://fac-staff.seattleu.edu/staleyj/web/publications.html.

For further investigations into a particular film's Christology or a director's image of Jesus, *Savior on the Silver Screen* by Richard Stern, Clayton Jefford, and Guerric DeBona (New York: Paulist, 1999) is highly useful. For a supplement in a historical-critical direction, we recommend W. B. Tatum's *Jesus at the Movies: A Guide to the First Hundred Years*. Revised and Expanded (Santa Rosa: Polebridge, 2004). For those who wish a more literary-ideological approach to film and to the Gospels, we recommend Richard Walsh's *Reading the Gospels in the Dark: Portrayals of Jesus in Film* (Harrisburg, PA: Trinity Press International, 2003). For those interested in Jesus films as biopics, we recommend Adele Reinhartz's *Jesus of Hollywood* (New York: Oxford University Press, 2007).

Coincidentally, we finished our book manuscript the same week that *The Da Vinci Code* opened in theaters across the United States. Although *The Da Vinci Code* (2006) is not a Jesus film, the media blitz that surrounded its release reminded us once again of the power of the Jesus story in popular American culture and of what meager knowledge of the Christian tradition the average American viewing public has. Not surprisingly, the American viewing public has even less knowledge of the Hollywood Jesus-film tradition.

We continually had to remind newspaper, radio, and television interviewers that in 1973 *Jesus Christ Superstar* created a furor with Mary Magdalene's refrain "I don't know how to love him," sung to a still-sleeping Jesus the morning after she had shared the night in his tent. Fifteen years later, theaters showing *The Last Temptation of Christ* were picketed because of its concluding hallucinatory sequence that showed Jesus and Mary Magdalene getting married and having sex. Now, eighteen years later in *The Da Vinci Code* we discover that the lovely (singular?) descendant of Jesus and Mary Magdalene is living in contemporary France, blithely ignorant of her divine DNA. What was hinted at in 1973 and what became a full-blown fantasy in 1988 became "history" and "biological fact" in 2006.

We hope we live long enough to see what Jesus / Mary Magdalene fantasy the 2020s will give us. Whatever it will be, we are convinced that future Jesuses, like those of the past one hundred years, will tell us much more about ourselves and American culture than anything about "the real" Jesus. And surely by 2020 we will have placed *The Da Vinci Code* within the cultural context of the early-twenty-first century. In this latter regard, we note that it is perhaps not insignificant that Jesus' living descendant is depicted as being upper-middle class and northern European. Perhaps most importantly, *The Da Vinci Code* suggests to its viewers that Christianity is, at its very roots, *not* a story about loving one's enemies—nor even a story about loving one's neighbors. It is instead a story about the purity of bloodlines. We think we have heard *that* story before as well.

Our study of one hundred years of Jesus films has taught us much about the deeply rooted connections between Christianity and American history and identity. Surely it is an oversimplification to say that in Hollywood, Jesus = America. Yet the equation is not far from the mark, and those who work with Jesus films must continually come back to the troubling implications of that equation. In this regard, perhaps the most important questions we have learned to ask with each Son of DVD are these: Why *this* Jesus film? And why this Jesus film at this particular juncture in American (or world) history?

# Chapter 1

# Watching Jesus Films

The suggestions listed below are just that: our own suggestions. But we have watched these Jesus films many times (some of them far too many times!), and we know that we have more questions than can be answered about any one film on just one viewing. Doubtless some of our questions will be more important to you than others, and some may seem to "suit" one particular film more than others.

Critical analysis is essentially a comparative process. Think about the questions you learned in kindergarten: How are these things alike? How are they different? With respect to Jesus films, we may analyze a film critically by comparing it to another film or text (like a Gospel or the canonical Gospels), to a particular genre or era, to a particular ideology (like Christian orthodoxy or Protestant evangelicalism), or to some modern ideology or methodology (like feminism, Marxism, or postcolonialism). Your critical abilities will become more sophisticated as you learn to articulate clearly that text, ideology, and so forth to which you are comparing the film.

## Film Medium: Camera, Editing, Set, Lighting

1. When watching film critically, always consider the camera. The camera, direction, and editing of the film are analogous to the narrator—the perspective and voice—of a literary piece. When watching the film, then, consider who sees and who tells the story. Is this perspective omniscient or limited? Consider, in particular, the way that the camera approaches Jesus. Does it look up to Jesus? Down? Is Jesus always on center stage? Is he lighted differently than other characters? Is the visual perspective realistic? Fantastic? Reliable? For example, is it significant that the audience's first glimpse of Jesus in DeMille's *The King of Kings* is filmed "through the eyes" of a little girl?

2. Another important question has to do with setting. Does the film production attempt to recreate first-century Palestine? If it does, how "accurately" is this done? If the setting is not first-century Palestine, what is the setting? What might a Jesus film gain by using a setting other than a replica of first-century Palestine? For example, why is Pasolini's *The Gospel According to St. Matthew* set in the small villages of southern Italy? Or why is Stevens's *The Greatest Story Ever Told* set in the American Southwest?

3. What kind of sets does the film employ? Are the film sets "on location," or is the

1

set a stage? If "on location," is that location modern Israel or elsewhere? If not Israel, why did the production company choose a different site? Are the sets minimal or detailed? If the set is detailed, what model did the film production rely on to create the set? Historical analysis of the first century? Illustrated Bibles? Christian art? The staging of passion plays?

4. If the film employs a number of images from traditional Christian art, does the film take on an iconic quality? See especially Hayes, *The Miracle Maker*, and Stevens, *The Greatest Story Ever Told*.

5. Does the film use lighting or color to present its viewpoint? Stevens is a master at the use of lighting. Do the characters wear particular clothing? Does the clothing change during the film? For example, in Saville's film, which "only" uses the Gospel of John as its text, costumes become crucial markers of identity and change. Why are Zeffirelli's three kings dressed in red, white, and blue in *Jesus of Nazareth*?

6. Sound is also important in film. Do the characters speak English? A particular kind of English? Do they have accents? Do Jesus and his opponents sound different from one another? Is this interpretative? Why do birds begin to chirp just before Lazarus is raised from the dead in Scorsese's *The Last Temptation of Christ*? Why is there absolute silence just before Jesus begins his triumphal entry into Jerusalem in Stevens's *The Greatest Story Ever Told*? Close your eyes and just *listen* to Mary giving birth to Jesus in Zeffirelli's *Jesus of Nazareth*. What does this scene actually *sound* like? What might Zeffirelli be implying about the birth of Jesus (if anything)?

7. If the film is silent, what interpretative aids does the film employ, other than words on-screen? Note especially the hand motions in Zecca, *The Life and Passion of Jesus Christ*, and in Olcott, *From the Manger to the Cross*.

8. Does the film use voice-overs? If so, what effect does this have?

9. What kind of background music and sound does the film employ? Does it add to the film's overall effect? For example, note Stevens's use of the "Hallelujah Chorus" after Lazarus is raised from the dead in *The Greatest Story Ever Told*. Consider also Pasolini's use of interpretive background music in *The Gospel According to St. Matthew*.

10. If a film scene represents a Gospel pericope, how do the lengths of the film scene and the Gospel pericope compare? Many film scenes are much longer than the Gospel texts they represent. Matthew 2:19 reads, "When Herod died. . . ."; Mark 6:22 reads, "When his daughter Herodias came in and danced. . ."; yet those directors who choose to film Herod's death or Salome's dance spend *minutes* depicting the scenes. Why? Mark 15:29–30 reads, "'Aha! You who would destroy the temple and build it in three days, save yourself, and come down from the cross!'" Yet Scorsese spends thirty-one minutes with these words. Why?

## Story, Plot, Causation

1. With respect to the film's story, consider the beginning of the film. What does this introduction lead you to expect about the rest of the movie? Ends are as important as beginnings. How does the film end? What sense or feeling does this end create? Greene's *Godspell* is a particularly good study here, as are Arcand's *Jesus of Montreal* and Stevens's *The Greatest Story Ever Told*.

2. Generally, Jesus films rely heavily on passion plays and the Gospels for their incidents. Is the film a passion play, or does it also include a treatment of Jesus' youth and/or ministry?

3. What Gospel incidents does the film include? Are there notable omissions? If so, can you imagine why they might not be included? Are there obvious gains or losses as a result of the omissions? For example, why does Sykes and Krisch's *The Jesus Film* leave out so many stories about women when most biblical scholars note that Luke has *included more* stories about women than any other Gospel? Why does that same film omit the parable of the Prodigal Son?

4. Typically, Jesus films include little of Jesus' teaching. Teaching is difficult to dramatize. If the film includes teaching, how does it show it? For example, how does Young's *Jesus* show Jesus' teaching about "turning the other cheek"? How does Stevens's *The Greatest Story Ever Told* show Jesus' teaching about "sharing your cloak"?

5. Can you summarize the film's presentation of Jesus' teaching? For quite diverse presentations, see Ray's *King of Kings*, Stevens's *The Greatest Story Ever Told*, and Saville's *The Gospel of John*.

6. With respect to the story incidents, does the film rely only or primarily on one Gospel? Does the film rely on all four canonical Gospels? If the film relies on all four canonical Gospels, can you determine when and why the writer/director moves back and forth between the various Gospels? Zeffirelli's *Jesus of Nazareth* is interesting in this regard.

7. Does the film include incidents (or characters) that come from the apocryphal Gospels or from Christian legends? If so, why? Gibson's *The Passion of the Christ* is particularly notable here.

8. Hollywood film has clearly defined patterns (including romantic interests, violence, melodramatic ends, special effects, and spectacle). Are any of these elements present in the film? If so, how do they transform the Gospel presentation(s) of Jesus? Ray's *King of Kings* is a good study here.

9. Typically, film establishes its characters and situations early, introduces a problem or conflict, moves that problem/crisis through conflict to a climax, and then provides a denouement-creating closure. Does the Jesus film that you are watching work in this fashion?

10. If you can identify the film's problem, conflict, climax, and denouement, you are beginning to describe the film's plot. Consider also the issue of causation. What drives the movie from incident to incident? Are there clear connections between the scenes? For example, compare the plot movement of Sykes and Krisch's *The Jesus Film* with that of Ray's *King of Kings*.

11. How does the film move from scene to scene? Does it use dissolves? Fades to black? Pasolini's *The Gospel According to St. Matthew* and Greene's *Godspell* can be valuable study guides at this point.

12. Does the film manipulate the time of the story? That is, are there significant anticipations of the story or are there flashbacks? Hayes's *The Miracle Maker* creates an interesting effect with flashbacks, as does Gibson in his use of flashbacks during the depiction of the crucifixion in *The Passion of the Christ*.

13. With causation, what motivates or causes Jesus' death? Compare Gibson's *The*

*Passion of the Christ* with Arcand's *Jesus of Montreal* for an idea of the wide range of possibilities.

14. Does the movie include Jesus' miracles? His resurrection? If so, how are these elements portrayed? Is there a modern reluctance or suspicion about the miraculous and the supernatural? Are there supernatural characters (or voices) in the film? Note the change from the early-twentieth-century films to those at the end of the century. Where have all the angels gone?

## Characters

1. Is Jesus the central character? If so, how would you concisely describe his character? Is he a figure drawn from Christian orthodoxy (e.g., the divine son of God)? Is he a more-human character? If so, is he a religious or philosophical figure? If so, what kind? Is he a teacher or a miracle worker? Does he advocate love and nonresistance, or does he advocate revolt against the powers-that-be? Is he a historical or contemporary person?

2. Is the Jesus of the film a typical Hollywood character? Is he a leading man? If not, why not?

3. What other characters are prominent in the film? Are these characters drawn from the Gospels and Christian tradition? Are they more-developed, round characters in the film than they are in the Gospels? If so, how does the film develop them? Are there novel (invented) characters in the film? If so, how important are they to the film? Do they help articulate the film's "message?" Do they help make the transition between an ancient story and modern viewers? Consider Ray's use of Lucius in *King of Kings* or Stevens's use of Lazarus in *The Greatest Story Ever Told.*

4. Which characters side with Jesus in the film? Which characters oppose him? Who provides the impetus that leads to the passion? Are Jews or Romans responsible for Jesus' death? Are leaders or the people responsible?

5. Are Jesus and his followers Jewish? Christian? How do you know?

6. What does Jesus look like? European? Semitic? Middle Eastern? Does he look like the intended viewing audience? Like a figure drawn from Christian art?

7. What do Jesus' opponents look like?

## Genre, Tone, Ideology

1. Would you describe the film as a documentary? An epic? A visualization of the Gospel? If so, which Gospel? Is the film a fictionalizing of the Gospel? If so, how so? Does the film change the setting of the story? The plot? The characters? The "message"?

2. What is the overall tone of the film? Is it reverent? Nostalgic? Humorous? A parody? Demythologizing? Can humor also be serious? If so, how? Does the film expect its audience to "believe" its presentation?

3. It may not always be appropriate to speak of the "message" of a film, but if we do, what is its message? Does it have a religious or secular message? If religious, does it advocate a particular interpretation of Christianity (creedal, evangelistic, Catholic, Protestant, liberal, fundamentalist)? If it is secular, what ideology provides the mes-

sage? For a marked contrast, compare Arcand's *Jesus of Montreal* with Sykes and Krisch's *The Jesus Film*.

4. When was the film produced? By whom? Who directed the film?
5. Who is the intended audience of the film?
6. Does the film have a clear cultural context?

## Motifs and Symbolism

Much of what is "said" in a film is not stated explicitly but is there subtly in the props, setting, or background action. Usually, motifs and symbolism are hard to pick up on one viewing. The more often you watch the film, the more you will "see" because you are no longer just thinking about the plot. For example, it is significant that just at the moment Judas asks Jesus, "How will you ever pay for your sins?" (Scorsese, *The Last Temptation of Christ*, 5:51), the viewer sees two children herd a flock of sheep through the open door behind him. Here crosses, sins, and sheep—perhaps even the door—are all juxtaposed in such a way as to evoke the symbolism of Jesus as the Lamb of God, the door/way to God. The symbolism "works" because of Judas's words and because images of slaughtered lambs appear elsewhere in the film.

Stevens places Jesus' Judean "Sermon on the Mount" under a bridge over which Roman soldiers have just walked, while the more traditional Sermon on the Mount is on an open mountain in Galilee. Why the difference? Stevens also depicts Jesus' anointing in Bethany (John 12:1–8; *The Greatest Story Ever Told* [22] 2.03:35) as if it were a burial, with Jesus being wrapped in a shroud, and with the triumphal entry beginning in total silence. Why?

For a motif or symbolism to "work" you need more than one or two examples, and ideally you should be able to "hear" as well as "see" the motif. What is the significance of the images of play and games in Young's *Jesus*? Of children in Pasolini's *The Gospel According to St. Matthew*? Of white cloth in Gibson's *The Passion of the Christ*? Why does Zeffirelli's Jesus raise his hand in a blessing like the Infant of Prague when the family returns to Nazareth, and later on make a fish symbol on the ground when a woman is about to be stoned for adultery?

Reflecting on Jesus films using our suggested questions is, as we have said, an exercise in critical analysis. The activity may prove to be far more than a mere academic exercise. After all, as we analyze the Gospels or films, we bring our own position/culture into relief and possibly even into the critical conversation. Historical scholars reading the Gospels find the Gospels reveal as much about the communities in which they were written and read as they do about Jesus. Similarly, in critically analyzing the Jesus-film tradition, we discover as much (and perhaps much more) about ourselves and American values as we do about Jesus. If studying the Jesus-film tradition helps us distinguish more carefully between these four worlds (Jesus and the early church; Christianity and America), then perhaps Hollywood has done us all a great service.

Chapter 2

# The Life and Passion
# of Jesus Christ

*Ferdinand Zecca and Lucien Nonquet,
directors. 44 mins. Not rated. 1905. Image
Entertainment, 2003*

### Plot Summary

This film is a series of scenes displaying the life of Jesus Christ from the announcement of his birth to his ascension to the right hand of God in heaven. The scenes
are enactments of moments in popular pageants and passion plays that draw from
Christian paintings and the illustrations in Bibles like those of Gustave Doré and
James Tissot. Ferdinand Zecca and Lucien Nonquet introduce each scene with an
intertitle. But unlike later silent films, these do not include Scripture references or
snippets of dialogue.

In the opening annunciation, Gabriel appears to Mary quite dramatically in a superimposed shot. He stands on clouds with wings and a cross halo as he speaks to the virgin.[1] A similarly dramatic, yellow star appears to the shepherds in the fields and leads
them to the Christ child,[2] while a multicolored angelic chorus appears with a scroll
announcing, "Gloria in excelsis deo." The wise men follow the same star. Then, as the
yellow star appears over the empty crib beside which Joseph and Mary kneel, the baby
Jesus appears suddenly and miraculously in the crib. After everyone arrives at the
manger, Mary holds aloft the naked baby Jesus before the entire crowd arranged around
her and faces the audience as though on a stage. Curiously, Mary, Joseph, and baby Jesus
do not leave Bethlehem before the slaughter of the innocents. While the slaughter is still
in progress, a band of heavenly angels protects baby Jesus, and their sweet singing keeps
him from crying. After an angel appears to Joseph in a dream, he leaves with his family, and a sword-wielding angel protects them from Herod's mayhem as they are on their
way to Egypt.

Two scenes represent Jesus' childhood. In the first, entirely invented scene, Jesus
works with his father at the carpentry shop in Nazareth while his mother spins. In

6

the second, an adolescent Jesus teaches the scribes in the Temple, with hand held aloft, prefiguring his authoritative teaching ministry and his knowledge of his heavenly parentage.

Jesus' official ministry begins with his baptism by John. Except for the story of Mary Magdalene's anointing the feet of Jesus and the story of the Samaritan woman at the well,[3] Jesus' ministry is miraculous. Although Jesus does not teach in words from the Gospels, his heaven-pointing gestures seem to reflect a Johannine perspective. His miracles are also signs of his connection to his heavenly father. Jesus' public ministry opens with the wedding at Cana, and he walks on water twice. In the stilling of the storm, Zecca and Nonquet dramatically raise Jesus from the watery depths, superimposing a shot of Jesus over the stormy sea. In that there are no other people in the scene, it functions purely as a cinematic hierophany for the viewing audience.[4] The second time Jesus walks on water is when he tells his disciples to let down their nets for a catch of fish (Luke 5:1–11). After raising Lazarus from the dead, Jesus' ministry ends with his transfiguration, where he appears in blinding white light, surrounded by a yellow nimbus.[5]

The triumphal entry and Temple cleansing open the passion narrative. At the Last Supper, Jesus and his disciples all stand to drink the wine, and then Jesus virtually chases Judas from the room. At Gethsemane, an angel appears again, this time holding out the cup that Jesus must drink. The betrayal, arrest, denial, and trials happen swiftly and accentuate the animosity of the Jewish crowds. Zecca and Nonquet show Jesus flogged—tied with his back to the post—but the whipping draws no blood. After Jesus appears before a wall inscribed with "ecce homo," Pilate washes his hands and turns Jesus over to the Jewish crowd. Women with babies in their arms raise their fists in anger (Matt. 27:25), but other women, including Veronica, Mary his mother, and Mary Magdalene, tearfully watch Jesus on the Via Dolorosa and at his crucifixion. The audience sees Jesus and the INRI placard affixed to the cross from afar. As women grieve at the foot of the cross, lightning and then supernatural darkness accompany Jesus' death.

Like Jesus' infancy and public ministry, his resurrection is quite miraculous. With Roman soldiers looking on, four angels lift the lid from a coffin, and then Jesus rises over the open hole.[6] The Roman soldiers thus become the first witnesses to Jesus' resurrection. But they flee, Jesus disappears, and another angel informs Jesus' followers of his resurrection. The ascension comes next, as a decorated cloud raises Jesus from the ground. The film ends with the disciples and audience looking into heaven itself, where Jesus is seated at the right hand of God, amidst adoring angelic throngs.

## Memorable Characters

- Jesus: Jesus is the Christ, the Son of God. He is always supernaturally attended and is always on the verge of transfiguration.
- Angels: The most important character group in the story, they pave the way for Jesus and give him supernatural attention and aid.
- Soldiers: Both Herod's soldiers and Pilate's soldiers play important roles in the story. Although Herod's soldiers attempt to kill the baby Jesus and Pilate's soldiers watch over the crucifixion, Pilate's soldiers also protect Jesus on the Via Dolorosa and are the first witnesses to the resurrection.

- Babies: From the naked baby Jesus who miraculously appears in the manger and who is held aloft for the magi to adore, to the slaughter of the innocents and the mothers of Jerusalem carrying their children and shaking their fists at Jesus, babies add a natural touch to a story that is otherwise largely lacking a connection to common humanity.

## Memorable Visuals

- The baby Jesus appearing miraculously in the manger, and Mary later holding him aloft for the wise men and shepherds to adore in a naked, full frontal view (yes, he is really a boy!)
- A choir of angels singing lullabies to the sleeping baby Jesus while Herod's soldiers look for him
- Slaughter of the innocents
- A sword-wielding angel protecting the vanishing holy family from Herod's soldiers
- Jesus rising from the waters to walk on the sea
- The deus ex machina resurrection, ascension, and seating in heaven

## Key Scriptures

Miracles dominate the story, but no one Gospel takes center stage. Perhaps the angelic proclamation "Gloria in excelsis deo" (Luke 2:14) is the dominant scriptural theme.

## Cultural Location/Genre: Christmas Pageant/Passion Play, Illustrated Bible

The film clearly comes from a Christian culture. Made in France and shown internationally, it assumes that its audience will know the story of Jesus by heart and, perhaps, even recite the appropriate Scriptures with each scene.[7] The directors also assume that the audience will expect a supernatural Christ, not a historical Jesus, even though the nineteenth century is famous for its liberal theologies and its quests for the historical Jesus.

Since this cinematic rendering of Jesus' life stands at the very beginning of film history, the film owes nothing to film tradition. It depends primarily on passion plays, Christmas pageants, Christian art, and the illustrated Bibles of the nineteenth century. Seen now, one hundred years later, the film does not look like a movie but like a stage play caught on film by one stationary camera. Its visual strangeness, however, lends an iconic effect to it—even today. In a sense it is Christian art and the illustrated Bible raised (almost) to life.

## Director

Although Ferdinand Zecca and Lucien Nonquet's *The Life and Passion of Jesus Christ* was first presented to the public in 1902, Nonquet continued to expand the film over the next few years until it reached its culminating forty-four minutes in 1905.[8] Given the fact that prior films consisted of one ten-to-fifteen-minute reel, *The Life and Passion* was quite impressive in its day. The hand-colorized scenes also add to the film's impact.

The acting is visually dramatic to compensate for the lack of conversational or Gospel text intertitles. Jesus, for example, repeatedly stands imperially and gestures emphatically (usually with one hand thrust upward) to indicate his command of the situation and his divine authority.

The camera is (generally) stationary and the players act before it as if they were on stage. Painted backdrops provide different scenes; and the deus ex machina devices, particularly in the resurrection and ascension scenes, also suggest the theater rather than the cinema. Zecca and Nonquet do, however, make extensive use of superimposed shots and dissolves to heighten the film's supernatural quality. Those devices and the use of familiar scenes from Christian art render the film quite iconic. The film becomes, like an icon, a material device through which one might encounter the spiritual.

## DVD Extras and Technical Features

This film is included on the same DVD with Olcott's *From the Manger to the Cross* (1912).

## DVD Chapters

1. Main Title: The Annunciation
   The annunciation, 0:20
   The arrival of Joseph and Mary in Bethlehem, 1:29
2. The Wonderful Star, 2:39
   Following the star, 4:05
   The nativity and adoration of the wise men, 4:41
   Slaughter of the innocents, 6:52
   The flight into Egypt, 7:30
   > Water from the rock nourishes the family (like Israel in the wilderness, Exod. 17:6; 1 Cor. 10:4), 10:25
   The holy family at Nazareth, 12:03
3. Miracles, 13:54
   Jesus and the doctors, 13:55
   Baptizing Christ, 14:41
   The wedding feast, 15:26
   Mary Magdalene at the feet of Jesus, 16:49
   Jesus and the woman of Samaria, 17:56
   Raising of the daughter of Jairus, 18:58
   Christ walks on water, 20:23
   The wonderful draught of fishes, 21:01
   > Jesus again walks on water.
   The raising of Lazarus, 22:16
   The transfiguration, 23:38
   Entering Jerusalem, 24:33
   Jesus driving out the money changers from the Temple, 25:16
4. The Last Days, 26:17
   The Last Supper, 26:19

The disciples stand to drink, then after Judas leaves, half of the disciples leave two-by-two.

Jesus on the Mount of Olives; the kiss of Judas, 27:22

An angel comes to strengthen Jesus (Luke 22:43).

A remorseful Judas laments and runs off.

Jesus before Caiaphas, 29:13

Peter denies Christ, 29:59

Jesus before Pilate, 30:30

Jewish authorities bring in a person to accuse Jesus, but the Romans keep him back; another person comes forward to accuse Jesus, but the Romans also keep him back.

The scourging; the crowning with thorns, 31:33

Jewish people put the crown of thorns on Jesus' head and mock him; Roman guards intervene and lead him away.

Jesus given over to the people, 32:45

"Ecce Homo," 33:06

Pilate washes his hands.

Jewish crowd beats Jesus; they bring the cross.

Women with babies and fists in air follow to Calvary (Matt. 27:25).

5. The Crucifixion, 34:13

Jesus falls under the weight of the cross, 34:15

Veronica's veil

Roman guards struggle hard to keep Jewish crowds away from Jesus.

Calvary, 35:25

Faithful women grieve as Jesus walks by.

Christ put on the cross, 36:43

Mary grieves at the foot of the cross.

Roman guards keep angry Jews away.

Agony and death of Christ, 38:25

Casting lots for his garments

Grieving women

Lightning, darkness

The Roman who pierces Jesus' side is the one who recognizes him as "Son of God."

Jesus taken from the cross, 39:15

The other two crosses are already empty; the Roman guard does not object.

Jesus put into the tomb, 40:32

The women enter the tomb with the disciples.

6. The Resurrection and Ascension, 41:13

The resurrection, 41:13

Four angels appear while Roman guards sleep inside the tomb.

Angels lift off the stone in the ground; Jesus rises from the grave.

The Roman guards are first to see Jesus.

The ascension, 42:31

Jesus, seated at the right hand of God in glory

7. End Credits, 44:06

# Chapter 3

# From the Manger to the Cross

*Sidney Olcott, director. 71 mins. Not rated. 1912. Image Entertainment, 2003*

## Plot Summary

Sidney Olcott's cinematic presentation of the life of Jesus selects scenes and motifs from the four Gospels to present a magisterial Christ's love for the world. Olcott divides his episodic plot of Jesus' life into three, roughly equal parts—birth and early life, public ministry, and last days—with Scripture intertitles that precede each scene.[1] Olcott opens the story with a young woman, Mary, dressed in Arab peasant clothing, carrying a jar of water to her house. In the subsequent annunciation scene, she is dressed like a nun, ready to receive the angelic message. But Olcott never shows the angel Gabriel— or any other heavenly messengers. In fact, the viewer never even reads anything about the angel's message that promises a child to the virgin. Olcott presumes his audience knows the story well enough to be able to complete the unseen angel's message. All of Olcott's subsequent angelic scenes will be equally restrained, revealing only brief, bright light and the characters' surprise and fear.

Olcott then draws from Matthew's Gospel, turning to Joseph in his carpentry shop. He watches Mary as she passes by him, carrying a water pot on her head. Joseph is contemplating what to do with his betrothed, although the viewing audience has not even been told she is pregnant. In the angel's message to him, the viewing audience reads for the first time that Mary, his betrothed, is to have a son who will save the people from their sins.

Following the composite structure of most Christmas pageants, both shepherds and wise men follow the star to the manger in Bethlehem to worship the newborn. But Olcott is most creative in his scenes of Jesus' childhood in Nazareth. In one scene, Mary reads from a scroll to Jesus (who wears a yarmulke) while Joseph watches from the background, working a piece of wood. And in perhaps his most famous scene, Olcott imagines the carpenter boy Jesus carrying a board across his shoulders in such a way that its shadow makes a cruciform on the ground. His mother sees the shadow and covers her mouth, thus bringing to an end the opening third of the film.

The story then moves to Jesus' public ministry, opening with John the Baptist

11

identifying Jesus as the Lamb of God (John 1:36). However, there is no actual baptismal scene, and Jesus is just barely observable off in the distance, walking on the horizon. The location then moves to the Sea of Galilee, where Jesus calls some fishermen to follow him. Not coincidentally, this is the point at which the viewing audience (playing the role of the disciples?) sees the adult Jesus in close-up for the first time. Despite teaching scenes on the lake and in homes, no Scripture intertitles help viewers identify Jesus' words. Instead, his ministry is a series of wavy-hand miracles and domestic tableaus with women, including two anointing scenes. Notably, the women are always at Jesus' feet, and they are among the few characters that Jesus looks at directly. The turning point of the plot comes with Jesus' "I am" statement in the Jerusalem Temple (John 8:58), after which Jesus walks away from the stone-wielding priests, who huddle together, apparently beginning to plot against him.

Thereafter, Judas's dissatisfaction with the anointing at Bethany provides the first clear, dramatic counterpoint to the film's magisterial Christ. Judas emerges from the group of disciples and the undefined crowds to take on the adversarial role that moves the plot toward its climax. After the triumphal entry, more healings, and the cleansing of the Temple; Judas, now in dark clothing, haggles with the priests over the betrayal price. In the extensive upper-room material—including footwashing, meal, and communion—Judas's identification and departure (notably before communion) are prominent.

In Gethsemane, Judas brings the soldiers by lamplight. After the kiss, Judas and the soldiers fall back in revelatory awe before the Johannine Jesus.[2] Olcott completes Judas's story—the repentance and the hanging—before turning to Jesus' Roman trial and his mockery by Herod. There is no trial before the Sanhedrin, but the Jewish priests point accusingly at Jesus from the background as Pilate questions Jesus. Likewise, the murderous crowd repeatedly demands Jesus' execution despite the scourging (which Pilate watches), the *ecce homo* scene, and Pilate's hand washing. After mocking Jesus as he sits on a stone pillar,[3] Pilate's soldiers take Jesus to Golgotha. He falls three times on the Via Dolorosa, and the second and third falls include incidents with Mary and Simon.[4] Simon is whipped in order to force him to carry Jesus' cross.

The audience sees Golgotha from afar, sharing the distant perspective with the watching women. Then the camera moves closer and looks down on the head and torso of a fully clothed Jesus. He writhes in pain as soldiers nail him to the cross and raise it into the air. As the soldiers gamble and fight beneath him, Jesus promises paradise to the good thief. Mary wails beneath the cross, and after darkness and an earthquake, Jesus dies. A fade to black leads to a final Scripture card: John 3:16. The closing art intertitle returns to the motif of wise men following the star, perhaps suggesting that the wise still seek him. Notably, there is no Easter morning scene at the empty tomb.

Olcott's film is an excellent example of the difficulties involved in transforming the Gospel stories into celluloid. Olcott stages select scenes from the Gospels in a manner reflecting Christian art and nineteenth-century illustrated Bibles. Using a stationary camera, the film resembles a photographed stage performance, despite being filmed on location in Palestine and Egypt. We see all the characters as if on a stage, and usually at a distance. They walk toward or away from the camera or completely offstage. But Olcott does effectively use lighting and clothing to distinguish his characters. Jesus is, of course, in white and bright light. His opposition—primarily Judas—is increasingly dressed in dark colors and ends up literally in the dark. As a result, while Olcott never cites the Scripture verse, the film in many ways is a visual interpretation of John 1:5.

## Memorable Characters

- Jesus: He is an ethereal, supernatural figure—the skinniest Jesus ever shown on the silver screen. He causes miracles often by just waving his hand over people. He rarely looks at them and faces the camera rather than the person healed. His left hand is often on his heart (most notably at 37:34ff.; 42:13ff.; and 44:16), signifying his great love for everyone and helping to mark a magisterial, authoritative pose. The character effect reflects a Jesus whose miracles are primarily demonstrations of God's love for the world and moments of revelation for the viewing audience rather than individual acts of compassion for those he encounters. Notably, he looks most often at the women who come to him for help or who anoint him.
- Judas: As in the Gospels, Judas is the lynchpin connecting the revelation from above with its rejection by earthly powers. The anointing of Jesus' feet "for burial" results in Judas's angry tirade against Jesus, and he runs off, eventually betraying Jesus and asking for thirty pieces of silver by clasping and unclasping his hands three times. Judas reaches for the sopped bread at the Last Supper, seizing it from Jesus' hand and running off into the night. He slinks away into shadows that then turn into a blackened screen, signifying his satanic plot. He repents and returns the money to the priests, who refuse it, laughing at him. He then runs out and hangs himself.

## Memorable Visuals

- The shadow of the boy Jesus, carrying a piece of wood. The shadow takes the form of a cross, and his mother gasps.
- The paralytic, pushed up onto a housetop, then dropped through the roof to be healed
- The various women at Jesus' feet
- Judas haggling with the high priest for the price of betrayal
- Simon of Cyrene being whipped to force him to carry the rear portion of Jesus' cross
- Jesus writhing in pain as he is being nailed to the cross
- Roman soldiers, fighting over Jesus' garments
- The absence of a resurrection scene

## Key Scriptures

John's Gospel is the theological subtext, particularly John 1:5, as evident in the black/white clothing in the film and the use of lighting (but see also John 1:36; 3:16; 8:58). However, the Scripture intertitles quote Matthew and Luke most often.

## Cultural Location/Genre: Illustrated Bible, Travelogue

The third intertitle of Sidney Olcott's *From the Manger to the Cross* states, "The scene of this history is the Holy Land." A map of Palestine follows, identifying all "on location" towns where the film was shot. A fourth intertitle concludes the film's preface with the words "With scenes filmed at Jerusalem, Bethlehem and other authentic locations in Palestine."

By the late nineteenth century, travel to the far corners of the world was becoming more easily accessible to a wide range of upper-middle-class Europeans and Americans. But the vast majority of Americans were unable to spend the money or time to travel abroad and thus depended on touring lecturers who would describe their exotic adventures to rapt audiences. Or Americans would attend the traveling exhibitions of "uncivilized heathens from distant lands" often presented by church mission societies or city museums. Sidney Olcott's *From the Manger to the Cross* combines his viewing audience's curiosity about exotic peoples and places (Egypt and Palestine) with the familiar—their knowledge of the Jesus story. The result is a film that adds elements of the travelogue genre to the traditional passion play and Christmas pageant. The travelogue genre is most evident in the exterior shots of Mary and Joseph resting in front of the Sphinx and pyramids of Egypt, of Jesus and his disciples traveling out of Jericho toward Jerusalem and of Jesus praying over the city of Jerusalem, and in such details as the goatskin flask used to fill the purification water jars at the wedding at Cana and the Turkish rugs on display when Judas is betraying Jesus to the Jerusalem priests.

The film also represents an important period in the history of religious film—and of film in general—in its presentation of Jesus as one who visually reflects the domestic (late Victorian) piety of early-twentieth-century American religion. The portrayal of women at the feet of Jesus throughout the film marks Jesus as a domestic, feminized figure. He belongs to women, and they and religion belong to the home. As a result, Olcott uses little of Jesus' teaching and explains Jesus' death in terms of religious infighting, not in terms of Roman imperialism.

## Director

Sidney Olcott was one of the early directors intent on establishing an audience for religious film. Early directors did so by advertising their reverence for the Bible and by marketing exotic spectacles. Olcott, who had already made films on location in Ireland, was the first to film the story of Jesus on location in Palestine, and the film has the feeling of a travelogue at various points. His company had gone to the Middle East in order to film spectacles, and his Jesus film was an afterthought, the brainchild of a woman, Gene Gauntier, already well known for her work with Olcott. She wrote the scenario for the film and plays the role of Mary, mother of Jesus.

Olcott established a reverential tone for the film by offering audiences a Jesus with whom most were accustomed. Accordingly, many of the scenes reflect the illustrated Bibles of the time, most notably the Tissot Bible, and mirror the story line drawn from popular Christmas pageants and passion plays.[5]

## DVD Extras and Technical Features

This film is included on the same DVD with *The Life and Passion of Jesus Christ* (1905). A four-page insert comes with the DVD and is titled *Filming "From the Manger to the Cross": The First Moving Picture of the Life of Christ Made in the Land Where He Lived and Died*, and was "condensed from a 1927 reminiscence by a major player and scenarist of the film."

## DVD Chapters

1. Main Title: The Infancy of Christ
    The annunciation and the infancy of Christ, 1:01
        (Luke 1:27–28), 1:27
            Only the faintest shape of something can be seen as white light at the extreme left.
        (Matt. 1:19–21), 3:00
            A bright light shines on Joseph.
        (Luke 2:4–10), 4:30
        (Matt. 2:1–12), 7:36
            Burning frankincense
    The flight into Egypt (Matt. 2:13), 13:17
2. The Period of Youth, 15:29
        (Matt. 2:19–23), 15:34
        (Luke 2:40–52), 16:44
            Mary reads a scroll with Jesus; Joseph listens.
            Jesus rides the donkey; his parents walk.
            Jesus points upward when teaching.
        Carpenter boy Jesus (shadow of a cross), 21:25
        Mary looks down at the shadow and covers her mouth, 21:31
3. The Calling and Miracles, 21:33
        After years of silent preparation: heralded by John the Baptist (John 1:23, 36), 21:35
        The calling of the disciples (Matt. 4:18–21), 23:23
        The beginning of miracles, 25:23
            Multiple miracles (Matt. 4:23; compare DeMille's opening scene)
            Wedding at Cana (John 2:1–7), 26:25
            Cleansing a leper (Mark 1:40), 28:24
                Healing the blind
            Healing the paralytic (Mark 2:2–11), 29:08
            Raising the widow's son (Luke 7:12–14), 31:31
            Anointing woman (Luke 7:37–50), 32:30
4. Scenes in the Ministry 33:45
        Teaching beside the sea (Mark 4:1)
        Walking on the water (Matt. 14:25), 34:21
        (Mark 6:56), 34:34
        Mary and Martha (Luke 10:38–42), 35:15
        Teaching in the Temple (John 8:20, 58), 36:56
        Raising of Lazarus (John 11:1–48), 37:57
        Departing from Jericho (Matt. 20:29), 41:02
        Healing blind Bartimaeus (Matt. 20:34), 42:16
        Anointing in Bethany (Matt. 26:1–12), 42:55
        (This woman has no veil and has loose flowing hair, unlike the woman of Luke 7:37–50; see above, 32:30.)

> Judas is incredibly angry and stomps out.

5. Last Days in the Life of Jesus, 45:11

> Triumphal entry to Jerusalem (Luke 19:37), 45:18
>
> Hosanna (Matt. 21:9), 45:43
>
>> The donkey and the foal
>
> Cleansing the Temple (Matt. 21:12), 46:27
>
> The plot to destroy Jesus (Mark 11:18), 47:24
>
> Healing in the Temple (Matt. 21:14), 48:24
>
> On the Mount of Olives (Luke 21:37), 48:58
>
> Judas plans the betrayal (Mark 14:10), 49:34

6. The Last Supper, 51:19

> Washing the disciples' feet (John 13:5), 51:28
>
> Reclining and prophecy of betrayal (Mark 14:18; John 13:26–30), 52:29
>
>> Judas leaves.
>
> The first communion (Luke 22:19–20), 54:08
>
>> Judas is seen walking down a street; then the screen turns black.

7. The Crucifixion and Death, 55:50

> Going to the Mount of Olives (Matt. 26:47), 56:01
>
>> Kneels and prays (Luke 22:41), 56:45
>>
>> Betrayer is at hand (Matt. 26:46), 57:55
>>
>> "I am he" (John 18:6), 58:33
>>
>> Peter cuts off the high priest's servant's ear.
>
> Judas repents and hangs himself (Matt. 27:3-5), 58:59
>
> Jesus led to Pontius Pilate (Matt. 27:2), 1.00:01
>
> Herod's men mock Jesus (Luke 23:11), 1.01:12
>
> Sent back to Pilate (Luke 23:11), 1.01:44
>
>> Jesus scourged (John 19:1), 1.02:10
>>
>> "Behold the man" (John 19:5–6), 1.02:52
>>
>>> No people in the crowd sympathize with Jesus.
>>>
>>> Pilate washes his hands.
>>>
>>> Even after Jesus is gone, the crowd still clamors.
>
> Crown of thorns (Matt. 27:28–30), 1.04:06
>
>> People also dump other stuff on his head.
>
> Led away to be crucified (Matt. 27:31; John 19:17), 1.04:45
>
>> His mother runs out of the crowd to try and help him.
>>
>> Another woman (Mary Magdalene? Veronica?) pulls her back.
>
> Simon of Cyrene (Mark 15:21), 1.05:51
>
>> Simon has to be whipped to actually help; he carries only the rear part of the cross.
>
> Women watch from afar (Luke 23:49), 1.06:26
>
>> *Very* far!
>
> Crucified (Mark 15:25), 1.06:57
>
>> A person is on top of Jesus holding him to the cross, Jesus appears to be trying to get off.
>
> Parting his garments (Luke 23:34), 1.07:22
>
>> A big fight; crowd watches passively in background
>
> The penitent thief (Luke 23:42–43), 1.07:48
>
> "I thirst" (John 19:28), 1.08:12
>
> His mother grieves (John 19:25), 1.08:40
>
> Earthquake (Matt. 27:51)
>
>> Then Jesus dies.
>
> "For God so loved the world" (John 3:16), 1.09:52

8. End Credits, 1.10:08

# Chapter 4

# Intolerance

*D. W. Griffith, director. 177 mins. Not rated. 1916. Kino, 2002*

### Plot Summary

D. W. Griffith's classic film *Intolerance: Love's Struggle Throughout the Ages*[1] is not a Jesus movie. In fact, only about seventeen minutes of the three-hour film have anything to do with Jesus at all. However, because Griffith's innovative cinematography, technique of interweaving stories, and conscious evocation of American values have influenced later Jesus films, it is important to include this film in our handbook of Jesus movies on DVD.

The film has five segments related to the story of Jesus, although Jesus only appears in four of these.[2] In the first segment, the viewer is introduced to two places—Jerusalem and Cana (a city and a rural village)—and to a hypocritical Pharisee. But "the Man of Men" (unnamed) who was "from the carpenter shop in Bethlehem [*sic*]" and "the greatest enemy of intolerance" is not shown on-screen.

The second and longest Jesus segment is the wedding at Cana, where the shadow of a cross is superimposed on the figure of Jesus as he performs the miracle of turning water to wine. One of the intertitles states, "Wine was deemed a fit offering to God; the drinking of it a part of the Jewish religion." The third segment focuses on the woman caught in adultery.[3] Jesus is accused of being a drunkard, even though he refuses to drink wine when offered it. The fourth segment is the briefest. Here Jesus blesses little children who surround him. The final segment, crosscut into three fragments and ending with Jesus hanging on the cross, shows Jesus on the Via Dolorosa. The segment is introduced by an intertitle stating Pilate's decision to have Jesus crucified.

The power and creativity of Griffith's film does not lie in these snippets of the Jesus story that New Testament scholars might want to cut from the three-hour film and analyze as free-standing segments. Instead, the power of the Jesus scenes lies precisely in the way that Griffith juxtaposes them to three other simultaneously told stories. In fact, *Intolerance* tells four versions of one story—intolerance's battle with love—beginning with the modern story of two young people who are forced into desperate economic straits as the result of progressive women reformers'/"uplifters'" grandiose plans to save society. The other three stories, in order of their appearance, are Jesus' life and death (a death precipitated by Pharisaic hypocrisy); the sixteenth-century persecution of the

Protestant Huguenots (caused by the Roman Catholic Catherine de Medici); and the fall of Babylon (caused by the treason of the pagan priests of the god Bel). The villains in each story are religious leaders and uncompromising moral reformers. The innocent victims are Jesus and various young lovers.

Griffith crosscuts the four stories as he develops his common theme. Comparisons and contrasts, narrative comments, and most importantly, a recurring scene with a woman rocking a cradle, connect the independent stories. The intertitle attached to the cradle scenes quotes Walt Whitman: "Out of the cradle endlessly rocking."[4] The woman, along with three fates standing ominously in the background, symbolizes the common human history that connects the stories.

The three historical stories provide the interpretative backdrop for the modern story.[5] In this story, the reformers/uplifters,[6] led by Miss Jenkins, seek funds for their goal to suppress vice in American society. Two young people, simply called "the Boy" and "the Dear One," depend on Mr. Jenkins's mill (Miss Jenkins's brother) for their livelihood. A cut to scenes in ancient Jerusalem and Cana establishes connections between the reformers/uplifters and the hypocrites among the Pharisees,[7] one of whom thanks God that he is better than other men.[8] Griffith's uplifters are cast from their mold.

The increasing demands of Miss Jenkins's charities lead Mr. Jenkins to cut wages at the mill. A strike for higher wages ensues, and after strike-breaking violence, the Boy and the Dear One (still unaware of each other's existence) move to the city. Due to continued economic hardship, the Boy becomes a member of a criminal gang led by "the Musketeer." He eventually meets the Dear One and tries to seduce her. The Dear One's father manages to protect her from the Boy's improper advances, but the father eventually dies, leaving the Dear One to fend for herself. The Boy, now sensing an opening, comes to her "rescue." The second cut to the Jesus story identifies Jesus as a comforter. At the wedding in Cana, Jesus supplies needed wine, but the Pharisees watch disapprovingly as the guests dance.

The Boy courts the Dear One and asks her to marry him, while the uplifters become the "most influential power in the community." The intertitle for the third cut to the Jesus story announces, "Equally intolerant hypocrites of another age." Now the Pharisees denounce Jesus as a glutton, a friend of sinners, and a wine bibber. Much to the Pharisees' chagrin, Jesus forgives the woman taken in adultery, who weeps in joy—or in repentance.

An ironic question segues back to the modern story —"How shall we find this Christly example followed in our story of today?" The answer appears quickly: the reformers/uplifters have managed to close all brothels, dance halls, and taverns in the city; however, unbeknownst to the naïve uplifters, shutting down these businesses has simply allowed the Musketeer to develop a black market for vice.

The Boy forsakes crime when he marries the Dear One, but the Musketeer frames the Boy. The Boy is falsely convicted of theft, and while he is in prison, the Dear One bears his child. When she leaves the baby for a moment to procure an "illegal" remedy (whiskey) for her cold, the uplifters accuse her of being a negligent mother. They take her baby from her and put it in an institution. The intertitle "Suffer little children" leads to the fourth and briefest cut to the Jesus story. Therein, the film simply shows Jesus with his hands on the heads of children, with men and women crowded around him.[9]

Released from prison, the Boy returns to his broken family. When the Musketeer tries to seduce the Dear One, promising her that he can get her baby back, the Boy fights the Musketeer. In the tumult, the Boy and the Dear One are knocked unconscious. While they lie unconscious on the floor of their apartment, the Musketeer's jealous mistress shoots him. She plants the gun in the Boy's hand, and he is convicted for the Musketeer's murder. The fifth cut to the Jesus story establishes a connection between the innocent Jesus, condemned and carrying his cross toward Calvary, and the Boy convicted of a crime he did not commit.

A judge sentences the Boy to hanging, but a kindly policeman decides the evidence is inconclusive and tries to procure a pardon from the governor. As the gallows are prepared and the end nears, the Musketeer's mistress finally confesses to the crime. The policeman, the mistress, and the Dear One start to chase down the governor, who has boarded a train. Only he can avert the Boy's execution. The Boy receives last rites, and it looks as though he will die, falsely convicted of the Musketeer's murder. The sixth cut to the Jesus story finds Jesus still struggling on the Via Dolorosa.

The policeman, the Musketeer's mistress, and the Dear One finally manage to stop the governor's train, and he grants a pardon to the Boy. The three then race to the gallows to try and stop the execution. In the seventh cut to the Jesus story the viewer sees Jesus' crucifixion in the darkening distance as a light streams from Calvary.

In the final scene, the policeman, the Musketeer's mistress, and the Dear One manage to arrive at the gallows just before three men (the three fates?) cut the threads that would hang the Boy. The Boy and the Dear One joyously embrace each other, and the story ends.

A fantastic epilogue imagines the end of war and the abolishment of prisons. Soldiers put down their weapons, innocent children hug and kiss, and a cross of light unites an angelic chorus and earthly throngs.

Griffith's Jesus is Love crucified by intolerant people. Although this Jesus hardly teaches, light (moral influence) from his cross offers hope for tolerance despite the Pharisees of all ages. That hope stands in tension, however, with Griffith's critique of reform movements and with his three tragic stories (Griffith's story of Jesus ends without the resurrection). Only the modern story ends happily, with the Boy and the Dear One reunited in love. And despite his rapid crosscutting between stories at the climax, Griffith establishes no causal connection between Jesus' story and the modern couple's escape from an unjust death.[10]

## Memorable Characters

- Jesus: Jesus is the ultimate innocent victim in human history. Compared to Zecca's, Olcott's, and DeMille's Jesus characters, Griffith's Jesus seems more human for several reasons. First, Jesus simply does not appear many times in the film. The longer a Jesus character is on camera, the more difficult it is to sustain a believable image of him. Secondly, the crosscuts connect Jesus to other tragic stories in human history, thus naturalizing him in the process. Nevertheless, Griffith still produces a Jesus of whom his audiences will approve. Jesus can turn water into wine and watch wedding guests dance without casting a disapproving look; but he does not dance with them, and he looks on from a distance. Later, when offered a cup of wine, he refuses it. Jesus does not condemn the woman caught in adultery (the scene is juxtaposed to the uplifter women who raid brothels and close taverns and dance halls because they have lost their ability to attract males), but Jesus does not get close to the adulterous woman or touch her.

- The Boy and the Dear One: They are the real protagonists, the ones who manage to survive despite the hypocritical uplifter women and the sloppy justice system. In fact, the movie's characters—the innocent and their hypocritical oppressors—are quite abstract, flat characters, capable of appearing in various cultures and at all periods of time.

## Memorable Visuals

These are from the Jesus story only:

- Woman[11] rocking the cradle
- Young mother and child seated in a Jerusalem doorway
- Various people stopping their activities when the Pharisee prays
- The shadow cross superimposed on Jesus at the wedding at Cana
- Dissolve from the woman caught in adultery to Jesus writing on the ground
- Cross of light and angels that stop the fighting soldiers and bring peace to the world

## Key Scriptures

The crosscut style is at times reminiscent of Mark's intercalations. The four versions of one story also resemble the canonical "the Gospel according to . . ." pattern, which transforms four disparate Gospels into one, canonical-Gospel message. The theme of Jesus opposing hypocrisy recalls Matt. 5–7 and Matt. 23. The character of Jesus comes from Matt. 11:19 (according to the intertitles; but also from John 2:1–12; 7:53–8:11).

## Cultural Location/Genre: Epic Spectacle

The contemporary story of the Boy and the Dear One uses early-twentieth-century progressive and New Woman reform issues to build a dramatic and scathing indictment of religious hypocrisy. The "white slave trade," alcoholism, and child abuse were social concerns especially of white, middle-class Protestant women. Through such organizations as anti-prostitution "purity leagues" and the Woman's Christian Temperance Union, these women sought to correct societal injustices by advocating for the urban poor and the recent immigrant. In Griffith's film, however, the women who advocated for such social reforms were unknowingly creating the very problems they sought to correct.

Griffith's story of the Boy and the Dear One is a powerful portrayal of capitalism's brutal exploitation of labor, a frontal attack on capital punishment, an indictment of upper-middle-class child rescue and welfare agencies, and a critique of governmental control of alcohol and drug use. Griffith's Jesus, however, does not address any of these social issues. His Jesus celebrates the family unit, but he is never found in the company of the physically disabled or the poverty stricken. The only people who are found with this type of folk are the women uplifters, whom Griffith ridicules as naïve, sexually unattractive, deceptive, misguided moralists.

## Director

Griffith secured the place of film in American culture.[12] He campaigned relentlessly to have film accepted as an art form and was tireless in his fight against those who would censor film. His famous *The Birth of a Nation* (1915) begins with intertitles arguing for his position.

That film and *Intolerance* both advocate pacifism in the face of the increasing international tensions of the late 1910s. Both films also reject "radical" reformers, exposing their hypocrisy, selfish motivations, and ineffectiveness. In *Intolerance*, Griffith's ideology is conservative. In *The Birth of a Nation*, his ideology is reactionary and racist.

*The Birth of a Nation*, Griffith's most famous film, has several elements in common with *Intolerance*: epic scale; focus on romantic couples (humanizing the epic scale); crosscutting to build suspense; and fantastic, spectacular epilogues. Griffith based *The Birth of a Nation* on *The Clansman*, a novel by a Southern preacher.[13] Like that novel, *The Birth of a Nation* presents the Ku Klux Klan as the savior of a ravaged South downtrodden by mercenary carpetbaggers and vindictive blacks. In fact, Griffith opens the Reconstruction section of the film with this intertitle: "The agony which the South endured that a nation might be born."

In short, the South becomes a suffering Christ figure, and the KKK represents that figure's vindictive resurrection. Not surprisingly, Northern unionists, abolitionists, carpetbaggers, and vindictive blacks are the film's villains.[14] For Griffith, blacks are helpless children, manipulated by evil Northerners, and unfit for public office. They are at their best when they are loyal to their "masters."[15] Accordingly, the film is fraught with concerns for whites' "Aryan birthright" and whites' fears about intermarriage and miscegenation. Black gangs run riot in the streets, and various black men pursue and force themselves on white women. In Griffith's typically spectacular finale, the KKK, bearing the cross, rides to the rescue and saves the threatened whites.[16] The blacks are disarmed in the midst of a victorious KKK parade, and without visible disjoint, the film concludes with a fantastic vision of the establishment of Christ's peaceful kingdom on earth.[17]

Both films use the figure of Jesus (and the cross) to support conservative and/or reactionary ideologies. The similarities between the two films raise important questions about the moral simplicity of Griffith's vision in *Intolerance* and whether he is able to distinguish neatly between those in need of judgment and those in need of salvation. While preaching peace and toleration, the canonical style[18] of *Intolerance* and the KKK parade that leads to Christ's peaceful kingdom in *The Birth of a Nation* both suggest Griffith's vision is quite imperial. As the Christ figure (i.e., the American South and the KKK) demonstrates, Griffith's Jesus is troublingly white, American, and intolerant of others.

## DVD Extras and Technical Features

"The Real Story of *Intolerance*," by Henry Stephen Gordon. Excerpted from *Photoplay Magazine*, October 1915 (one-page insert).

Special Features:

Introduction by Orson Welles

Excerpt of *The Last Days of Pompeii* (1913), an Italian epic that inspired D.W. Griffith

Excerpt of *Cabiria* (1914), which inspired the scale and production design of D.W. Griffith's Babylon

Excerpt of *The Fall of Babylon* (alternate ending), a less downbeat resolution to the Mountain Girl's predicament

Pamphlets

About the Score

The Book: the text of the book that is used as an intertitle background. It provides a concise summation of the structure and ideology of the film.

## DVD Chapters

Jesus story excerpts only:

7.  Jerusalem the Golden City, 8:40–11:39

(Jesus does not appear in this segment.)

"From the carpenter shop in Bethlehem [sic] . . . the Man of Men, the greatest enemy of intolerance"

Near the Jaffa Gate

(Jerusalem)

The house in Cana of Galilee

Certain hypocrites among the Pharisees

Prayer of the Pharisee (Matt. 6:5–6; Luke 18:9–14), 10:04

11. The Wedding in Galilee, 1.01:56–1.06:20

(John 2:1) The ceremony according to Sayce, Hastings, Brown, and Tissot

"Be ye harmless as doves" (Matt. 10:16)

Shadow of a cross over Jesus as he turns water to wine

13. Cast the First Stone, 1.13:28–1.16:15

(Matt. 11:19; John 8:1–11)

16. Modern Motherhood, 1.30:15

"Suffer little children" (Mark 10:14), 1.36:58–1.37:19

24. The Verdicts, 2.34:09

"Let him be crucified," 2.34:13–2.34:49

On the Via Dolorosa

27. The Massacre, 2.52:06

"Let him be crucified" (Via Dolorosa)—cont'd, 2.56:37–2.57:00

29. On the Gallows, 3.10:41

"Let him be crucified" (Calvary)—cont'd, 3.11:21–3.12:00

30. Epilogue, 3.14:37

Angelic Hosts, 3.15:22

With a cloudy cross, 3.16:28

## Chapter 5

# The King of Kings

*Cecil B. DeMille, director. 155 mins. Not rated. 1927. Criterion, 2004*

### Plot Summary

Cecil B. DeMille's *The King of Kings*[1] represents a significant break from the episodic plot structure of earlier Jesus films, in that DeMille attempts to structure the public ministry of Jesus around the integrated plot device of Mary Magdalene's unrequited love for Judas and Judas's thirst for power and glory.[2] While DeMille fails to accomplish his goal of a unified plot, his intuitive sense of how best to tell the story of Jesus on film sets the parameters for future directors of Jesus films.

DeMille's film opens with an incredible scene shot in full color: the opulent brothel of Mary Magdalene, where leering old men surround the scantily clad prostitute. A monkey scampers about the room while Mary strokes a friendly leopard. Mary is despondent because her lover, Judas, has disappeared. But then she hears that Judas is with another man—"a carpenter from Nazareth and his band of beggars."[3] Convinced that her womanly wiles can win back her lover, the mocking, decadent Mary zooms off to find him in her private chariot pulled by four zebras.

After Mary Magdalene leaves the brothel to find Judas, the viewer is taken to a house surrounded by people in need of healing.[4] A little blind girl tries to get help in finding Jesus, while Judas proclaims Jesus to be the next king of the Jews and points out to the crowds where Jesus is. Roman soldiers basking in the sun take note of Judas's proclamation, but suddenly a young boy squeezes through the crowds to announce that Jesus has just healed him of lameness. The boy is Mark, the future author of the Gospel by the same name, and he will follow Jesus from Galilee to Jerusalem, witnessing the raising of Lazarus from the dead, Jesus' triumphal entry into the Temple, his crucifixion, and his ascension. Reports of Jesus' healing powers have spread widely, and Caiaphas the high priest also has his spies in town (a priest, a scribe, and a Pharisee), who are investigating reports of Jesus' activity.

The film then introduces the disciples—all but Matthew—as they gather inside the house, listening to Jesus. But the viewer is not given a glimpse of Jesus or a hint of his words. As Sabbath nears, Mark leads the little blind girl to Mary, Jesus' mother, who introduces the girl to Jesus. After an intertitle, "I am come a light into the world that whoever believes in me shall not abide in darkness," Jesus heals the girl, and the audience sees Jesus for the first time through the little girl's slowly focusing eyes.[5] In future scenes, DeMille will often film Jesus in a gauzy, ethereal light,[6] and his interactions with children will show the most human side of his character.

Mary Magdalene eventually arrives to confront her lover, Judas, and take him back. But she finds him with Jesus, whose piercing eyes mesmerize her. He casts the seven deadly sins from her, and the seductive, scantily clad Magdalene quickly covers her body. She disappears from the story until near the end of Jesus' life, when she reappears in the Jerusalem crowd scenes as one of Jesus' most vocal supporters.

Despite (or because of) his many miracles,[7] Jesus faces opposition from Caiaphas the high priest, who cares "more for [the Temple] revenue than for religion."[8] Judas, who believes Jesus will be Israel's next king, also wishes to use Jesus to procure money and power for himself. But Caiaphas is more devious in his strategizing to maintain power. He first attempts to trap Jesus by forcing him into paying taxes to Caesar, thus introducing the viewer to Matthew the tax collector and note taker.[9] In this notable sequence, DeMille manages to connect the Temple tax story (Matt. 17:24–27) with Jesus' "Render unto Caesar" saying (Matt. 22:15–22), Judas's empty money bag (John 12:6), the call of Matthew (Matt. 9:9), the healing of the "lunatic" boy (Mark 9:14–29), and the demon-possessed man's cry, "I know who you are, the Holy One of God" (Mark 1:24).[10] To these Gospel materials DeMille adds a setting that functions both as flashback and foreshadowing. As the high priest's servant challenges Jesus about the Temple tax, Jesus takes up the carpenter tools of the "lunatic's" father—who, unbeknownst to Jesus, is making crosses for the Romans, "who pay him well." For Jesus, the carpenter's "tools of the trade" take him back to his former life. But when a cloth falls down and exposes the full form of the wood he is working on (with doves sitting above it) Jesus finds himself staring at a cross. As he poses, contemplating his future, Judas looks on bewilderingly.

When Caiaphas's tax trap fails to catch Jesus and when Jesus' fame continues to spread due to his raising of Lazarus from the dead, Caiaphas decides to use the adulterous woman (John 8:1–11) to force Jesus' libertine views into the open.[11] This attempt to trap Jesus also fails, and after Jesus cleanses the Temple courtyard and then triumphantly enters the Temple precincts, Judas and Satan make a final offer of kingship to Jesus.[12] But Jesus, holding a lamb, responds to the Temple crowds by speaking to them of an ethereal kingdom and repeating the Lord's Prayer. As a result of Judas's public attempt to make Jesus king, Caiaphas makes death threats against Judas. Desperate to save himself, and knowing that Jesus has rejected his ideas of an earthly kingdom, Judas offers to betray Jesus for money. Ironically, Judas had become a disciple of Jesus precisely because he saw Jesus as a way to make money. He had hoped to get rich from Jesus' healing ministry. Now, finally, Caiaphas has found a way to get to Jesus; and Judas has found a way to make money from Jesus' career.

At the Last Supper, however, a haunted Judas refuses to partake of the bread and wine and leaves the table. After Jesus and the other disciples depart for Gethsemane, DeMille's camera lingers on the cup, surrounded by a hazy, heavenly light as a dove lights upon it. Judas brings the Temple police to Gethsemane by lamplight to arrest

Jesus,[13] and then Caiaphas, seeking the death penalty, takes Jesus to Pilate.[14] Pilate's wife tells her husband of her dream of Jesus' innocence, so Pilate refuses to condemn him.[15] Nevertheless, Caiaphas is able to bribe evil men in the crowd to call out for Jesus' death.[16] Pilate finally washes his hands of the affair; Caiaphas claims sole responsibility for the death sentence; and a remorseful Judas repents of his betrayal.

As the disciples hide in the upper room, Jesus walks the Via Dolorosa. He heals the infirm along the way, is encouraged by his mother, and then the boy Mark shames Simon of Cyrene into carrying Jesus' cross. As Jesus is crucified, Judas watches from afar, making preparations for his own death. Caiaphas mocks Jesus, but Jesus asks for forgiveness for others and tells the repentant thief that the two of them will enjoy paradise together. As a supernatural darkness falls on Calvary, Jesus dies—declaring it finished and commending his spirit to God at the very moment Judas hangs himself. The grieving mother of the unrepentant thief finds loving forgiveness in the arms of Jesus' mother,[17] and as a cataclysmic earthquake begins, Judas's tree falls into the split-open earth. Finally, the Roman centurion declares Jesus to be the Son of God. Caiaphas is then seen standing before the torn, burning Temple veil and confessing his solitary guilt; while back at Calvary, Mary, the mother of Jesus, prays for light. Miraculously, light bathes the cross as the crucifixion scene ends.

The resurrection follows *in color*.[18] As Roman guards watch, a bright light falls on the gravestone. It rolls away, the guards flee, and Jesus emerges. He appears first to his mother, and then after Mary Magdalene enters the tomb, he appears to her as well. Later, "behind closed doors,"[19] he appears to the disciples (including Thomas), his mother, Mary Magdalene, and the boy Mark. He then sends them all forth as his witnesses.[20] In the epilogue, Jesus ascends over a modern city with an accompanying intertitle, "Lo, I am with you always."[21]

## Memorable Characters

- Jesus: He is an ethereal healer, uninterested in earthly power, wealth, or glory. He is God's supernatural light who has entered the human world, but viewers are given no explicit clues as to how or why he heals. There is no hint of his virginal conception or of his baptism by John, with the Holy Spirit descending upon him. He is most human when interacting with children—almost grandfatherly in age and demeanor.

- Mary Magdalene: She provides erotic interest and provides the sin-to-salvation story. However, in DeMille's film she is not the nameless woman caught in adultery—a role that will become her primary character marker in future Hollywood films. She is visible during Jesus' triumphal entry into the Temple and leads the vocal opposition to the crowd that is shouting for Jesus' crucifixion. She is at the foot of the cross and is the only one to enter the tomb of Jesus on Easter morning.

- Judas: He is the follower who fails. Interested in wealth and earthly power, he bears most of the weight of the disciples' misconceptions and failures. For example, Judas takes on the role of the unnamed disciples by being unable to perform a miracle and by sending the children away from Jesus. With Peter, he is a witness to almost all of Jesus' miracles, but in his case they do not evoke reverence, faith, or love.

- Caiaphas: He is the lone Jewish culprit, minimizing the anti-Semitic tendencies of the Gospels. Caiaphas's interest in getting rid of Jesus is motivated by specific monetary concerns. The Temple with its revenue in taxes will be lost to him if he cannot control Jesus. Thus he sends the tax collector Matthew to ask Jesus the question about paying taxes to Caesar. When that fails, he uses the woman caught in adultery to try and expose Jesus' loose interpretation of Jewish law.
- Mark: The future author of the Second Gospel is portrayed as a lame boy healed by Jesus (Mark 2:1–12). He is a child evangelist, leading other children to Jesus. He witnesses the healing of the blind girl, the exorcism of the "lunatic" spirit, the raising of Lazarus, Jesus' response to the adulterous woman, the triumphal entry, the agony in the Garden of Gethsemane, the Via Dolorosa (at Mark's impetus, Simon of Cyrene takes up Jesus' cross), the crucifixion, and Jesus' final resurrection appearance and ascension.

## Memorable Visuals

- Mary Magdalene racing in her chariot to find her lover, Judas, with Jesus
- The blind girl (and the audience) seeing Jesus for the first time (nearly nineteen minutes into the film)
- The exorcism/conversion of Mary Magdalene
- Roman soldiers catching fish and looking for gold coins
- The father of the lunatic boy (Mark 9:14–29) making crosses for the Romans
- Jesus "healing" a child's broken doll
- Jesus raising Lazarus from the dead
- Jesus, holding a lamb, rejecting Judas/Satan's crown
- Angle shot of Jesus' cross, scraping across the ground, with a dog and people's feet walking around it
- Jesus' ascension over a modern city

## Key Scriptures

Jesus is the Johannine light from above (John 8:12; cf. 3:19–21; 12:46).[22] The Temple cleansing, depending primarily on John 2:13–22 and configured as a choice between prayer (Jesus) and money (Judas/Caiaphas), is the Scripture on which DeMille hangs his plot conflict and his good guy/bad guy characterizations. Despite the ever-present intertitles from the King James Version (or surreptitiously parroting the KJV), DeMille's sin-to-salvation story is fully Americanized in its narrative impetus and characterization.

## Cultural Location/Genre: Illustrated Children's Bible, Epic Spectacle

According to the 1920 U.S. census, for the first time in American history more people lived in metropolitan areas (defined as towns with a population over 2,500) than in rural areas. Immigration was at its height, and large cities like New York and Chicago had foreign-born populations of over fifty percent. Thus, DeMille's portrayal of Jesus' activity in "cities" with large crowds of begging children and desperately needy adults would have resonated deeply with his viewing audiences.

Hollywood had also recently gone through a number of financial and sex scandals, and filmmakers were turning to moralistic projects to curry favor with their American audiences. The Hays Code, which would regulate the parameters of morality for the Motion Picture Association of America for over thirty years, was barely three years in the future, but DeMille was ahead of the morality game, having already produced several reverent spectacles, notably *The Ten Commandments* (1923)[23] and *The King of Kings* (1927). The latter became the quintessential American Jesus film until Nicholas Ray finally made his *King of Kings* in 1961. But DeMille's *The King of Kings* set the standard narrative pattern for subsequent biblical epics with its interwoven sin-to-salvation plot and its immense visual spectacle.

DeMille's film, unlike Griffith's *Intolerance*, also provided Americans with an easily consumable Jesus. Accordingly, DeMille's Jesus would become the model for Hollywood Jesus figures until Pasolini's Jesus finally broke the mold forty years later (with his *The Gospel According to St. Matthew*). DeMille's sentimentalized Jesus is an eminently nice, nonthreateningly divine figure. His Jesus offers the comfort of a divinity who accepts all except the greediest of bastards. In particular, DeMille's Jesus utters none of those troubling sayings about the rich and their wealth. Such pronouncements might discomfort American capitalists—the sort of people who underwrote the project. In DeMille's first-century world there is nothing wrong with wealth unless it becomes one's ultimate focus, replacing religion (Caiaphas) or personal relationships (Judas, Mary Magdalene). Although DeMille's Jesus is often in the company of socially outcast women and children, he does not condemn the wealthy or those in power. Ironically, DeMille's profitable spectacle aligned him more closely with his villainous Judas and Caiaphas than with the Jesus of his film.

## Director

DeMille made a number of successful "sexy" comedies in the late 1910s and early 1920s. Reportedly, he thought that only sex and money interested American audiences. After the Hollywood scandals of the early 1920s, DeMille moved on to produce blatantly "moral" tales. Nonetheless, as the opening scenes with Mary Magdalene in *The King of Kings* illustrate, he continued to titillate his audiences. His sin-to-salvation trope repeatedly provided him the vehicle for toying with issues of illicit sex and its moral comeuppance or redemption.

DeMille's 1932 film, *The Sign of the Cross*, opens with Nero's persecutions—an opportunity for sadomasochistic spectacle—and with the decadence of imperial Rome. Nero's wife, Poppaea (Claudette Colbert), lolls in a famous, revealing milk bath. She loves the prefect of Rome, Marcus Superbus (Frederic March), known for his own frequent dalliances. But Marcus, in the course of his Christian-hunting duties, falls in love with Mercia (Elissa Landi). His refusal to turn over this Christian for execution places him in a precarious position in Rome's power politics, and a jealous rival, Tigellinus (Ian

Keith), seeks to undo him. Having saved Mercia from death twice, Marcus takes her to an orgy in his home, hoping to convert her to his decadent lifestyle. One of his many women, Ancaria, hastens this conversion with a sensual dance. While Marcus leers, Christians march by on their way to death, singing hymns. Transfixed, Mercia asks Marcus to return her to the arena. In the finale, after failing to rescue Mercia a third time or to convince her to recant her faith, Marcus joins Mercia, marching upstairs with her to death in the arena (cf. the finale of *The Robe* [1953]). In short, morality trumps titillation, for the last shot in the film is of a cross formed of light on the closed door leading to the arena.

DeMille's second *The Ten Commandments* (1956) is equally moralistic, but here jingoistic patriotism takes center stage. In the midst of fighting the Cold War and wishing to assure militant, imperialistic Americans of the justice of their cause, DeMille presents the story of the exodus as Moses' quest for freedom from tyranny and the birth of freedom (cf. *Braveheart* [1995]).[24] The glorious finale presents Moses (Charlton Heston) in a Statue of Liberty pose, intoning, "Go, proclaim liberty to all lands."

*The Ten Commandments* is exemplary of the spectacle genre that was DeMille's other trademark. In fact, critics have often castigated his films as postcard pageants. Thus, in the spectacular exodus and sea crossing, DeMille simply lets his cast of thousands move before his camera. The penultimate scene at Sinai also offers DeMille yet another opportunity for titillation and its moralistic redress. Here, DeMille crosscuts repeatedly between the divine pillar of fire that gives the law to Moses and the orgy transpiring at the foot of the mountain, which DeMille narrates. Moses, of course, ends the orgy with divine judgments when he comes down from the mountain. Thereafter, the movie ends precipitously, with Moses taking his leave and offering one last statement of the DeMille Gospel.

As in *The King of Kings*, DeMille often quotes biblical stories but ignores the stories' own narrative impetuses. Instead, he clothes biblical stories in his own narrative conventions: a sin-to-salvation story, the hero's choice between good and evil women, political struggles, contemporary ethical concerns, and spectacle.

## DVD Extras and Technical Features

Special-edition, double-disk set. Disk 1 (1927), 155 minutes; disk 2 (1928), 112 minutes. Black & white and color. Silent. New musical scores commissioned by Criterion for each version.

### *The King of Kings* (booklet, 36 pages)

"Showman of Piety," by Peter Matthews

"The King of Kings," by Robert S. Birchard: "The following provides a glimpse into the production history of *The King of Kings*. It is excerpted from Birchard's book *Cecil B. DeMille's Hollywood*."

"Hollywood Moves to the Holy Land," by Grace Kingsley: "The following article originally appeared in the March 1927 issue of the Hollywood monthly *Picture-Play*."

"The Screen as a Religious Teacher: How the much-discussed filming of *The King of Kings*, the new religious drama, was produced with reverence and accuracy," by Cecil B. DeMille: "This essay by DeMille was originally published in the June 1927 issue of *Theatre* magazine."

DVD Extras (Disc 1)

Supplements
    Opening Night
        Newspaper Ads
        Stills
        Telegrams
    Original Program
    Press Book
    Blessings from the Clergy (Roman Catholic, Protestant denominations, and a Jew, a Muslim, and a Buddhist)
    Trailers
The Score
    About Sosin

DVD Extras (Disc 2)

Supplements
    Scenes from the Making of *The King of Kings*
        Behind the Scenes (outtakes, etc.)
           Jeanie Macpherson, who wrote the screenplay, is on set for much of the filming
    Stills Gallery
    Sketches by Dan Sayre Groesbeck
    Portraits by W. M. Mortensen
The Scores
    Original 1928 Score by Hugo Riesenfeld
    Alternate 2004 Score by Timothy J. Tikker

## DVD Chapters (Disk 1, 1927)

Where there are multiple Scripture references for an individual scene (below), the references are in canonical order, not in the order that the references appear on screen.

1. Logos/Opening Credits
2. Prologue, 1:14
    The opening scenes are shot in color (up until 8:32).
3. The House of Mary Magdalene, 1:52
    "A beautiful courtesan"; Judas is her lover
4. "Take me to Him," 8:32
    Lame boy healed (Mark 2:1–2), 10:26
        The boy is Mark, the eventual author of the Second Gospel.
        "This man is not of God" (John 9:16), 11:55
    Peter first appears, 12:16
5. Jesus the Great Physician, 13:47
    The remaining disciples are named—except for Matthew, 13:50
    Mary, mother of Jesus, 14:50
        She is weaving, and there is a shimmering dove in the background.
    A Sabbath Healing (of a blind girl) (Mark 3:2), 15:20–20:37
        Mark, then Mary brings the blind girl to Jesus; Peter and Judas observe.
        The blind girl's point of view, 17:42
        First view of Jesus (through the eyes of the girl), 18:44
        Jesus' and Judas's response (Luke 8:39), 19:45–20:37
6. Seven Deadly Sins, 20:38
    Mary Magdalene arrives in her chariot to see Jesus, then meets Judas, 21:30

(Matt. 7:7), 21:53

Cleansed of seven deadly sins, 22:15-26:45

(Matt. 8:3; Luke 8:2; Matt. 5:8)

7. House of Caiaphas, 26:47

Why the large spider art piece sitting on Caiaphas's desk? (27:10, 28:21; see also 52:24)

(Luke 19:47; cf. Mark 3:6)

(John 12:19), 27:50

"He broke the Sabbath! And said that God was his Father" (John 5:18)

"We feared the multitude" (Matt. 21:45)

Caiaphas's tax plan to catch Jesus involves Matthew, the future disciple, 29:22

8. Judas Fails to Heal, 30:22

(Luke 8:1; see also Mark 9:14–29; the boy Mark is in the background)

"Thy disciples could not cure him!" (Matt. 17:15–16)

"All things are possible" (Mark 9:23)

"The Holy One of God!" (Mark 1:24)

"Why could not I cast out the devil?" (Matt. 17:19–20)

9. "Follow me, Matthew," 35:16

Jesus the carpenter (with a dove nearby, cf. 41:35)

Tribute to Caesar (the coin in the fish's mouth) (Matt. 17:24–27)

Peter is asked by the high priest's servant; Peter goes to Jesus.

Peter asks Judas, who has the money bag.

"Is it lawful to give tribute?" (Matt. 22:17–21)

"Matthew—follow me!" (Matt. 9:9)

A covered cross—Jesus stares at it, 41:35.

"I make many crosses for the Romans—they pay me well."

Judas watches.

10. "Suffer little children," 42:46

Face set toward Jerusalem (Luke 9:51)

Children pick olives; Judas sends the children away from Jesus (Mark 10:14)

Jesus fixes a child's broken doll, 44:22–45:36

Mark again is in the scene.

11. The Tomb of Lazarus, 45:37

(John 11:21–22, 17, 25, 43–44)

Mark is in the scene, as is Judas.

12. The Adulteress, 52:06

"The High Priest was filled with madness and pondered what he might do to him" (Luke 6:11).

The adulteress becomes Caiaphas's second trap for Jesus (John 8:1–11).

13. At the Temple, 54:30

Animals slaughtered; veil of the Temple, 55:16

White doves fly across in front of the veil.

The adulteress (Luke 18:11; John 8:1–11), 55:45

Mark is there, but is politely shielded from viewing the woman. Notice how much of the adulteress's leg is exposed as she stands up!

14. Den of Thieves, 1.01:10

(Matt. 21:13; Mark 11:15; John 2:14–19)

Caiaphas meets Jesus (Matt 21:23), 1.05:00

15. "He is our King," 1.06:12

(Mark 11:10; Luke 19:37–38; John 6:15, 68–69; 14:6)

Triumphal entry takes place in the Temple.

Mark is there, as are Peter, John, and Mary Magdalene; Judas finds a "crown" to put on Jesus.

The Devil tempts Jesus (Matt. 4:8–9; Luke 4:8), 1.08:48

A lamb in the Temple, 1.10:53

16. Thirty Pieces of Silver, 1.11:14

    A kingdom not of this world (John 18:36), 1.12:30

    The Lord's Prayer, 1.13:10

    Thirty pieces of silver (Matt. 26:14–15; Mark 14:2), 1.13:42

17. The Last Supper, 1.15:28

    "Take, eat" (Matt. 20:28; 26:22, 27–28; Luke 22:19, 21, 33–34; John 13:27, 33–34; 16:33)

    Peter, John, and Judas are next to Jesus; and Jesus' mother is outside the door; Judas does not eat.

    The dove and the glowing chalice, 1.25:20

18. The Garden of Gethsemane, 1.25:50

    (Matt. 26:36–38, 40–42, 48–49, 52, 55; Luke 22:42–44, 48; John 17:1–4; 18:18)

    Mark is with them.

    Judas meets the temple police, 1.26:55

    Healing High Priest's servant's ear, 1.33:30

19. Peter Denies Jesus, 1.35:12

    (Matt. 26:57–58, 71–72; Mark 14:71; John 18:19, 25–26)

    Jesus continually looks down at Peter in the courtyard, but Peter's eyes do not meet Jesus' until 1.39:00.

    Jesus before the Sanhedrin, 1.39:46

20. Hall of Judgment, 1.40:00

    Jesus before Pilate (Mark 15:1)

        Caiaphas brings him in to Pilate (Matt. 27:20; Luke 23:2–3, 14–22; John 18:37–38; 19:10, 12)

        Hordes of people are clamoring outside.

        Pilate's wife (Matt. 27:19), 1.45:16

        "Bring Barabbas" (Mark 15:7)

21. The Crown of Thorns, 1.47:38

    Roman beatings, with Judas watching

22. "Crucify him!" 1.51:46

    High priest's servant bribes people in the crowd to shout "Crucify him," but not all the Jews can be bribed.

    Barabbas and Jesus are brought before Pilate, 1.52:54

    "Behold the man" (Matt. 27:22; Luke 23:18; John 18:39; 19:5), 1.53:47

    "Crucify him" (Mark 15:14; John 19:6, 15),1.55:25

        Said by Caiaphas to Pilate

        Mary Magdalene in defense of Jesus, 1.56:58

    Pilate washes his hands (Matt. 27:24), 1.58:52

    Judas returns Caiaphas the thirty pieces of silver (Matt. 27:4), 1.59:33

23. The Way of the Cross, 2.01:26

    A dog walks by as the cross scrapes across the pavement.

    The two thieves (Luke 23:32)

    Peter and the other disciples watch Jesus pass by, 2.03:32

    Mary his mother and John the beloved disciple, 2.03:57

    White doves fly by, 2.04:28

    Jesus heals a lame man, 2.04:35

    Simon of Cyrene and Mark (Mark 15:21), 2.05:05

24. Calvary, 2.07:53

    (Luke 23:33)

    Judas readies himself for death, 2.09:18

        The view of Jesus' cross is from Judas's distant perspective.

    Caiaphas stands below the cross, 2.10:40

        "Jesus of Nazareth, King of the Jews" (John 19:20), 2.11:00

(The Greek word for "king" is misspelled.)

"Come down from the cross" (Matt. 27:42; Mark 15:29–30).

Last words of Jesus (Luke 23:34, 39–43), 2.11:56

The mother of the unrepentant thief (Gestas) meets Mary, the mother of Jesus, 2.14:05–2.15:18

25. God's Wrath, 2.15:19

Darkness (Matt. 27:45)

A dog at the foot of the cross, 2.15:50

"He trusted in God" (Matt. 27:43), 2.16:27

"It is finished" (Luke 23:46; John 19:30), 2.17:00

Judas hangs himself, 2.17:37

A crow sits on Gestas's cross, 2.18:49

The Beloved Disciple at the foot of the cross, 2.19:00

Earthquake (Matt. 27:51), 2.19:09

Judas's hanging body falls into the abyss, 2.20:07

The Roman centurion and the spear thrust (Mark 15:39; John 19:34), 2.20:18

Veil of the Temple (Matt. 27:5), 2.20:53

Caiaphas says "I alone am guilty!" 2.21:15

A white dove flies to the cross, 2.22:15

26. The Resurrection, 2.22:42

(in color)

Roman guards hear a sound coming from within the sealed tomb.

White doves, 2.23:32

Roman guards witness the glowing stone.

Mary Magdalene and Jesus' mother come to the tomb (white doves), 2.25:55

Jesus meets his mother outside the tomb.

Mary Magdalene enters the tomb.

"Woman, why weepest thou?" (John 20:13, 15–17), 2.27:36

(Matt. 28:6)

Jesus stands in their midst (Mark 16:15, 17–18; Luke 24:39; John 20:19; 21:15–17, 28–29); 2.29:25

(black and white again)

The boy, Mark, bursts into the room, 2.31:26

Then Thomas enters; then Mary his mother and Mary Magdalene.

Ascension over a modern city, 2.36:25

"Lo, I am with you always" (Matt. 28:20).

# Chapter 6

# King of Kings

*Nicholas Ray, director. 168 mins. Not rated.*
*1961. Warner Home Video, 2003*

### Plot Summary

In the thirty-five-year gap between DeMille's *The King of Kings* and Nicholas Ray's *King of Kings*, some directors made Jesus movies, but major Hollywood studios released none. Hollywood had turned instead to quite profitable "sword and sandal" spectacles like *Quo Vadis* (1951), *Salome* (1953), *The Robe* (1953), and *Ben Hur* (1959). These "biblical" epics were important precursors to Ray's *King of Kings*.

Ray apparently learned from these Bible-related spectacles of the 1950s, for he is the first Hollywood director to make a clean break with the episodic plot structure of earlier Jesus films and the Gospels. He does so by framing the story of Jesus in the larger context of first-century Jewish and Roman politics and by developing into full, round characters two men only briefly mentioned in the Gospels. The first character is the Roman centurion at the foot of the cross (Mark 15:39), whom Ray develops into Lucius, an officer who serves Herod the Great, Herod Antipas, and, later, Pontius Pilate.[1] The second character is Barabbas, the prisoner whom Pilate releases instead of Jesus (Mark 15:6–15). By Ray's hands he becomes a Judean insurgent, attempting to instigate a military revolt in Palestine. In developing the story of these two characters, Ray displaces Jesus from his traditional central position in the Christian story. Dramatic voice-overs often replace the voice of Jesus; most of the miracles are reduced to Lucius's reports of them; and, at the end of the film, the audience is left with only the shadow of the cross. The historical context of the Jesus story, as the opening voice-over by Orson Welles explains, is Rome's oppression of the Jews (seen as a forest of crosses outside Jerusalem) and the Jews' survival through the promise of a coming messiah. Accordingly, Ray contrasts the subsequent Christmas story with the murderous, false kingships of Herod the Great and his son, Herod Antipas. Lucius, the Roman centurion, is responsible for the slaughter of the innocents and later travels to Nazareth as a representative of Herod Antipas, registering people for the tax rolls. There he meets the twelve-year-old Jesus and to his surprise learns that the young boy was born in Bethlehem, about the time of the massacre.

33

Years later, the cruel, ambitious Pilate arrives to govern Judea, hoping to impress his father-in-law Tiberius and to return to Rome with an impressive record of government service. Barabbas, with his band of insurgents and with Judas by his side,[2] plans an attack on Pilate's forces as they are on their way to Jerusalem. Lucius, Herod Antipas, Herod's wife Herodias, and her daughter Salome are on their way to meet Pilate when they see John baptizing people in the Jordan. Lucius tells Herod that John talks about a coming messiah, and Herod tells Lucius that he will have to arrest John before long. Then, in the film's first spectacle, Barabbas and his men attack Pilate's entourage. But Lucius and Herod come to Pilate's aid, and Barabbas and Judas escape into the wilderness.

In the next scene, Jesus meets John and is baptized in the Jordan while Jesus' mother watches. Here, for the first time, Ray presents one of several extreme close-ups of Jesus' startlingly blue eyes. Leaving John, Jesus goes into the wilderness for his trials, where he examines his soul and concludes that the Satan (whom the audience never sees) will not force him to put God to the proof. Although easily overlooked after the film's first spectacle, this scene is the biopic hero's generative conflict. As the hero has now overcome the desire to "test" God, the rest of the film is denouement.[3]

While Jesus is in the wilderness, John the Baptist and one of his disciples (later identified as John, who becomes Jesus' "beloved disciple") travel to Nazareth to find out more about Jesus. John the Baptist tells Mary that Jesus is "without sin" and that although he himself preaches in the desert, "the word must be brought to Jerusalem." Mary tells him that Jesus will do that, in his time.

Soon, however, John does go to Jerusalem where he publicly criticizes Pilate for bringing Tiberius's medallions into the Temple and condemns Herod for his marriage to Herodias. After Herod has Lucius arrest John, Jesus begins his ministry—a ministry that the narrator reports as the "time of miracles." Here, Ray offers the audience visuals that privilege Jesus' healing shadow and his compassionate eyes. Judas reports Jesus' success to Barabbas, who is looking for a prophet to inspire revolt. Barabbas and Judas find Jesus standing between a mob and Mary Magdalene, the woman taken in adultery. Jesus, with a little help from Barabbas, stops the stoning, but Barabbas flees from approaching Romans. Left alone in the street, Judas puzzles over the uncast stone, as the narrator states the movie's central dilemma: Should Judas follow Barabbas, the messiah of war, or Jesus, the new messiah of peace?

Jesus visits John in prison and in the process meets Lucius yet again. Jesus tells Lucius that he wants to "free John," but he is talking about "spiritual" freedom, not liberation from "these stone walls." Ominously, Lucius warns Jesus that he will be Jesus' merciless enemy if Jesus breaks Caesar's law. John, who has been in Jerusalem preaching about God's coming judgment, asks Jesus to give him a blessing. When Jesus refuses, John falls to the ground, heartbroken. Before John dies, Lucius also visits John in prison, and John asks him to take a message to Jesus, asking if "his coming was the one foretold." Before Lucius has a chance to return with Jesus' answer, Herod executes John at the request of young Salome.[4]

Having heard Lucius's reports about Jesus' miracles, Pilate sends Lucius as a spy to listen to Jesus' Sermon on the Mount.[5] The sermon, with an audience of thousands (including Judas and Barabbas; Claudia, Pilate's wife; and Mary, Jesus' mother), is the film's central spectacle.[6] The sermon is delivered in response to the crowd's questions, and it borrows widely from the Gospel teachings of Jesus, including the Gospel of John. Notably, it includes another warning not to test God—this in response to someone telling Jesus to destroy the Romans. Lucius summarizes the sermon later for Pilate as a message of "peace, love, and the brotherhood of man." In short, Jesus is a religion teacher and not a threat to Rome's empire. Similarly, Caiaphas does not see Jesus as a serious threat to Jewish politics in Judea. He simply says he will take a wait-and-see approach to Jesus. But Jesus' disciples do not understand so quickly, so Jesus takes them into the wilderness to dispel their desires for a political kingdom and to instill in them his spiritual message. Satisfied with their progress, he sends them out by twos and promises to meet them in Jerusalem. Meanwhile, Barabbas, who has misled Judas about his revolutionary plans, prepares an insurrection at the upcoming Passover celebration.

Before he leaves for Jerusalem, Jesus returns home to Nazareth to see his mother. She has a premonition of his death in Jerusalem, so she decides to join his entourage. Jesus triumphantly arrives in Jerusalem for the Passover and apparently preaches a message of peace in the Temple (although this is not shown).[7] Meanwhile, the Romans crush Barabbas's attempted revolt in the Temple courts. Devastated by Barabbas's failure, Judas decides to "test" the supernatural power of this messiah, forcing Jesus to establish an earthly kingdom by betraying him to the authorities. When Jesus dismisses Judas just before his eucharistic words at the Last Supper, Judas gathers Caiaphas, the Temple police, and a Roman cohort to Gethsemane to arrest the praying, agonizing Jesus.

The film only hints at the Sanhedrin trial and concentrates on the Roman trial. Before Pilate, Jesus stands with bowed head, unconcerned with the events transpiring around him. Pilate appoints Lucius as Jesus' advocate, who defends Jesus against Pilate's charge that he was sent by God to liberate the "Hebrew nation" from Rome. Lucius claims that Jesus spoke only of a spiritual, peaceful kingdom (not one in opposition to Rome).[8] Pilate turns Jesus over to Herod, and after Herod mocks King Jesus, he sends him back to Pilate, who quickly decides to crucify him simply because Jesus is "different" and refuses to obey.[9] As Jesus makes his way to Golgotha, Lucius reviles Barabbas in the dungeons with the story of a better one who dies for him. Lucius then releases Barabbas, who, along with Judas, follows Jesus to Calvary. Although Judas's motives are not clear at this point, he and Barabbas follow Jesus on the Via Dolorosa possibly with the hope that Jesus will reveal his supernatural powers and overthrow the Roman occupation of Judea.

During the remarkably nonviolent crucifixion,[10] which occurs against a forest of crosses (recalling the opening scenes of the film), Jesus utters all but one of the seven last words (omitting only the Johannine "I thirst"). Both Judas and Barabbas watch Jesus die, hoping against hope that Jesus will pull off some last great miracle. But he doesn't. And as Judas walks away, he picks up a stone (just as he did after the attempted stoning of Mary Magdalene) and disappears. After Jesus' death and during the supernatural darkness, Lucius (with Claudia at his side) confesses that Jesus is the Christ. When Barabbas leaves the site of Jesus' crucifixion he finds Judas's corpse hanging from a tree. The limb breaks, and Barabbas holds Judas in a bleak pietà. After Jesus' deposition and entombment, Mary Magdalene waits at the tomb, and on Easter morning, Jesus appears to her. The narrator reports other appearances, and then Jesus appears (one supposes) to the eleven at the shore of the Sea of Galilee.

The audience hears his Great Commission but sees only a cruciform formed by a shadow stretched across a net lying on the ground (recalling the disciples who were called to be fishers of men [*sic*]).

## Memorable Characters

- Jesus: The most human Jesus in film up to its time, Ray's Jesus reflects the liberal Christ of nineteenth-century Protestant historical criticism, preaching "peace, love, and the brotherhood of man." He apparently teaches in the Temple, but does nothing to disturb its economy (cf. Mark 11:15–19; 13:1–2; John 2:13–20) or the priesthood. Jesus does not confront his opponents or call them hypocrites, nor does he say anything objectionable about Roman taxation (cf. Mark 12:13–17). He makes no embarrassing apocalyptic pronouncements. Although there are many reports of his spectacular miracles, the Sermon on the Mount functions as his failed inauguration because he rejects all attempts to turn him into a political leader. If it weren't for Judas and Pilate, Jesus would not have died.
- Barabbas: He provides Jesus' foil as the violent messiah, with Judas being the link between the story of the two messiahs.
- Judas: He resembles the Judas imagined by Thomas de Quincey (1785–1859). Judas is a compatriot of Barabbas who attempts to force Jesus into a corner where he will have to reveal his supernatural powers. He and Barabbas follow Jesus on the Via Dolorosa and watch him die, waiting for Jesus to do something, but he doesn't. The disconsolate Judas commits suicide, and his death is mourned by Barabbas.
- Mary, mother of Jesus: She is surely the oldest cinematic Mary ever to give birth to the Christ child. She knows more of Jesus' purpose than Jesus does, is there for all the important turning points of his life, and completes Jesus' ministry when he is absent (welcoming the sinner, Mary Magdalene, and offering her a place at her table).
- Pilate: Ray offers one of the most politically ambitious, coldly calculating Pilate figures in film. Only Scorsese's Pilate in *The Last Temptation of Christ* comes close, but that Pilate is only on screen for a few minutes. Notably, Ray's Pilate never says that Jesus is innocent, nor are there any Jewish crowds "manipulating" his emotions or his judicial decisions.
- Lucius: He is the most important character for the secular audience of the film's day. He is the eyes and ears of the imperial audience. He is a cynical political realist and an atheist through much of the film, but he tries to "rule" fairly, functioning as Jesus' advocate in Jesus' trial before Pilate. With Claudia, Pilate's wife, Lucius kneels at the foot of Jesus' cross saying, "He is truly the Christ" (cf. Mark 15:39). Curiously, this is the last time Lucius is seen in the film. Perhaps, like the modern-day liberal Christian, he simply does not need to see the resurrected Christ in order to believe.[11]

## Memorable Visuals

- Hillside of crosses, the dead rolling down the mountain to pyres
- Herod's death
- Jesus' blue eyes in extreme close-up (as well as Judas's)
- The shadow of Jesus (numerous times)
- The (expanded, dialogic) Sermon on the Mount
- Jesus letting go of John the Baptist's hand, allowing John to fall back into the dungeon
- Salome's dance, with a leering Herod Antipas. The jeweled ornament in Salome's navel ensures the film will make it past the Hays Code censors, who prohibit showing navels on-screen.
- Jesus with bowed head, as Pilate and Lucius decide his fate
- Jesus' agony in the garden
- Pilate's men dragging off the corpse of one of Barabbas's insurgents just as Jesus is led to Pilate
- Judas looking down from rooftops on Jesus as he walks the Via Dolorosa—most of which is shot from Judas's point of view
- Mary Magdalene looking at "the place where they laid him"
- The shadow-cross resurrection appearance (cf. DeMille's concluding, modern, risen Jesus)

## Key Scriptures

Ray's tale of the two messiahs hints at the two men named Jesus mentioned in Matt. 27:16–17. Nonetheless, the Sermon on the Mount (Matt. 5–7, with additions from the other three Gospels), which Lucius summarizes as a message of peace, is the Scripture around which the film's plot revolves. With Luke 2:1–2; 3:1–2, Ray sets the story of Jesus firmly within the context of Roman and Jewish political history.

## Cultural Location/Genre: Biblical Epic, Sword-and-Sandal Spectacle

Following the heyday of the successful biblical epics (particularly, the 1930s and 1950s), Ray decided to present the story of Jesus as a spectacle with an integrated plot line. He does so with two major battle scenes, Salome's dance, a spectacular Sermon on the Mount,[12] and the two central fictitious characters: Lucius and Barabbas.

Unfortunately, Ray's film was too late to be well received. American culture was beginning to change in the early 1960s, with racial concerns at home and concerns about how best to curtail Soviet power in Cuba and Asia starting to divide the nation. Perhaps, aware of the changing times, Ray tailors his film for his more "modern" audience in three important ways. First, he presents the film through the filter of Orson Welles's "historical" narration, which recognizes the distance between the Jesus story and the viewing audience.[13] Second, Ray provides a way for secular audiences to connect with the film through the decent but somewhat skeptical Lucius. Third, in a nod to the postwar baby-boomer generation, Ray provides his viewing audience with a far-more-youthful Jesus (Jeffrey Hunter) than any of his predecessors. Likewise John, the Beloved Disciple, fills the role of the responsible teenage boy while Salome fills the role of the sulkily rebellious and sexually dangerous teenage girl.

Faced with an America troubled by issues of war, violence at home, and growing imperial oppression, Ray's film—like the biblical epics of the 1950s—continues to fight the Cold War while hinting at the growing "generation gap." Thus, Ray's film sets Jesus in the violent context of empire rather than in the sexual context of DeMille's *The King of Kings* or Scorsese's *The Last Temptation of Christ*. For example, Ray's Mary Magdalene (the woman taken in adultery) is far more demure than DeMille's Magdalene, and Ray keeps her at a safe distance from Jesus throughout the film. Jesus' mother, not Jesus, is the one who "converts" the Magdalene. The teenage girl, Salome, on the other hand, becomes the dangerous female, who, of her own volition, asks for the head of John the Baptist.

If DeMille offered his viewing audiences a Jesus with whom American capitalists would be comfortable, Ray offers his audiences a Jesus with whom American imperialists would be comfortable. Ray does this by focalizing Jesus through Lucius, the American imperial audience's eyes and ears. Yet Ray's Pilate character seems to echo the McCarthy-inspired fears of the 1950s motion picture industry with his jaded reasoning for crucifying Jesus. "He is different and refuses to behave like others," says Pilate. Notably, "democracy" (the Jewish crowds) is not involved in crucifying Ray's Jesus. Rather, that role belongs to the bureaucratic Pilate, a life-long politician who hopes soon to get back to the center of power (Rome). If he can control these Jews on the eastern edge of the Roman Empire (or the eastern seaboard of the United States?), he just might become the next emperor.

## Director

Nicholas Ray was protected from being blacklisted in the 1950s by Howard Hughes, who bankrolled a number of his films. But Ray was a left-leaning liberal throughout much of his life, and his perspective can be seen in his tales of tortured, alienated figures—often adolescents (e.g., Judas and Salome in *King of Kings*). Of course, his most famous version of the alienated adolescent is in his film *Rebel Without a Cause* (1955).

*Rebel Without a Cause* opens with Jim Stark (James Dean), the new kid in town, publicly drunk. Taken to the police station, he sees the two other troubled youths, Judy (Natalie Wood) and Plato (Sal Mineo), who eventually form his surrogate family. None of the three has a satisfactory father figure. Jim quickly runs afoul of Buzz, Judy's boyfriend, and finds himself in an afternoon knife fight and an evening "chicken run" with Buzz.[14] When Buzz dies accidentally in the race, Buzz's gang turns murderous. Jim, Natalie, and Plato seek refuge from Buzz's gang in a deserted mansion where they pretend to be the happy family they do not have. When the gang finds Plato there, he defends himself with his father's gun and seeks refuge from the gang and the police in a nearby planetarium. Although it seems that Jim is able to take Plato out of the standoff, the police shoot and kill Plato as he comes out of the planetarium holding an unloaded gun.

Compared to the Jesus characters of earlier films, Ray's Jesus is, like Jim Stark, quite youthful. In fact, critics lampooned the film when it was released by dubbing it *I Was a Teenage Jesus*. The film fits the emerging youth culture of the 1960s and American social anxieties about young people. Unlike Jim, however, Ray's Jesus is unusually calm and submissive to his (divine) father.[15] That calmness gives *King of Kings* a serenity that *Rebel Without a Cause* never attains. Like Jim, Jesus provides a surrogate family for his disciples in tumultuous times. But it is Ray's Judas, who is the alienated figure struggling to find a father figure (between Barabbas and Jesus), that resonates most strongly with Ray's *Rebel Without a Cause*. In fact, Judas is another version of Ray's Plato.

## DVD Extras and Technical Features

Cast and Crew
The Camera's Window to the World (3:57 minutes long)
    Planning for the Sermon on the Mount scene
*King of Kings*—Impressive Premiere on Two Coasts (1:45 minutes long)
*King of Kings*: Egyptian Theater Premiere, Hollywood, CA (1:09 minutes long)
Theatrical Trailer (1:39 minutes long)
Languages
    Spoken: English, French
    Subtitles: English, French, Spanish

## DVD Chapters (The appearances of Lucius are in italics)

1. Overture
2. Credits, 3:47
3. Fallen Jerusalem, 6:12
    Rome captures Jerusalem, 63 BCE.
4. Herod's Forests, 10:50
    Fifty years later. Herod, king of the Jews
    Jewish rebellions, forests of crosses, 12:14
    A promised messiah
5. A Bethlehem Stable, 12:53
    Note the fleeting view of a pregnant Mary (14:18), as befitting Hays Code restrictions.
6. Crown of Murder, 16:02
    Slaughter of innocents (Matt. 2:16–18), 16:50
        (*Lucius* in charge)
7. The Census, 20:50
    In Nazareth, when Jesus is twelve
        (*Lucius* meets Jesus)
8. Pontius Pilate, 23:11
    Twenty years have passed; Barabbas the zealot
        Judas is with Barabbas's band of insurgents, but is not named.
    John the Baptist, 26:55
        (*Lucius* sees John.)
9. Ambushing the Romans, 28:33
    Judas is with Barabbas's band of insurgents, but is not identified.
10. John Meets Jesus, 33:00
    Mary, Jesus' mother, watches the baptism.
    John the Baptist meets Mary—"he is without sin."
        John, a young man, Jesus' future disciple, is with the Baptist.

11. Desert Temptation, 36:48
12. Fisher of Men, 41:16
    John's disciples, John and Andrew, follow Jesus, 41:26.
    Calling of Simon, "who shall be called Peter," 42:05
13. Voice of an Agitator, 43:09
    Caesar's plaques in Jerusalem (*Lucius* and Pilate)
14. John Imprisoned, 48:06
    *Lucius* arrests John the Baptist.
15. Healer at Work, 51:58
16. Uncast Stone, 54:48
    Judas introduced in conversation with Barabbas.
      "Jesus speaks only of peace."
    Mary Magdalene, 57:03
    Two messiahs for Judas—one of peace, one of war
17. Familiar Face, 59:47
    Jesus, wanting to see John the Baptist, meets *Lucius.*
    "You place faith in nothing but your sword."
18. Blessing through Bars, 1.02:18
    Jesus meets John, who is in prison.
      "Give me your blessing."
19. Madman and Magdalene, 1.04:01
    Magdalene meets Mary the mother of Jesus, 1.05:35
20. So It Is Reported, 1.07:52
21. John's Request, 1.10:38
    *Lucius* visits John the Baptist in prison.
22. Whatever Salome Wants, 1.12:30
    Pilate is present.
23. Salome's Dance, 1.15:29
24. Head on a Platter, 1.17:41
25. Message to John, 1.19:50
26. A Great Multitude, 1.21:51
    *Lucius*, Pilate, and Herod: "All over Galilee the disciples of Jesus are calling for a gathering to hear him speak."
    Pilate tells *Lucius* to go hear Jesus' Sermon on the Mount.
27. Sermon on the Mount, 1.25:09
    Barabbas's insurgents are there, as well as *Lucius.*
    (A combination of Matthew 5–7 and Luke 6)
    "Give us a sign from heaven" (Luke 11:16).
    Mary, his mother, and Mary Magdalene are there.
    "When is the kingdom of God coming?"
    "The Kingdom of God is within you." (Luke 17:20–21), 1.27:42
    "What must I do to inherit eternal life?" (Mark 10:17), 1.27:57
      (Greatest Commandment)
    "Who can I call neighbor?" (Luke 10:29), 1.28:24
    "Are you the messiah?" 1.28:35
    "I am the good shepherd" (John 10:1–18).
    "Why do you eat and drink with sinners?" (Mark 2:16), 1.29:14
    "No man can serve two masters," 1.29:37
    "Come to me all you who labor" (Matt. 11:28), 1.30:50
    "The Son of Man comes to serve" (Mark 10:45), 1.31:15
    "Whoever will be first must be slave of all" (Matt. 20:26; Mark 10:43–44; Luke 22:26–27).
    "A kingdom divided against itself" (Matt. 12:25–26; Mark 3:20–21; Luke 11:17–18), 1.31:36

"If I am not doing the deeds of my father, do not believe me" (John 10:37–38), 1.32:06

"Destroy the Romans and free our people!" 1.32:28

"Thou shalt not tempt the Lord thy God" (Matt. 4:7).

"Faith of a mustard seed" (Matt. 17:20; Luke 17:6), 1.32:44

"Do not judge," 1.33:04

"This is the law *of* the prophets."

28. The Lord's Prayer, 1.35:05

29. Reactions, 1.37:44

*Lucius* to Pilate and Herod: "He spoke of peace, love, and the brotherhood of man."

Caiaphas and Nicodemus, 1.38:46

30. Jesus and the Apostles, 1.39:16

Choosing the twelve (Matt. 10:1–4)

"Why not a messiah to strike Judea free?"

Jesus' task: to keep his disciples from the doubting cities.

"Receive without payment" (Matt. 10:8, 16–23), 1.41:13

31. Fire and Water, 1.41:54

*Lucius* uncovers Barabbas's weapons "factory."

Judas (with Barabbas) has a plan to make Jesus king.

32. Intermission, 1.45:30

33. Entr'acte, 1.46:15

34. Eyes toward Jerusalem, 1.50:35

*Lucius* and Pilate: The work of Barabbas and Jesus

Jesus and his mother, 1.51:56

Peter and John stop by.

"The chair will never be mended."

35. Entry into the City, 1.53:28

36. To the Slaughter, 1.55:58

37. "I will force His hand," 2.01:02

Judas and the insurgents

38. The Last Supper, 2.02:49

Judas, the last to arrive, 2.03:09

Judas leaves before the Eucharist.

39. Garden Torment, 2.08:38

Judas at Caiaphas's house, 2.08:42

Judas, the Temple police, and the Romans join together, 2.09:49

Judas, the Temple police, and the Romans, 2.12:10

40. Betrayed and Denied, 2.13:00

Judas arrives with Temple guards and the Romans.

41. On Trial, 2.16:16

"He has been judged by Caiaphas guilty on two counts," 2.16:58

*Lucius* as Jesus' advocate

"Jesus' claim to a divine mission does not challenge the authority of Rome."

Recalling the Sermon on the Mount

42. "What is truth?" 2.20:52

43. Still Made of Clay, 2.22:25

Before Herod (priests are present)

44. Scourged and Crowned, 2.25:41

Claudia to Pilate: "What is his crime?"

"He is different and refuses to behave like the others."

(A black man involved in scourging Jesus)

Judas listens to the scourging and watches crosses being made.

45. Free Men, 2.28:27

*Lucius* asks Barabbas if he knows Jesus.

Barabbas is released.

Why? "Your followers yelled the loudest."

46. Procession to Calvary, 2.32:05

Mary, his mother, Mary Magdalene, and John, the beloved disciple, watch.

(Silence; there are no shouting crowds)

47. Crucifixion, 2.35:27

Judas and Barabbas watch

Claudia, Pilate's wife, watches, as do Mary and John.

48. "It is finished," 2.38:36

49. Bodies Claimed, 2.41:00

*Lucius* and Claudia kneel: "He is truly the Christ."

Thunder (Herod had asked Jesus to "Make it thunder.")

Barabbas finds Judas's body after he has hung himself.

50. "He is risen," 2.44:31

51. With You Always, 2.46:33

52. Exit Music, 2.48:39

## Chapter 7

# The Gospel According to Saint Matthew

*Pier Paolo Pasolini, director. 142 mins. Not rated. 1965. Waterbearer Films, 2003*

## Plot Summary

Pasolini released this film in Italy in 1964. He consciously rejected the 1950–60s Hollywood conventions of the biblical epic with their integrated plotlines by producing a Jesus film in black and white, using an untrained cast, and following one Gospel "exclusively." Pasolini shot the film in southern Italy because the terrain and villages reminded him of first-century Palestine.[1] He used a neorealist documentary style exemplified by long periods of silence and sharp cuts between scenes that mimics Matthew's own episodic structure. In fact, Pasolini follows Matthew so closely that the film is difficult for viewers to follow without having some knowledge of the Gospel.

Skipping over the genealogy of Jesus (Matt. 1:1–17), Pasolini opens his film with a close-up of a pregnant peasant girl.[2] She looks at an older man who turns away from her and leaves. Later, as he sleeps, another peasant girl in white (an angel) tells him to take Mary as his wife. As he goes back to Mary, a narrator quotes Isa. 7:14, and the reunited Joseph and Mary smile. Except for the angel, the characters do not speak. The visuals, the narrator (and angel), and the background music carry the message *for the viewer who knows Matthew.* After the wise men's visit, the angelic peasant girl tells the holy family to go to Egypt. As a result, the holy family escapes Herod's slaughter of the innocents. After Herod's gruesome death,[3] the young peasant angel sends the holy family back to Israel.

The subsequent John the Baptist scene establishes a major theme of the film: the man of the people is one who opposes oppressive leaders. John's repentance harangue targets, in particular, religious leaders whom the camera watches as they pass by. After John's words about "the one who will baptize with fire," Pasolini offers the first close-up (and appearance) of the adult Jesus. After his baptism, Jesus goes into the wilderness where a richly dressed Satan tempts him. Having dispatched Satan, Jesus begins his ministry as John languishes in prison.

In the film's second major departure from Matthew's script,[4] Pasolini opens Jesus' ministry with Jesus warning his new disciples that they will be sheep in the midst of wolves and that he will bring a sword to their world (10:16–20, 22, 28–31, 34–37, 39).[5] Omitting much of the "religious" material in Matt. 10, Pasolini's Jesus prepares his followers for a fierce, political struggle. Jesus himself is agitated, angry, confrontational, and alienated. Pasolini films the speech sequence with Jesus walking down a road and looking back at his followers only intermittently. After healing a leper, an isolated Jesus delivers the Sermon on the Mount. No audience appears on the screen except at the beginning and end of the sermon. Pasolini presents the sermon as a series of disconnected teachings by reordering the sermon and by filming Jesus speaking the words in various clothing, with various lighting, and against various backgrounds. Once again, Pasolini's version is less religious and more political than Matthew's sermon. As a result, Jesus' offer of liberation differs from that of Matthew (Matt. 11:28–30).

Miracles[6] and conflicts with the religious leaders over matters of the law follow, and as a result, the religious leaders decide that Jesus is demonic and should be killed. Meanwhile, Jesus also becomes more confrontational: "Whoever is not with me is against me," he says; he pronounces judgments on various cities and dismisses his family and hometown in favor of those who do the will of God;[7] and he sends a rich man and other would-be disciples away. The increasingly angry, violent Jesus is happy only with children (whom Pasolini adds to the film at every opportunity). Ominously, during this section of the film, Herod kills John.

Part 2 opens with the narrator's words about judgment—words found nowhere in the Gospel of Matthew. Peter then makes his confession, and Jesus repeatedly predicts his upcoming death. Pasolini's Jesus speaks selections from Matt. 18 that emphasize humility and forgiveness, and children are again present. After the triumphal entry, Jesus cleanses the Temple under the religious leaders' watchful eyes. While confrontational with the leaders, Jesus smiles when he is among the crowds and with the children, who offer their hosannas to Jesus.

Outside the city, Jesus curses a fig tree, which withers immediately (as Judas notes). And after further controversies with the religious leaders, Jesus delivers a final harangue (Matt. 23, a passage which Pasolini follows more faithfully than any other Matthean discourse). On this occasion Jesus has an audience, and Pasolini films Jesus from a vantage point behind the crowd. Pasolini moves the camera away from Jesus to show approaching soldiers and to focus on the crowds and the city as he speaks about righteous blood (Matt. 23:25) and Jerusalem's desolation (Matt. 23:37–38).[8] Subsequently, and not surprisingly, the leaders plot Jesus' death while Pasolini offers another shot of the withered fig tree. After a woman anoints Jesus and Judas complains,[9] Jesus' response sends an angry Judas to the Temple for a traitorous deal that leaves him smiling.

Jesus' betrayal and arrest are followed by the Jewish trial, which Pasolini shoots from the crowd's perspective with a hand-held camera.[10] As a result, the viewer sees Peter's denial clearly but can hardly see or hear Jesus. The established powers have devoured Jesus, and Judas, in remorse, repents and hangs himself (from yet another barren tree). During Jesus' trial before Pilate, Pasolini includes the heinous "let his blood be on us and on our children," but the speaker is not on screen. On the Via Dolorosa and at Calvary, Pasolini emphasizes Mary's suffering,[11] rather than Jesus'. In fact, Pasolini presents the viewer with more visuals of Mary during Jesus' passion than any of his precursors.

At the cross, the film fades to black, and a narrator reads Isa. 6:9–10. As a result, the words address the audience as well as Jesus' contemporaries. After Jesus' death, an earthquake destroys the city. Following the deposition and entombment, Mary mourns. The mourners return on the third morning. The rock falls away; Mary smiles; and the mysterious peasant (angel) girl from the opening announces the resurrection. The audience hears the Great Commission, and then sees Jesus with his disciples.[12]

## Memorable Characters

- Jesus: This is the angriest Jesus shown on screen to date. Jesus (and perhaps John the Baptist) is the Gramscian intellectual/artist[13] who provides the downtrodden with a revolutionary myth. Jesus is young, meticulously groomed, and clean—unlike the peasants and poor who are attracted to him. He does not appear to have ever worked outdoors at hard, physical labor; yet his opening message, unprecedented in the history of Jesus films, is one full of challenges and struggle.
- Peasants: Jesus' family, his disciples, and the children are merely abstractions of Pasolini's ideology. They represent the oppressed.
- The Jewish leaders: They represent those who oppress the people. However, their outlandish hats do not evoke a Jewish context but rather the Christian hierarchy, as they are the hats of Christian leaders in a series of medieval frescoes from Piero's *Legend of the True Cross* cycle, found in the Church of San Francesco in Arezzo, Italy. According to Christopher Fuller, Pasolini's hats evoke the context of the medieval Christian crusades and Piero's depiction of Emperor Heraclius's return of the cross to Jerusalem.[14]
- Mary (the mother of Jesus): She alone is more than a flat character. She has multiple traits and expresses a variety of emotions.
- Judas: Aspects of his character are drawn from the Gospel of John. He keeps the money bag and is upset at the extravagance of ointment used at Jesus' anointing in Bethany. He watches Jesus' trial before the Sanhedrin and afterwards repents and commits suicide.
- John, the disciple: Aspects of his character are drawn from the Gospel of John. He is the Johannine Beloved Disciple—young, effeminate, drawn from the ranks of John the Baptist's disciples to follow Jesus, and held close by both Jesus and his mother.

## Memorable Visuals

- Jesus' peasant family
- Slaughter of the innocents in Bethlehem; Herod's death
- Jesus' angry, violent, confrontational face (with the leaders)
- Jesus smiling with children
- Three-shot healings (the problem, Jesus, the cured)
- Barren trees
- Jesus lost from view (devoured, if you will) by the powers behind his Jewish trial

- The medieval headgear of Jesus' adversaries
- Jesus' failure to touch any of the people whom he heals

## Key Scripture

Pasolini uses Matthew as his script,[15] interpreting it with visuals and music. His removal of Matthew from the canon—along with his selections and his rearrangements of Matt. 5–7; 10; 23—present the viewer with a strikingly materialist, political Gospel. Accordingly, his Jesus is a violent prophet—by far the most violent Jesus on film, railing against the establishments of all times. Pasolini himself claimed that it was Jesus' words about bringing a sword (Matt. 10:34) that led him to make the film. Matthew 23—the only discourse included in its entirety in the film—is particularly important for Pasolini. It is the peasant leader's denunciation of the established powers, and it exposes the established powers' rationale for killing Jesus.

## Cultural Location/Genre: Docudrama

Pasolini felt that Marxism had failed to liberate the Italian people. He made *The Gospel According to St. Matthew* to reinvigorate Marxism with the new Catholicism of Pope John XXIII, to whom Pasolini dedicated the film.[16] The attempt to construct a new myth for the common people also locates Pasolini with Antonio Gramsci's Marxism. For Gramsci, artists and intellectuals can create national-popular myths that will lead the people to social reform. Pasolini reinvents Matthew as such a Gramscian Gospel. Of course, Pasolini also reinvents Jesus as the people's intellectual leader, a social reformer, and an artist (poet) like Pasolini himself.

Pasolini's documentary-style treatment of his Matthean national-popular myth allowed the Roman Catholic Church to embrace the film as a "documentary" treatment of its truth. In fact, a recent Vatican list of the best films of all time included *The Gospel According to St. Matthew*—the only Jesus film on the list. Religious academics also often describe Pasolini's film as the best Jesus film ever produced. Perhaps it is because Pasolini's angry social reformer—who criticizes society but does not actually induce social reform—mirrors some academics' own perception of their role in society. This mirror is particular apt for the American historical Jesus critics of the last third of the twentieth century who abandoned an apocalyptic Jesus for a social prophet/cynic Jesus.

## Director

Pasolini's early films (for example, *Accattone* [1961], *Mamma Rosa* [1962]) depict the fate of the people at the hands of a callous establishment in a "reverential," mythologizing style. The style reached its height and an ironic treatment in Pasolini's *La ricotta* [1962], the short that Pasolini directed to be included in *RoGoPaG* (which was composed of shorts by three other important European directors: Rossellini, Godard, and Gregoretti [1962]).

In Pasolini's segment, Orson Welles directs the filming of a passion play. Pasolini contrasts the abundance of food for the crew with the chronically hungry Stracci, who plays the good thief. Ironically, Stracci dies not from hunger but from gorging himself on ricotta cheese. Even more ironically, he dies on the cross—during the supernatural thunder and lightning intended for the filmed passion—while the crew, with their backs to Stracci on the cross, discuss matters related to the filming. The contrast between the fake (filmed) passion (in color) and the real passion of the hungry people like Stracci (in black and white) is dramatic. The crew does not notice the passion (suffering) of Stracci—who represents the suffering of the downtrodden. After all, their suffering is too common to be noteworthy. The film crew knows that Stracci has died only when he fails to follow the film (and Gospel) script and ask Jesus to remember him.

Jesus' death in *The Gospel According to St. Matthew* is somewhat different. Those in power "notice" him and deliberately dispatch him. But, as noted, Pasolini's camera does lose sight of Jesus somewhat at this point. Pasolini films the trial from behind the crowd, from the perspective of the people. Thus, the bureaucratic machinery seems to devour Jesus, just as it does Stracci. Jesus' resurrection also distinguishes him from Stracci. Pasolini obviously hoped that Jesus' liberating message might still make a difference for the oppressed. The uncaring power establishment continues, however, as Stracci's fate illustrates. Sadly, Jesus' successors are the victims of a capitalist, consumer society.[17]

## DVD Extras and Technical Features

Widescreen. Italian with English subtitles. No English dubbed track. No DVD chapters.
*Pier Paolo Pasolini: A Filmmaker's Life,* thirty minutes, English. Documentary. Includes some of Pasolini's reflections on the making of *Il Vangelo secondo Matteo.*

> On *The Gospel of Matthew,* 12:50–14:50
> On religious experience and the power of the Catholic Church in Italy, 21:15-24:10
> On his fascination with the Italian peasantry, 26:00-27:00
> Credits 27:58

## DVD Segments

There are no DVD chapters, so the DVD segments that follow are those of the authors. Wherever possible, the titles of the DVD segments are from the *HarperCollins Study Bible* (NRSV). Numbers in parentheses are chapters and verses in Matthew. The italicized phrases denote motifs in the film that are drawn from the Gospel of John.

1. Birth of Jesus the Messiah (1:18), 3:04
2. Visit of the Wise Men (2:1), 6:40
3. Escape to Egypt (2:13), 14:55
4. Massacre of the Infants (2:16), 17:20
5. Return to Nazareth (2:19), 20:00
6. Proclamation of John the Baptist (3:1), 22:47
     *John (the youngest disciple) is there, as is his brother James,* 23:41
7. Baptism of Jesus (3:13), 26:25
8. Temptation of Jesus (4:1), 28:35
9. Jesus Begins His Ministry in Galilee (4:12), 32:00
     John the Baptist in prison, 32:03
     "Repent, for the kingdom of heaven is at hand" (4:17), 33:37
10. Jesus Calls the First Disciples (4:18), 33:55

Peter, Andrew

James, John, 34:45

11. Harvest is Great, the Laborers Few (9:35), 35:45

12. Twelve Apostles (10:1), 36:00

   13. Coming Persecutions (10:16)

   14. Have No Fear (10:26)

   15. Cost of Discipleship (10:34), 38:35

   16. Jesus Cleanses a Leper (8:1), 38:44

   17. Beatitudes (5:1), 41:35

   18. Instructions on Conduct and Prayer (7:7)

   19. Fulfilling the Law and the Prophets (5:17)

   20. Salt and Light (5:13)

   21. Orientation to God (6:19)

   22. Piety that God Rewards (6:1)

   23. Jesus' Teaching Alters the Law (5:38)

   24. Instructions on Conduct and Prayer (7:1)

   25. Piety that God Rewards (6:5)

   26. Orientation to God (6:25)

   27. Jesus as Wisdom's Spokesperson (11:25)

28. Plucking Grain on the Sabbath (12:1), 48:00

   Eating olives on the Sabbath

   *Judas keeps the money bag.*

29. Man with a Withered Hand (12:10), 50:02

   Jesus heals a lame man on the Sabbath rather than a man with a withered hand (cf., 11:5; John 5).

30. God's Chosen Servant (12:15)

31. Man with the Withered Hand (12:14), 51:50

   But the Pharisees went out and conspired against him, on how to destroy him.

32. Feeding the Five Thousand (14:13), 52:07

33. Jesus Walks on the Water (14:22), 54:20

34. Messengers from John the Baptist (11:2), 55:47

35. Woes to Unrepentant Cities (11:20), 58:52

36. Sign of Jonah (12:38), 1.00:00

37. True Kindred of Jesus (12:46), 1.00:46

   The disciple John introduces the subject.

   His mother Mary is there.

38. Rejection of Jesus at Nazareth (13:54), 1.02:34

   His mother Mary is there.

39. Rich Young Man (19:16), 1.05:20

40. Jesus Blesses Little Children (19:13), 1.07:17

   "Christ, bless our children."

   Judas tells children to "leave him in peace."

41. Death of John the Baptist (14:1), 1.07.55

   Salome, her mother, and the dance, 1.08:40

42. Would-be Followers of Jesus (8:18), 1.13:00

   "Howl O gate, cry out O city

   Suffer, Palestine, for a river is coming . . ."

   43. The Narrow and the Wide Gates (7:13)

44. Peter's Declaration about Jesus (16:13), 1.14:50

45. Jesus Foretells His Death and Resurrection (16:21), 1.16.11

46. Jesus Again Foretells His Death and Resurrection (17:22), 1.17:10

47. True Greatness (18:1), 1.17:23

"Unless you become like little children"
48. "If your hand or foot offend you" (5:29–30)
49. Parable of the Lost Sheep (18:10), 1.18:45
50. Forgiveness (18:21), 1.19:07
51. Jesus Again Foretells His Death and Resurrection (17:22), 1.20:00
52. Triumphal Entry into Jerusalem (21:1), 1.20:50
    Lots of children
53. Jesus Cleanses the Temple (21:12), 1.24:19
    Followed by children into the Temple, shouting "Hosanna!"
54. Jesus Curses the Fig Tree (21:18), 1.26:14
    Praying over Jerusalem
55. Authority of Jesus Challenged (21:23), 1.29:00
56. Parable of the Two Sons (21:28), 1.29:55
57. Parable of the Wicked Tenants (21:33), 1.30:44
    58. Parable of the Wedding Banquet (22:1)
    Parable missing but included is "Many are called, few are chosen" (22:14), 1.32:15
59. Question about Paying Taxes (22:15), 1.32:50
60. On the Resurrection of the Dead (22:23), 1.33:40
61. Greatest Commandment (22:34), 1.34:54
62. Jesus Denounces Scribes and Pharisees (23:1), 1.35:26
    Soldiers come to listen.
    Jesus' words create a riot.
63. Lament over Jerusalem (23:37), 1.40:50
64. Destruction of the Temple Foretold (24:1), 1.41:50
65. Plot to Kill Jesus (26:1), 1.42:00
    Another view of the dried-up fig tree (21:19), 1.42:50
66. Anointing at Bethany (26:6), 1.43:00
    *John (the "Beloved Disciple") is next to Jesus, on his right.*
    *Judas is the disciple who challenges Jesus about the poor.*
67. Judas Agrees to Betray Jesus (26:14), 1.45:45
68. Passover with the Disciples (26:20), 1.46:20
69. Institution of the Lord's Supper (26:26), 1.47:25
70. Peter's Denial Foretold (26:30), 1.48:56
    *John is beside Jesus as the disciples leave the "upper room."*
71. Jesus Prays in Gethsemane (26:36), 1.49:50
    *Jesus hugs John.*
72. Betrayal and Arrest of Jesus (26:47), 1.53:38
    Judas hugs Jesus—*no kiss.*
    Peter follows from a distance.
73. Jesus before the High Priest (26:57), 1.56:25
    Guilty of blasphemy, Jesus should die.
    Jesus is beaten on the way to Pilate.
74. Peter's Denial of Jesus (26:69), 1.57:58
75. Jesus Brought before Pilate (27:1), 1.59:50
    Judas watches as the high priest condemns Jesus to death.
76. Suicide of Judas (27:3), 2:01:05
    Judas apparently hangs himself near where John the Baptist was baptizing.
77. Pilate Questions Jesus (27:11), 2.02:33
    *Mary, the mother of Jesus, looks on; John ("the other disciple" [cf., John 18:15–16]) weeps, and is*
        *hugged by Mary. She tries to hold him back as he goes into Pilate's chambers.*
    "His blood be on our children!" (27:25), 2.04:08
78. Soldiers Mock Jesus (27:27), 2.04:15

*Roman soldiers mock Jesus.*
*John and Mary follow Jesus to Calvary.*
*Mary hugs John again.*

79. Crucifixion of Jesus (27:32), 2.06:48
    *John and the three Marys watch Jesus being crucified.*

80. Death of Jesus (27:45), 2.10:00
    Quotation from Isaiah 6:9–10 (13:14–15)
    Earthquake
    Darkness

81. Burial of Jesus (27:57), 2.12:01
    *John, the three Marys, and two others (Joseph of Arimathea? Nicodemus?) watch the deposition.*
    John, Mary the mother, and another Mary(?) wrap the body.

82. Guard at the Tomb (27:62), 2.14:11

83. Resurrection of Jesus (28:1), 2.14:35
    The three Marys, *Peter, and John are there when the stone is rolled away* (albeit without the Matthean angel).

84. Commissioning of the Disciples (28:16), 2.15:55

85. Credits, 2.16:19

Chapter 8

# The Greatest Story Ever Told

*George Stevens, director. Not rated. 194 mins.*
*1965. MGM Home Entertainment, 2001*

### Plot Summary

Stevens's epic film returns Jesus to his central position as portrayed in the canonical Gospels. But Stevens attempts to tell the story of Jesus' life through an integrated plot that emphasizes the broad scope of Jewish and Roman politics in Palestine and the fulfillment of prophecy; and develops Jesus' personal relationship with his friends, Mary, Martha, and Lazarus, and with his disciples Judas and Peter. All this he sets against the grand landscapes of the American West.

The film opens with the camera panning the interior of a Byzantine church. The camera finds a priestly icon of Christ, and a narrator reads John 1:1–5 (to which Jesus' voice adds, "I am he"). The screen then fades to a night sky, and the narrator speaks of light shining in the darkness. A bright star becomes the flame of a flickering oil lamp in a cattle stall,[1] and thus the Christ child arrives in a dark world[2] as the narrator intones, "The greatest story ever told."

Surprisingly, the first characters Stevens introduces are not Mary and Joseph but Herod the Great and his son, Herod Antipas. Herod is a cold, calculating ruler, and so after the magi meet him and tell him of a newborn king's star, Herod's men follow the magi to Bethlehem. As the shepherds look on the Christ child, Herod's soldiers appear on the horizon. Joseph has also seen Herod's men, and an internal voice tells him to take the child and flee to Egypt. When the soldiers return to Herod and give him the message that the magi were in Bethlehem, Herod says that he also knows the Scriptures, and he intends to fulfill Jeremiah's tragic prophecy of "Rachel weeping for her children" (Jer. 31:15; cf. Matt. 2:18).

After Herod dies, Herod Antipas rules his father's kingdom with even greater recklessness and oppression. But hearing only that Herod the Great is dead, the holy family returns to Nazareth by way of Jerusalem, where Antipas has hung hundreds of crucified victims along the roadside. Mourners chant excerpts from Psalms 61, 103, and 22, while the baby Jesus looks out from his mother's arms in wonder. As a result of Herod Antipas's ruthless reign, the Romans demote him to Galilee, where Jesus will grow up.

Years later in Jerusalem, as the adult Jesus watches from the shadows, people are still crying for a deliverer. Then John the Baptist begins his prophetic ministry. Jesus goes to him to be baptized and afterwards fasts in the wilderness where the Dark Hermit[3] tempts him with the possibility of an "easy life." Stevens restructures the three familiar Gospel temptations, ending with Jesus' statement "Not by bread alone," in order to focus on what will be an important element of Jesus' message: Don't worry about food or clothing; God will provide if you have faith.

As dawn breaks, Jesus hears John's message prophesying the coming of a messiah who will turn the land to fruitfulness, who will give light to the blind and joy to the meek and poor, and who will make sure that the needy are not forgotten. Jesus resolutely stands, then climbs on up beyond the hermit's cave to the top of the mountain to embrace the calling of his "hard life."

The scene then shifts back to the Jordan River, the site of John's baptizing, where soldiers come to tell John that the Sanhedrin has ordered him to stop preaching. Judas (not yet identified) tells the soldiers that they ought to repent, because they are the ones who do Caesar's bloody work. Jesus then appears and stands with John the Baptist. John tells his disciples that Jesus is the shepherd, but Jesus brushes him off, saying that those who know him will follow him. Ironically, Judas is the first to follow—but he will never be convinced that Jesus is anything more than a great leader and teacher.

More than any previous director of Jesus films, Stevens focuses on Jesus' teaching. But there is little emphasis on Jesus' picturesque parables or his provocative aphorisms. Nor does Jesus make his death a subject of his message. Instead, as Roman boots tramp on a bridge over his head, Jesus teaches his first followers to "labor for the food of eternal life, which comes from heaven."[4] He encourages them to put away all anxious thoughts about food and clothes, and to stop worrying about the arrival of the kingdom of God, because it is here now, within them (Luke 17:21).[5] Jesus' first teaching session ends the next morning with a humorous conversation between Peter and Jesus about Peter's stolen coat. Unable to persuade Peter of the greater importance of spiritual matters, Jesus finally silences him by offering Peter his own coat.

Soon thereafter, Jesus' conversation with Lazarus (whom Stevens recreates from all of the wealthy inquirers of the Gospels) establishes his long-term relationship with Lazarus and his sisters, Mary and Martha, and clarifies Jesus' rejection of wealth in favor of spiritual matters. However, Jesus' rejection of wealth is not absolute. He maintains that being wealthy is not a crime, but it *may* be burdensome if one is not willing to give up everything.[6] In a subsequent scene with Matthew the tax collector, Jesus teasingly says that because he has only God in his heart, he only has God's love to "declare." Matthew seems confused by Jesus' words but follows him anyway.

Throughout the ministry of Jesus, Stevens cuts repeatedly from Jesus' simple message of trust to images of the watchful, anxious political and religious leaders. Since Herod Antipas had lost most of his father's kingdom to the Romans, he particularly fears the loss of his political position. Jesus' public ministry begins in earnest in Capernaum, where he enters a synagogue and responds to a sermon on judgment (also a common theme in John the Baptist's preaching) with one of his own that emphasizes mercy and forgiveness (cf. Hos. 6:6). Jesus illustrates his point with his first miracle—healing a lame man through the man's own faith.

Back at the Jordan, Herod Antipas's men arrest John as a revolutionary, and John condemns Herod for his adulterous marriage.[7] By now Jesus' fame is spreading, and both Herod and Caiaphas the high priest are apprehensive about Jesus' activities. Herod asks John about Jesus, and Caiaphas sends Sorak (Stevens's invented character) and Nicodemus to gather information on Jesus, who speaks one Johannine "I am" metaphor after another. Caiaphas's informants see great crowds in Capernaum welcome Jesus as messiah and king; they see his miracles; and they witness him forgiving Mary Magdalene's act of adultery.

Herod Antipas, who continues to question John about Jesus,[8] finally executes John after John says that Jesus fulfills prophecy. Herod then sends his soldiers to arrest Jesus. Meanwhile, Jesus preaches the Sermon on the Mount, beginning with the beatitude directed at the persecuted. He enjoins the crowds again to trust in God and ends with the Lord's Prayer, which the crowds repeat. Pilate hears Jesus has instigated a rebellion in Capernaum, and some Pharisees warn Jesus that Herod is seeking to kill him.

Jesus returns to his hometown of Nazareth to preach, but his prophetic message is rejected there. He stops by to see his mother (cf. Ray, *King of Kings*), but Mary, Martha, and Lazarus interrupt the reunion, warning him that he is in danger. As he leaves town, he heals a blind man who will follow him to Jerusalem and who will eventually be called as a witness against Jesus at his Sanhedrin trial. Jesus returns to the site of his baptism, and while there is told that Lazarus is dying. He stays at the river, reciting the Lord's Prayer before returning to Judea and the home of Lazarus, Mary, and Martha. Jesus' subsequent raising of Lazarus from the dead is the climax of Jesus' public ministry. Witnesses to the miracle—including the cripple healed at Capernaum and the blind man healed at Nazareth—rush to the walls of Jerusalem proclaiming the arrival of the Messiah as Handel's "Hallelujah Chorus" resounds in the background.

The passion narrative opens with the Jerusalem authorities fretting about what the resurrection of Lazarus might mean for their political positions. Meanwhile, at the home of Lazarus, Mary Magdalene (the woman taken in adultery) anoints Jesus' head and feet with oil.[9] Judas complains on behalf of the poor, but Jesus defends her action as a preparation for his burial.

Jesus enters Jerusalem in triumph and cleanses the Temple while the religious leaders attempt unsuccessfully to arrest him. In the Temple—as in the synagogue earlier—Jesus demands mercy, not sacrifice. Later, in the Temple at night, Jesus declares that he has come as a light *into* the world (recalling the film's opening) and demands an ethic of love (quoting 1 Cor. 13:13!). Jesus and his disciples leave before Pilate's soldiers can arrest them, but the soldiers menacingly encircle the Temple crowds as they prayerfully recite Ps. 23. Despite the fact that a Jewish leader turns the other cheek, the soldiers go on a rampage, killing many innocent people.[10]

Unaware of the events unfolding in the Temple, Jesus and the disciples gather in the upper room for the Last Supper.[11] Judas leaves before everyone arrives and passes the Dark Hermit in the shadowy streets as he makes his way to betray Jesus to Sorak and Caiaphas. Judas's betrayal finally brings together the film's two parallel stories—the story of Jesus and that of the murderous authorities.[12] At the supper, Jesus tells Judas to "do it quickly"; and as Judas leaves, Jesus declares that "the Son of Man is now glorified." Stevens then cuts back and forth between Jesus' agonizing prayer in Gethsemane and

Judas's receipt of the money and his arrival with the Temple police. In the garden, a non-violent Jesus saves the betrayer from Peter's sword.

At the Jewish Sanhedrin trial, the blind man refuses to help condemn Jesus (cf. John 9:24–34).[13] And although Nicodemus disputes the legality of the proceedings, Caiaphas is able to extract a blasphemous "I am" (God's son) statement from Jesus. The criminal charges brought to Pilate are sedition, sorcery, blasphemy, and open rebellion, but the only charge Pilate spends much time with is Jesus' claim to be "son of God." After Jesus recites the Shema, Pilate finally connects Jesus' claim to be son of God with the claim of kingship and asks him where his kingdom is. When Jesus declares that his kingdom is not of this world (it is universal), and that God loves Pilate,[14] Pilate is convinced Jesus is harmless and sends him off to Herod Antipas. Herod Antipas repeats the messianic prophecy of Mic. 5:2, and then returns Jesus to Pilate. As Jesus is led back to Pilate, the Dark Hermit lurks in the shadows, reciting John 3:16. Pilate tries to release Jesus, offering Barabbas to the crowd. But spurred on by the Dark Hermit, the crowd prevails, and Pilate sentences Jesus to crucifixion.[15]

As Jesus makes his way through the city, a black Simon of Cyrene helps Jesus with his cross. The audience finally views Golgotha, where crosses are being raised, when the Roman soldiers open the city gate.[16] As Jesus is crucified, Stevens crosscuts a number of times to Judas, who is climbing the Temple altar to throw himself into its fire. After reciting all seven last words from the cross, Jesus dies. During the subsequent supernatural events, the centurion declares Jesus to be the Son of God.

After the entombment, some of Jesus' disciples go to the Jordan River, but some remain behind in Jerusalem. The disciples at the Jordan absentmindedly throw stones into the river, recalling their life-and-death questions asked of Jesus at the river just prior to the raising of Lazarus.[17] After the resurrection (accompanied by a reprise of Handel's "Hallelujah Chorus"), a larger-than-life Jesus appears in the sky to his disciples in Galilee. He commissions them, repeating his message of universal salvation and love, and ends the way he began his ministry: he admonishes his followers not to fret, for he will be with them until the end of the world.[18] Then Jesus vanishes. The commissioning Christ in Galilee had assumed the posture of the priestly Christ of the Byzantine church, and Stevens returns to the Byzantine church with which he began the film—with a Jesus who remains available to people today through the church.

## Memorable Characters

- Jesus: He is the one foretold by the prophets—the heavenly light come into the world. Acclaimed as a kingly messiah in Galilee and in Judea, he heals the sick and infirm. He speaks of a kingdom within each person, given to those who accept it or repent of their sins. Jesus is both a Jew[19] and the Johannine "I AM,"[20] but his task is largely an enigma until his final days in Jerusalem. Notably, John the Baptist calls Jesus a shepherd—a term Jesus also later uses for himself. But John never calls Jesus the Lamb of God, and Jesus never speaks of dying for the sins of the world. Jesus seems most "normal" and carefree when he is either traveling to or in Galilee. However, beginning with the raising of Lazarus from the dead, Jesus seems to turn inward, with his prayer in the Garden of Gethsemane best expressing the internal struggle that culminates in his crucifixion.

- Mary: The mother of Jesus is memorable by her absence and silence.[21] There is no hint of a virginal conception, nor is Isa. 7:14 (Matt. 1:23) ever quoted in the film. Jesus meets his mother and hugs her when he returns to Nazareth as an adult, but their reunion is interrupted by Lazarus's warning, and Jesus and his mother exchange no words. Jesus kisses her hand and turns to look at her as he leaves for Jerusalem. Mary is at the tomb of Lazarus, on the Via Dolorosa, and at the foot of the cross; and in the upper room on Easter morning, she has a knowing look on her face.

- Herod Antipas: A ruthless tyrant, he is more violent than his father, Herod the Great. Because of his oppressive rule in Judea (historically, his brother Archelaeus ruled in Judea, but Antipas never did), Rome demotes him to Galilee. Antipas alone is responsible for John the Baptist's death (neither Herodias nor Salome request John's head). Herod tells his men to arrest Jesus, and they search for him throughout Galilee.

- The Dark Hermit: Stevens breaks with the tradition of early Jesus films by inventing a character found nowhere in the canonical Gospels. The Dark Hermit is clearly a Satan figure, being the one who tempts Jesus after his baptism and saying, "Hail, Son of David," in Capernaum. Later he quotes John 3:16 as Jesus is led from Herod to Pilate, and he incites the Jerusalem crowds to crucify Jesus. Other than Pilate and Herod, the Dark Hermit is the most important character opposed to Jesus.

- Lazarus: The unnamed rich man (Mark 10:17–22); with his sisters, Mary and Martha, he is a longtime friend of Jesus and warns Jesus that his life is in danger.

- Sorak: Sent by the high priest, Caiaphas, to investigate Jesus in Galilee; he travels with Nicodemus and reports back to Caiaphas on two or three occasions. He is at the Sanhedrin trial and in the background when Jesus is tried by Pilate.

- Judas: An important link between John the Baptist, Jesus, and those in political power. He is the first of Jesus' disciples, having previously been a disciple of John (perhaps Stevens intends him to be the unnamed disciple of John 1:37–40). Although he is not a fully developed character, he seems more concerned with Roman oppression and the poor than is Jesus, and he seems somewhat put off by Jesus' more spiritualized kingdom. It is not entirely clear why he betrays Jesus, whom he calls the "purest, kindest man" he has ever known.

- John the Baptist: A preacher of apocalyptic judgment, especially for those in power. He believes the messiah will bring hope to the poor and "level the mountains" (where Herod's and Pilate's soldiers are most often ominously poised). John does not passively submit to those sent out to arrest him, forcibly "baptizing" them in the Jordan. His voice echoes throughout Judea and Galilee, reaching Jerusalem and the courts of Herod Antipas and Pilate. Despite the fact that his message is different from Jesus', John's death provides an ominous foreshadowing of what the future holds for Jesus.

## Memorable Visuals

- The church at the beginning and end, with the priestly Christ as icon
- Jesus standing in the shadows surrounded by the afflicted
- The throne rooms of the oppressors
- Jesus introducing himself to his first disciples
- Jesus' opening sermon under the bridge
- John forcibly "baptizing" Herod Antipas's soldiers sent out to arrest him
- John the Baptist and Herod Antipas talking to each other. (Herod Antipas, the king, is viewed through prison bars; John, the prisoner, is mostly filmed without prison bars.)
- The western landscape (baptism, temptation, sermon)
- Jesus fingering his tzitzit as he talks of prayer and tells the lame man to get up
- Children playing "army" as Jesus walks into Nazareth
- Jesus being stoned in Nazareth
- Jesus' prayer at Lazarus's tomb
- Anointing in Bethany, surrounded by Mary, Martha, and Mary Magdalene, who then wrap Jesus as though for burial before he begins his triumphal entry to Jerusalem
- People reciting Ps. 23 in the Temple as Pilate's soldiers appear and a disciple turns the other cheek
- Calvary from afar (viewed through the city gate)

## Key Scriptures

Stevens uses Ps. 22 to set the stage for Jesus' life. He uses Luke 17:21 and Hos. 6:6 to distinguish Jesus' message, and Mic. 5:2 to emphasize the theme of prophetic fulfillment.[22] But by far the most important Scripture is the Gospel of John. Stevens uses most of the "I AM" sayings of Jesus, and the Johannine raising of Lazarus is the culminating miracle of Jesus' ministry. However, Stevens's Jesus is as much the one prophesied (cf. Matt. 2:6, 18) as he is the divine Son. Moreover, Jesus only talks about "his hour" at the end of his life,[23] and Stevens does not emphasize Jesus' task as one of "taking away the sins of the world."[24] Stevens thus largely substitutes a "kingdom within" message for the Johannine revelation of life from above. In this regard, the film moves toward the *Gospel of Thomas* and away from the canonical Gospels.

## Cultural Location/Genre: Epic Spectacle, Western

Stevens's film is another epic spectacle like those of DeMille and Ray before him. Nonetheless, it differs from its precursors by focusing more intensely on spiritual matters—on a universal kingdom and the divine within all humans. Stevens's Jesus replaces the transcendent God of earlier Jesus films with "the Father [who] is in me [as] I am in the Father," and with a Jesus who invites others to trust in the same, inwardly available God. The scene where Jesus "declares" the God within him to Matthew the tax collector and the scene in the synagogue where Jesus heals a lame man with the faith that resides within the man both speak eloquently to this point.

Stevens's film may have appeared too late in American culture to be successful as an epic, but it does reflect the self-expressive, self-enriching, self-concerned American individualism that began to dominate American society in the 1960s. Yet Stevens attempts to counter an overly individualistic interpretation of the "kingdom within" through his use of voice-overs, where groups of faithful people sing hymns and recite psalms, creeds, and prayers. Significant, too, is the fact that Stevens places people of all races in the crowds shouting for Jesus' crucifixion and among the mourners on the Via Dolorosa. For Stevens, all peoples—regardless of race—are capable of both senseless hatred and the kingdom's openhearted compassion.

Stevens's Jesus rejects the "easy life" for an almost ascetic trust in God, and it is notable that Stevens does not show Jesus at the wedding at Cana or eating with "tax collectors and sinners." Perhaps not coincidentally, the Dark Hermit tells Jesus that he can rule "all this" if he simply does "homage" to him—this on a night with a huge full moon dominating the sky. Is this scene an allusion to President John F. Kennedy's promise to "put a man on the moon by the end of the decade"?[25] It was a promise that, coupled with Kennedy's nomination speech (July 15, 1960) and his inaugural address (January 20, 1961), spoke of both the hard work and the sacrifice required of all Americans who should be asking "not what your country can do for you [but] . . . what you can do for your country." If Stevens's Jesus represents the ideal American, then like Jesus, America should shoulder the heavy load, climb the hard path, take the moon, and be the empire that "saves the world."

## Director

Stevens's early camera work was with Laurel-and-Hardy slapstick comedies of the 1920s. But by the 1930s he was directing full-length feature films like *Swing Time* (1936) and *Gunga Din* (1939). During the Second World War, he filmed the Allied armies' entry into the Nazi concentration camp Dachau; and in the 1950s he directed the critically acclaimed films *A Place in the Sun* (1951), *Giant* (1956), and *The Diary of Anne Frank* (1957).

Stevens chooses to familiarize the exotic story of Jesus in two ways. First, he introduces the audience to the story by beginning with the camera looking up into the dome of a Byzantine (Orthodox) church. As the camera works its way down from heavenly heights to the apse, Jesus comes into view and then fades into a night sky. The story thus belongs to the church; but it is also mythically available (in Stevens's film) to all of modernity.[26] Second, Stevens sets his Jesus story within the familiar, nostalgic landscapes of the American West. In fact, in many respects *The Greatest Story Ever Told* is an American western. Like many westerns, the film cinematically juxtaposes the wilderness/itinerant ministry of Jesus with the city/civilization and its rulers. Furthermore, Jesus resembles the self-reliant western hero, untroubled by his conflict with corrupt society. He is, after all, from another place. Of course, *The Greatest Story Ever Told* suggests these common western tropes most clearly through its broad, majestic landscapes.

Perhaps Stevens's highly acclaimed western, *Shane* (1953), has the clearest lines of connection to *The Greatest Story Ever Told*. The film opens with a lone frontiersman (Shane) riding out of the mountains into the settled valley below. Meanwhile, a young boy, Joey, playfully hunts deer until he sees the stranger arrive. On the farm, Joey's father, Joe Starrett, offers Shane a job, and his mother, Marian, provides him with food (and some pensive, longing looks). Abandoning his gun, Shane settles down to a new life.

Trouble, of course, has already been brewing in the valley, for Rufus Ryker, a cattle rancher, has been trying to drive farmers like Starrett from the valley. After various hostilities—and the arrival of gunslingers hired by Ryker —Starrett decides to confront the rancher. Shane, knowing Starrett is outmanned by the hired guns, fights with him, knocks him out, and goes to town in his place. There, in a saloon, where he has previously been humiliated, he defeats the outlaws and the head rancher as Joey watches. Then, of course, he leaves because, as he tells Joey, "a man has to be what he is."

The parallels with *The Greatest Story Ever Told* (and the Gospel of John) are obvious. Both protagonists are strangers from beyond. Both associate themselves with a small, endangered community that they educate and save (Shane educates Joey in self-reliant maturity). Both stories are told from the perspective of the "saved" community. And in both cases, only the saved community knows the hero's true identity. Of course, the protagonist of *The Greatest Story Ever Told* suffers and dies while the protagonist of *Shane* uses violence to deliver his community. Accordingly, Shane is a more apocalyptic Christ figure than Stevens's Jesus, where the latter's most apocalyptic moment comes after Jesus' wilderness triumph over the Dark Hermit.

## DVD Extras and Technical Features

Two-page descriptive insert of the film's production
Disk 2
"He Walks in Beauty" Documentary (about 40 minutes long): There are six separate parts to this documentary, but no chapters, and no way to move randomly from one part to the next. Each part is almost exactly eight minutes long, and the time resets to zero with each part. The title is an allusion to Changing Woman of Navajo mythology, for the film was shot near the Navajo Reservation and many Navajos were used as extras in the film.
1. George Stevens as director
2. Max von Sydow on "Jesus": Jesus the man; the new Christ; not a superman; an enigma
3. Philosophy of camera shots
4. Influence of Stevens's "Dachau experience"; ecumenical point of view; miracles should take "effort"
5. Production cost and time: the role of great art; critics and audience reaction
6. Credits
   Theatrical Trailer (3:29 minutes long)
   Still gallery
      1. Original production art
      2. George Stevens during pre-production
      3. Production camp and the Glen Canyon location
      4. Behind the scenes of the John the Baptist sequence
   Costume Sketches
   Deleted Scene (alternate version of the Via Dolorosa sequence; 2:09 minutes long)
   "Filmmaker" Documentary (about 26 minutes long): There are four separate parts to this documentary, but no chapters, and no way to move randomly from one part to the next. The first

three parts are each about eight minutes long. The fourth part is three and a half minutes long. The timer resets to zero with each part.

1. Lighting, composition; touring Israel, religious significance of the geography of the American Southwest
2. Costumes, planning Salome's dance and John the Baptist's death. Carl Sandburg's Jesus as the "ideal man," the "universal man." A story of man's inhumanity.
3. Filming the resurrection of Lazarus
4. Anointing of Jesus and film editing

Disk 1

   Languages
   French (dubbed)
   Subtitles: French, Spanish

## DVD Chapters

1. Main Title
2. In the Beginning, 4:48
      John 1:1
3. The Three Kings, 7:23
4. Jesus, Mary, and Joseph, 11:31
5. Escape from Bethlehem, 17:40
      A forest of crosses around Jerusalem, 22:54
         Baby Jesus looks at the forest of crosses, 23:20
         Jesus in the shadows, 25:30
6. John the Baptist, 26:15
      Sacrifice of lambs in the Temple, 26:22
      John does not know Jesus is someone special until Jesus says his name and his place of birth.
7. Jesus' Temptation, 31:52
8. Gathering His Flock, 39:30
      Teaching under the bridge, 41:17
         "Do not labor for food that perishes—but for the food of eternal life."
         "The bread of life is that which comes from heaven" (John 6:27–51).
         "Put away all anxious thoughts about food to keep you alive, or about clothes—think of the ravens" (Matt. 6:25–34; Luke 12:22–31).
            (Compare with the last of the three temptations.)
         "The kingdom of God is here, within you" (Luke 17:20–21), 44:15
         "Give him your cloak also—you must be their light" (Matt. 5:38–42).
      Work to start in Galilee, 46:53
9. "Love Thy Neighbor," 51:55
      The greatest commandment (Matt. 19:16–23; Mark 10:17–31; Luke 18:18–30)
      "What does it profit" (Matt. 16:26; Mark 8:36; Luke 9:24)
      Two masters (Matt. 6:24; Luke 16:13)
      The widow's two pennies (Luke 21:1–4)
10. "Bring the Baptist to me," 56:15
11. The Tax Collector, 57:55
      Matthew, Little James's brother, 58:38
      "He who sees the Son, sees the Father" (John 14:9), 59:57
12. "Do Unto Others," 1.01:34
      Judgment on sinners
         Jesus objects—Scriptures say, "I desire mercy" (Matt. 9:13).
         "Do unto others"—salvation, not revenge (Matt. 7:12; Luke 6:31).

"Knock, and it shall be opened—have faith, believe" (Matt. 7:7; Luke 11:9).

Walks by a burning lamp (walking in light . . .)

13. John before Herod, 1.07:58

John "baptizes" Herod's soldiers.

"I have no king."

Herod will burn in Hell for his adultery.

(Compare with Jesus and the adulterous woman)

14. The Flock Grows, 1.11:43

Simon (the Zealot) tells Jesus of John's arrest.

"Come unto me all ye who labor" (Matt. 11:28–30), 1.12:26

"I am the bread of life" (John 6:35), 1.13:02

"I am the good shepherd" (John 10:11, 16) 1.14:20

"If anyone wants to follow me—day after day take up his cross" (Luke 9:23), 1.17:50

Receiving the kingdom like a child (Mark 10:13–15)

15. "Cast the First Stone," 1.19:30

(Mary Magdalene)

The Dark Hermit, 1.20:14

"Hail, Son of David," 1.20:46

16. "I'm Cured," 1.23:25

Hemorrhaging woman, 1.24:07

Salome's dance, John's death, 1.25:27

Reports of Jesus' miracles

"He's the one prophesied, born in Bethlehem."

"Arrest the Nazarene," 1.31:12

17. "Blessed are the Meek," 1.31:20

Sermon on the Mount

Twelve disciples are seated around him.

Message to Pilate: What began as a riot in Capernaum is now a rebellion, 1.33:05

Reports to priests of Jesus' miracles

"Who do men say that I am?" 1.33:56

Mary Magdalene on the scene

"Who do you say that I am, Judas?"

Pharisees warn Jesus of Herod's intent to kill him (Luke 13:31–33), 1.35:35

"All that was written by the prophets will come true" (Luke 24:44)

18. A Prophet in His Home, 1.36:51

The blind man at a pool (John 9:6–8)

Children playing army

"How long will you keep us in suspense?" (John 10:24), 1.38:05

"The prophecy is now fulfilled—the spirit of the Lord is upon me" (Luke 4:18), 1.38:24

"You shall not tempt the Lord your God" (Matt. 4:7; Luke 4:12), 1.40:15

"You have ears, but do not hear" (Matt. 13:13; Mark 4:12; Luke 8:10).

"If I am not acting as my Father would, then do not believe me" (John 10:37–39), 1.40:39

"The Father is in me, and I in the Father," 1.40:49

Judas's reaction

Someone throws a stone at Jesus (John 10:31).

Jesus and his mother, 1.41:25

Mary, Martha, and Lazarus (who is ill) tell Jesus he will be arrested and taken to the city (John 11:1–3).

19. Restoring Sight, 1.43:25

No one is around (John 9:6–8).

Children return to play in the background.

"Lazarus is sick and dying" (John 11:1–3), 1.45:14

20. The Lord's Prayer, 1.46:00
>    The Lord's Prayer (in full), 1.46:39

21. Lazarus Comes Forth, 1.47:40
>    Black men on the scene

22. Jesus in Jerusalem, 2.02:52

23. Cleansing the Temple, 2.10:25
>    "It is written in the scriptures, 'I desire mercy'" (Matt. 9:13), 2.11:15
>> "I have not come to destroy the Law or the prophets" (Matt. 5:17).
>> "Do what the scribes and Pharisees tell you to do, but don't take their works as your example" (Matt. 23:3).
>> "There is only one teacher and one father."
>
>    Herod Antipas, the priests, and Pilate, 2.13:16
>> "He's telling people to love their enemies" (Matt. 5:43; Luke 6:27), 2.14:18
>
>    At night in the temple courts, 2.14:43
>> "I have come to bring salvation to the world."
>> "A light into the world" (John 8:12)
>> "I have not come to bring judgment" (John 3:17).
>> "While you have the light, walk in the light" (John 12:35–36).
>> "Faith, hope, and love abide" (1 Cor. 13:13).
>> "Gathered together in my name" (Matt. 18:20)
>>> People begin quoting, "The Lord is my shepherd" (Ps. 23).
>>> Roman soldiers appear, an unknown disciple turns his other cheek (Matt. 5:38; Luke 6:29), 2.17:50
>>> Slaughter in the Temple

24. Judas's Betrayal, 2.18:45

25. The Last Supper, 2.24:14
>    "If a grain of wheat dies" (John 12:24)

26. "Your Will Be Done," 2.33:51
>    "The hour has come" (John 12:23), 2.36:46
>    "All my life, I've walked in the light, and spoken in the light" (John 12:35–36).

27. Jesus' Trial, 2.38:55
>    Before the Sanhedrin
>> Aaron, the blind man, as a witness (John 9:24–34)
>> The Dark Hermit, 2.41:51
>> Nicodemus comes late and interrupts (John 7:49–52), 2.42:5

28. Pilate's Sentence, 2.45:40
>    First time before Pilate
>    To Herod, 2.48:23
>> "From you Bethlehem, shall he come forth."
>
>    The Dark Hermit, 2.51:22
>> "For God so loved the world" (John 3:16).
>
>    Second time before Pilate, 2.52:39
>> The Dark Hermit, "Crucify him!" 2.53:17
>> Scourging, 2.53:53
>> Release of Barabbas, 2.54:15
>> The Dark Hermit, "Crucify him!" 2.55:39
>> Simon of Cyrene, 2.55:53
>> The Dark Hermit, "No king but Caesar" (John 19:15), 2.56:34
>> Pilate washes his hands, 2.57:14
>> The Apostles' Creed, 2.57:21

29. Carrying the Cross, 2.57:28
>    Veronica, 2.58:50

Judas throws down the thirty pieces of silver, 3.00:00

Simon of Cyrene, 3.00:35

    A black man voluntarily takes Jesus' cross, Jesus holds on to him to stand.

30. Calvary, 3.02:16

Judas climbs the Temple altar ready to commit suicide, 3.02:55

Judas at the top of the altar, 3.03:55

Judas throws himself into the altar as Jesus is nailed to the cross, 3.04:19

The last words of Christ begin, 3.05:00

31. "It is Finished," 3.06:35

"Into thy hands" (Luke 23:46), 3.08:27

Thunderstorm

"Truly this man was the Son of God" (Mark 15:39), 3.09:14

Temple veil torn, 3.09:29

    A person kneels on the chair.

Laid in the tomb, 3.10:18

"Jesus tread the path of prophecy," 3.10:27

32. "He is Risen," 3.10:59

Disciples throwing stones in the Jordan River, as they did just before Lazarus's resurrection

The prophecy (Luke 24:6–8), 3.12:50

"Go now, and teach all nations . . . love one another [(Matt. 28:19; John 13:34), 3.15:05] . . . find the kingdom of God; and all things shall be yours . . .don't fret . . . [Matt. 6:25], I am with you always . . ."

# Chapter 9

# Jesus Christ Superstar

*Norman Jewison, director. 107 mins. Rated*
*G. 1973. Universal Pictures. DVD Special*
*Edition, 2004*

## Plot Summary

This cinematic version of the successful rock opera of the same name was filmed on location in modern Israel.[1] Like its contemporary *Godspell,* the film imitates the episodic plotting of the Gospels—since only a tenuous plotline connects the various songs.

The film begins as a play-within-a-play, with the camera following a tour bus as it arrives on set amidst the Byzantine ruins of Avdat in the Negev desert. A troupe of actors disembarks, unloads a cross and other props tied to the bus roof, dons costumes, and begins to dance around an actor playing Jesus. They have begun to enact an operatic version of a passion play.[2]

A black actor (whom the viewing audience will soon discover is Judas) walks away from the dancing troupe, and a group of vulture-like actors (later revealed to be the Jewish religious leaders opposing Jesus) mount scaffolding in the ruins of the ancient city. Alone on a desert mountain, Judas sings of his desire to strip the myth from the man Jesus, who, it seems, has begun to believe the things his followers are saying about him. Judas is worried about preserving Judea's precarious peace with the Roman occupation.[3] As in the opening song, the movie as a whole primarily follows the perspective of Judas.[4]

In the next scene, Jesus and his disciples are in a sunlit cavern,[5] where he tries to tell his dim-witted followers about his mission. Mary Magdalene anoints Jesus and sensually soothes him (she is a pastiche of the woman taken in adultery [John 8:1–11] and the anointing woman [Luke 7:36–50]), while Judas complains in exasperation and Caiaphas plots against Jesus.

From their scaffolding, the dark-robed priestly leaders nervously watch as Jesus enters Jerusalem with adoring crowds singing "Hosanna! Hey, Superstar." The crowds end their song with the question "Hey, J.C., would you die for me?" And the camera freezes on a suddenly somber, disturbed Jesus. Segueing to a desert city in ruins, Simon the Zealot and a crowd of frenzied dancers try to get Jesus to revise his message. But he rejects their revolutionary ideas, stating that they do not understand what real power is and that to conquer death one need only die.

63

The next three scenes juxtapose three images of power. In the first scene, Pilate's wife gives Pilate his crown after he describes a haunting dream he has had about a Galilean whom millions mourn. In the second scene, Jesus "cleanses the Temple" of modern-day merchants selling drugs, sex, automatic weapons, food, clothing, and postcards. And in the third scene, a weary, wary Jesus retires to the desert wilderness, frustrated that there is not enough of him to meet everyone's physical needs. He turns away from the crowds who clamor for him and his healing powers.[6] That night while Jesus sleeps, Mary Magdalene sings to him her signature song, "I Don't Know How to Love Him." The song, later repeated by Judas shortly before he commits suicide, poignantly affirms how much Jesus' followers need him, while repeating their belief that "he's just a man."

Fearful of Jesus' growing popularity, Judas outraces a group of threatening tanks to make a deal with Caiaphas. Caiaphas is more than willing to deal because he has also seen the political value of quickly dispatching Jesus. He wants his Jewish people to maintain their peace with the Romans. When Judas later rejoins the disciples, they are in a park, just sitting down to a final meal with Jesus. In a whimsical song, they describe their hope of one day being named apostles and writing famous Gospels. But Jesus declares that they will soon forget him and that for all they care, the food they are eating could be his body and blood. Jesus and Judas then go off by themselves and quarrel, with Judas railing against the fate/God that decrees he must betray Jesus. In Gethsemane, a frightened Jesus asks God (who "hold[s] every card") why he must die. As Jesus reluctantly submits to God, Jewison offers a montage of classic paintings of the crucifixion.

Jesus is then led to the high priest, and the "press" hounds him with questions befitting his celebrity status. The priests are able to extract a charge of blasphemy against Jesus, and then turn him over to Pilate. Apparently Jesus' disciples have deserted him, and after Peter denies having known Jesus, he meets Mary Magdalene in the wilderness, where Mary reminds Peter that Jesus had foretold his denials.

Pilate refuses to try Jesus when he first meets him. But after finding out who Jesus is, Pilate sends him off to Herod, who, in a slapstick scene, asks Jesus to walk across his swimming pool. Herod finds Jesus boring—he won't do any tricks for him—and so he sends Jesus back to Pilate. But before Pilate and Jesus meet again, Mary Magdalene and Peter lead the crowd in a nostalgic refrain about how things went wrong and how they wish they could start over. Judas is also reevaluating his role in Jesus' arrest, and he confronts Caiaphas, railing against the notoriety that will mark his name. Judas claims he was used by God for God's crime, accosts God for murdering him, and hangs himself.

As the crowd chants for Jesus' crucifixion, Pilate tries to release him. Jesus wonders if there is a kingdom elsewhere for him and dismisses Pilate's aid by telling him that it's all "fixed." Pilate has Jesus beaten, but when the crowd continues to chant for crucifixion, Pilate sentences Jesus, telling him to die if he wants to and saying, "You misguided martyr, you innocent puppet."

As Jesus goes to the cross, Jewison offers a contrasting heavenly song-and-dance routine, starting with the transfigured Jesus but featuring the resurrected Judas singing "Jesus Christ Superstar" with the troupe.[7] The music stops when Jesus arrives at Calvary and the soldiers nail him to the cross. Canned mockery begins as the soldiers raise the cross. Jesus whispers a few of the words from the cross ("Father forgive them, they don't know what they're doing"; "My God, My God, why have you forgotten me"; and "Father, into your hands I commend my spirit") while Mary Magdalene watches. After Jesus says his final words, he dies, and the music abruptly stops.

Instrumental music begins shortly thereafter, and a close-up focuses on the placard above Jesus' crucified body. It reads "*INRI.*" Everyone leaves Calvary, and the troupe, now out of costume, boards the bus. Mary Magdalene and Judas are the last on board and look back forlornly. As the sun sets, a lone cross stands on a hill in the distance, and a figure walks across the hillside below it, herding sheep.[8] The actor playing Jesus is not among those on the bus.

## Memorable Characters

- Jesus: This is one of the few Jesus films where Jesus' hair actually moves when he moves or when the wind blows. Not coincidentally, Jewison is one of the first filmmakers (cf. Jones, *Life of Brian*; and Arcand, *Jesus of Montreal*) to struggle with the dichotomy between Jesus the man (the one with the moving hair) and Jesus the Christ/Savior figure, which in Jewison's hands becomes Jesus Christ "superstar" or Jesus the celebrity.[9] This Jesus has "fans," and his opponents refer to the "Jesus mania" that they feel will soon pass. Despite Judas's desire to burst the bubble of myth-making crowds and despite Mary Magdalene's sensual love, the myth of "Jesus the celebrity" ultimately triumphs.
- Judas: Judas is at least as important a character as Jesus, and perhaps even more important, as the story is told from his perspective.[10] He is the 1960s antihero, whose self-appointed task is to keep Jesus "grounded" and "real," and to remind Jesus to be critical of the crowds' adulation and myth making.
- Mary Magdalene: Jesus' comforter and would-be lover is almost always within reach of Jesus. Both Judas and Mary Magdalene claim that Jesus is "just a man" yet seem to recognize an intangible quality about his character that makes Jesus different from other people they know.

## Memorable Visuals

- Mary Magdalene "comforting" Jesus
- Jesus cleansing the (very modern, market-place) "Temple"
- The crowds begging for healing
- The picnic-style Last Supper
- Jesus and Judas arguing face to face in the garden
- Jesus before Herod
- Judas's song-and-dance resurrection

## Key Scriptures

Jewison choreographs the passion narrative as a modern musical. His rendering turns important Gospel assertions such as "Jesus is the Christ" into questions and treats other themes ironically. But the key motif remains the mysterious fate that gives birth to the respective roles of Judas and Jesus. Judas is the oracular Judas of Mark 14:18–21 (cf. Ps. 41:9) and the fated betrayer of John 6:70, and Gethsemane becomes Jesus' defining moment (Mark 14:32–42).

## Cultural Location/Genre: Rock Opera Passion Play

The film *Jesus Christ Superstar* and the rock opera on which it is based reflect the counterculture youth movement of 1960s America. Countercultural voices that dispute tradition (here, the Jesus story) have most of the screen time, but the movie actually represents the domestication of the 1960s counterculture. That culture has been annexed by consumer capitalism. Accordingly, Jesus Christ becomes yet another troubled, money-making superstar or celebrity (rather than the Messiah, the Son of God). Traditionally, passion plays dramatize the stories associated with the holiest week of the Christian calendar. They also tend to turn the passion narrative into a set of moral lessons for the faithful by absolutizing the negative characteristics of the villains (usually "the Jews") and glorifying the heroes. Not surprisingly, Judas and "the Jews" fare quite badly in passion plays, and critics now often accuse the authors of the traditional passion plays of anti-Semitism. The traditional emphases and problems with passion plays are quite evident in the films of Griffith and Gibson.

Jewison skews the traditional passion play with "modernized" language, costumes, and sets, and by slightly displacing Jesus from the center of the plot. No longer the undisputed focus of attention, Jesus shares time with two other dominant characters, Mary Magdalene and Judas, neither of whom understand Jesus in traditional Christian terms. As a result, in the finale the absent Jesus is celebrated as a superstar/celebrity, but not as the Messiah or Son of God. "Christ" functions here more as a last name than as a descriptive title for Jesus' role in Christianity.

Jewison undoes some of the anti-Semitism of traditional passion plays with his concentration on the viewpoint of Judas and his depiction of both Jesus and Judas as "fated" to their roles; however, his Judas's end ultimately underscores a "Christian" perspective.[11] Jewison has flirted with a skewed view of the Jesus story by following the perspective of Judas and by inscribing Jesus as a celebrity instead of the Christ. But raising Judas from the dead to sing "Jesus Christ Superstar" with the choir reinstates the Christian perspective in a modern form.

## Director

Jewison has a long list of important films to his credit (*The Cincinnati Kid* [1965], *In the Heat of the Night* [1967], *Fiddler on the Roof* [1971], and *Moonstruck* [1987] are just a few). In his film *Agnes of God* (1985), Jewison offers a variant on the virgin birth story. Like *Jesus Christ Superstar*, the film struggles with the difference between modernity (reason, science, the human) and tradition (faith, religion, the myth). In a nunnery outside modern Montreal, a novice, Agnes, gives birth to a child that is subsequently found dead in the wastebasket of her room. The court appoints a psychiatrist, Martha Livingston, to investigate Agnes's sanity (Martha has a sister named Mary who died as a nun, and she herself is barren due to an abortion). The Mother Superior represents faith/religion, and Martha represents reason/science. After a long struggle between these two forceful women, Martha finally learns the "truth" about the baby after hypnotizing Agnes: Agnes thinks that she had been impregnated by God.

Jewison lends some credence to Agnes's view by filming the flashback of Agnes's memory of this event with doves and heavenly light. However, Martha believes that a passing field hand raped the incredibly naïve Agnes. More troublingly, Martha also discovers that Agnes believes she "returned the child to God." In the denouement, the court consigns Agnes to the guardianship of the nuns and to regular psychiatric treatments. One wonders if Jewison were to write his own script for a Jesus movie, would his Judas character be tempted to do the same with Jesus and his messianic complex? Would his Judas want to put Jesus away somewhere where he could not harm himself or anyone else, and would he order regular psychiatric treatments for him?

## DVD Extras and Technical Features

Languages
    Spoken: English, French, captioned for the hearing impaired (English)
    Subtitles: English, Spanish, French
Bonus Materials
    An exclusive interview with master lyricist Tim Rice
        Genesis, 0:00
        The Music Men, 0:55
        The Album, 2:49
        Rock Opera, 4:41
        Controversy, 6:26
        Cast, 8:26
            Comments about racial issues
        The Film, 10:54
        Legacy, 12:38
    Feature Commentary with Director Norman Jewison and actor Ted Neeley (To turn this on, go to
        "Languages," find "Feature Commentary," and click "on." Then start the movie.)
Photo Gallery

## DVD Chapters

1. Heaven on Their Minds, 0:20
    Judas goes off by himself, 3:42
    Title, 5:30
    Judas on a mountain by himself, 5:48
    Jesus is on a mountain with his disciples, apparently teaching them (6:39) but we hear nothing. Judas sings of Jesus' words being "twisted."
2. What's the Buzz? 10:56
    Mary Magdalene washes Jesus' feet (Luke 7:36–50; 10:38–42).
3. Strange Thing Mystifying, 13:17
    Plots against Jesus (Matt. 12:14; 26:1–5; Mark 3:6; 14:1–2; Luke 6:11; 13:31–33; 22:1–2), 15:54
4. Everything's Alright, 18:10
    Mary anoints Jesus (John 12:1–7).
    Caiaphas and the Council (John 11:48–53), 22:21

Triumphal entry to Jerusalem (John 12:12–19), 23:57
5. Hosanna, 26:03
Triumphal entry to Jerusalem (Luke 19:40)
6. Simon Zealotes, 29:40
Holds Mary Magdalene's hand, 34:33
Lament over Jerusalem (Matt. 23:37–39; Luke 13:34–35), 34:42
7. Pilate's Dream, 35:37
"Leaving me the blame" (Matt. 27:19)
8. The Temple, 37:21
Cleansing the Temple—"a house of prayer"
9. My Temple Should Be, 39:14
Miracles of Jesus, 40:39
Jesus and Mary Magdalene, 43:14
10. I Don't Know How to Love Him, 44:09
Mary Magdalene (cont'd)
Judas, 48:14
11. Damned for All Time, 49:24
Judas's betrayal (Luke 22:3; John 6:70–71; 13:27)
12. The Last Supper, 53:33
Judas's response to Jesus' "prophecy," 56:55
Jesus goes to Judas, 58:28
Gethsemane, 1.00:17
13. Gethsemane, 1.00:50
"I will drink your cup of poison," 1.05:51
Judas comes, 1:06:30
14. The Arrest, Part 1, 1.07:03
15. The Arrest, Part 2, 1.08:57
Reporters try to interview Jesus.
High Priest's trial, 1.10:12
16. Peter's Denial, 1.11:14
Mary Magdalene reproaches Peter, 1.12:17
17. Pilate and Christ, 1.13:54
Pilate meets Jesus, 1.14:03
18. King Herod's Song, 1.16:10
19. Could We Start Again Please? 1.19:29
Mary Magdalene sings (then others join in), 1:19:44
Judas looks at Jesus one last time, 1.22:43
20. Judas's Death, 1.23:14
"I don't know how to love him," 1.25:00
Death, 1.27:12
21. Trial before Pilate, 1.28:00
Mary Magdalene's grief during Jesus' scourging, 1.32:03
22. Superstar, 1.35:01
Judas's resurrection and descent to earth, 1.35:35
Via Dolorosa, 1.38:04
23. The Crucifixion, 1.39:07
Mary Magdalene lamenting, 1.39:49; 1.41:06
Death, 1.41:50
Mary Magdalene, 1.43:10
Judas, 1.43:14

# Chapter 10

# Godspell

*David Greene, director. 103 mins. Rated G. 1973. Columbia Pictures, 2000*

### Plot Summary

Based on a popular off-Broadway play that was first performed with Stephen Schwartz's new musical score in 1971, *Godspell*[1] returns to the early decades of Jesus films through its episodic plot and use of pantomime. But in contrast to the era of silent Jesus films, *Godspell* eschews miracle stories and instead emphasizes the teaching of Jesus, drawing largely from the Gospel of Matthew and presenting it in comic form.[2] The film opens with a voice-over from the Creator who says that God's plan is to make humans into gardeners for their own re-creation. Then John the Baptist appears, pulling a colorfully painted cart and strolling across the Brooklyn Bridge into New York City.[3] In the midst of the angry, clamoring metropolis, he finds eight disciples who follow him to Bethesda Fountain[4] in Central Park as he sings, "Prepare Ye the Way of the Lord." There he baptizes them, and suddenly a half-dressed, afro-coifed, Caucasian Jesus appears in the background. After John baptizes Jesus, Jesus appears in a Superman T-shirt, rainbow clown pants, and clown shoes. John's baptized followers are likewise dressed in crazy, mismatched clothing, and Jesus leads them throughout Central Park singing "Save the People."

Jesus and his disciples leave the park and move on to a junkyard where they play and gradually begin to clean up the place, turning old castaways into new toys.[5] Jesus paints his disciples' faces in gaudy colors, and the troupe begins to perform his teachings in a vaudevillian style.[6] The Sermon on the Mount provides the frame that Jesus and his disciples expand with various other teachings and parables.[7] The teachings stress righteousness (Matt. 5:17–20) and forgiveness (Matt. 5:24–26; 18:10–14, 23–24, 35). The disciples leave the junkyard singing "Day by Day."

Gamboling back through Central Park and out into the city again, the troupe performs other parts of Jesus' Sermon on the Mount. They also act out various parables, including the Sheep and the Goats (Matt. 25:31–46), the Good Samaritan (Luke 10:30–35), the Rich Man and Lazarus (Luke 16:19–31), and the Sower and the Soils (Matt. 13:1–9, 18–23). While some of the disciples play the role of opponents—particularly the John the Baptist character—Greene's universal kingdom leaves none

69

behind. Everyone is part of Jesus' new world. Greene films the troupe in various New York settings, including UN Plaza—and most poignantly, the unfinished World Trade Center's Twin Towers. But the city is eerily empty, even as they sing "All for the Best." At the Cherry Lane Theater, where the play *Godspell* had premiered, the troupe enacts the Lukan parable of the Prodigal Son to the accompaniment of clips from old black-and-white comedies and westerns.[8] In the parable's finale, unlike its Gospel source, the father reunites the two feuding brothers. After the troupe leaves the theater, they embark on a tugboat into the bay. With the Statue of Liberty and an American flag in the background, they sing, "You are the light of the world" and "You are the city of God."[9]

Arriving at a pier, a huge robot (operated by the disciples) emerges from a warehouse and confronts Jesus with the Matthean Jerusalem controversies (Matt. 21:23–27; 22:16–21, 36–40; 23:1–10).[10] In anger, Jesus and his disciples dismantle the robot. A suddenly somber Jesus laments the fate of Jerusalem (Matt. 23:37–39) and then silently walks away.[11] The passion has begun, and John the Baptist narrates the opening of the Judas story. Walking through the empty city and singing about creating a beautiful city of man (*sic*), the troupe returns to Central Park.

In the evening, in the junkyard, Jesus cleans the faces of his disciples and then sends John (who has become Judas) to betray him. After the Last Supper, Jesus moves away to pray alone. The disciples enact the temptation narrative (Matt. 4:1–11), and Judas arrives with the police (but the audience sees only the flashing lights of the cars). Judas pauses uncertainly, but Jesus encourages him—kissing *him* twice. Then, Judas, humming circus ringmaster music, ties Jesus to the chain-link fence surrounding the junkyard. Bound in blood-red ribbon, the body of Jesus is a cruciform. Jesus claims that this happens to fulfill the prophecies (recalling the opening words of Jesus to his disciples in the film, Matt. 5:17–20). In the film's most powerful moment, the disciples share Jesus' suffering as a community, screaming out and flailing against the fence with Jesus. The scene ends with light falling on the dead Jesus, and the disciples' words "Oh God, you're dead."[12]

The next morning, the disciples awake and sing, "Long live God," as they take the body of Jesus down from the fence. They walk through the park and into the lonely city, carrying the cruciform Jesus and singing a final medley of "Prepare Ye the Way of the Lord" and "Day by Day." They turn a corner ahead of the camera, and when the camera follows them, they are gone. But the New York City streets are suddenly busy again. Only the music lingers on.[13]

## Memorable Characters

- Jesus: The movie portrays Jesus as a happy teacher-clown, wearing a T-shirt that evokes a comic-book, fantasy character. It is a portrayal that subverts and complicates Gospel certainties. Coupled with the absence of any miracles and the lack of a resurrection scene, this makes for a most human Jesus.
- The Disciples: The clown's troupe is as important as Jesus. They perform his teachings with him and share in his suffering and death. Finally, they are the ones left singing "Day by Day."
- John the Baptist/Judas: He is the only other actor who plays a central role in

the film. As John, he opens Jesus' ministry. As a transitional figure he inaugurates the opposition to Jesus by pointing at Jesus and shouting, "Blessed are you when people revile you and persecute you and say all manner of evil against you falsely!" (Matt. 5:11). And as Judas, he ends the story by tying Jesus to the junkyard's chain-link fence.

## Memorable Visuals

- Jesus clad in Superman T-shirt and clown pants
- Baptisms in Bethesda Fountain, Central Park
- The parable of the Prodigal Son
- The troupe carrying the cruciform Jesus through the city

## Key Scriptures

The movie is a musical adaptation of Jesus' teaching in the Gospel of Matthew. While it includes Jesus' baptism and passion (omitting the trials), the focus is on the Sermon of the Mount (Matt. 5–7), restructured and added to from the Gospel of Luke. The end result emphasizes a quality of love and forgiveness that is more reminiscent of Luke's Sermon on the Plain (Luke 6:20–49) than Matthew's Sermon on the Mount. Greene also adds (and interprets) some Lukan parables in order to stress the theme of forgiveness.

## Cultural Location/Genre: Musical Comedy

*Godspell* inhabits a cultural location similar to *Jesus Christ Superstar*. Both are "plays within plays," both appeared in the early 1970s, and both bespeak the countercultural youth movements of the 1960s. However, *Godspell*'s setting is quite different from that of *Jesus Christ Superstar* in that it is filmed in a modern American city as opposed to the land of Israel. *Godspell*'s vaudeville style—one that gently mocks silent-era films—also gives it a more lighthearted tone than *Jesus Christ Superstar* with its angst-driven Judas.

*Godspell*'s notion of Jesus as clown had a precursor in *Parable*, a short film produced by New York City churches for the World's Fair of 1964–1965. Set in the circus surroundings[14] of the Circus World Museum in Baraboo, Wisconsin, *Parable* opens with a black screen and a voice-over that declares Jesus' parabolic message today might imagine the world as a circus of unconcerned people—until a man comes "who dared to be different." There is no narration in the remainder of the film, although there is a musical score playing in the background.

In the first scene, Magnus the Great, a circus puppeteer, sits before a mirror. The film cuts to a clown in white on a donkey, bringing up the rear of a circus parade. The clown follows the other performers around and takes on their various burdens. Those whom he helps follow him. At the circus, the clown angers a barker by entering a magic show without paying. He angers the magician by spiriting away his female assistant. Finally, the clown comes to Magnus's puppet show and disrupts it by wiping the feet of the children in the audience and interfering with the puppets' strings. The clown then takes a puppet's place in the harness. When Magnus and the clown's own followers beat him, a loud scream interrupts the otherwise-silent film. The clown dies, and the next day the clown's disciples help each other prepare for the day. The circus parade starts again; Magnus sits in his trailer and applies white face paint again; and a clown (Magnus?) on a donkey follows the parade once more.

Despite its silent format, *Parable*, like *Godspell*, imagines Jesus as a teacher who enlists disciples that continue his work after his death. Both movies imagine Jesus' teaching as a challenge to "the System." Both expect such challenges to be deadly for Jesus and risky for his followers. If Magnus is *Parable*'s second clown, that film is even more hopeful about the success of Jesus' teaching than is *Godspell*. It would imply that even "the ruler of this world" (John 12:31) finds redemption/salvation in the end. Nonetheless, in neither film is "the System" (the circus or the noisy city) completely displaced.

## Director

John-Michael Tebelak wrote the original play *Godspell* when he was a graduate student in drama at Carnegie-Mellon University in Pittsburgh, Pennsylvania. His intention was to liberate the message of Jesus from the stifling confines of the church.[15] David Greene directed the film version of the play and is best known for his television productions (he was a codirector of *Roots* [1977] and won Emmy awards for the TV features *The People Next Door* [1969] and *Friendly Fire* [1979]). Greene's strategy for liberating the message of Jesus from the confines of the church was to set the musical in the (not-so-mean) streets and parks of New York City. Much more so than the theater production itself, the movie thus imagines Jesus' message as one that remakes the human city as the garden of God or the new city of humankind.

Like Pasolini's *The Gospel According to St. Matthew*, Greene breaks the confines of the fourfold canon by focusing on one particular Gospel. Actually, of course, he only partly breaks that canonical mold, for he borrows rather freely from Luke.[16] Nonetheless, Greene turns his edited version of Matthew into a light, upbeat musical that is much further from the canonical mode than is Pasolini's somber docudrama.

The problem—or benefit—of removing a Gospel (or some collage of Gospel materials) from the canon is that it can easily become a free-floating text in search of an ideology. The various reconstructed Jesuses formed by those who quest for the "historical Jesus" have demonstrated this point repeatedly. These Jesuses end up sharing the ideology of the ones who produce the historical reconstruction. Given the fate of the arts and cinema in the United States, the ideology that dominates Hollywood's reconstructed Jesuses is clearly a capitalist consumerism. Like *Jesus Christ Superstar*, *Godspell*'s Gospel becomes a successful U.S. commodity, perhaps implying thereby that the United States—or its consumer capitalism—should (?) or has (?) taken on the Messiah's role in the modern world.

## DVD Extras and Technical Features

English, Spanish, Portuguese, Chinese, Korean, and Thai subtitles. Widescreen on side A.
Musical Numbers: Highlights

(These are simply songs lifted out of the film, functioning like music videos)
1. "Prepare Ye (The Way of the Lord)"
2. "Save the People"
3. "Day By Day"
4. "Turn Back, O Man"

Talent Files (text only)
David Greene (director)
Victor Garber
Katie Hanley
David Haskell

Bonus trailers
"Bye Bye Birdie"
"Oliver!"

## DVD Chapters

(Non-Matthean sources are in italics)
1. Start
2. Prologue, 1:15
3. "Prepare Ye the Way of the Lord," 7:34
    *Jesus' disciples were first disciples of John (John 1:35–37).*
    "I baptize you with water" (Matt. 3:1–15), 10:00
4. "Save the People," 10:37
    New York City is now strangely empty of people.
    "I have not come to abolish the prophets" (Matt. 5:17–20), 15:34
    *Parable of the Pharisee and the Tax Collector (Luke 17:9–14),* 19:58
    "What if your brother sues you?" (Matt. 5:25–26), 19:33
    Parable of the Unmerciful Servant (Matt. 18:23–35), 19:29
5. "Day By Day," 22:30
    "Turn the other cheek" (Matt 5:38–39), 25:55
    Parable of the Sheep and Goats (Matt. 25:31–46), 26:50
    The lamp of the body (Matt. 6:22–24), 29:21
6. "Turn Back, O Man," 30:36
    *Parable of the Good Samaritan (Luke 10:30–35),* 35:11
    "Your Father who sees in secret" (Matt. 6:2–5), 37:45
    *Parable of the rich man and Lazarus (Luke 16:19–31),* 38:53
7. "Bless the Lord," 41:40
    Beatitudes (Matt. 5:1–12), 44:32
        Opposition to Jesus first appears.
8. "All for the Best," 46:05
    The end of the song is sung from the top of the unfinished Twin Towers.
    "The speck in your neighbor's eye" (Matt. 7:3–5), 48:54
    "Love your enemies" (Matt. 5:44), 51:55
    Parable of the Sower (Matt. 13:3–8, 19–23), 52:48
9. "All Good Gifts," 55:03
    "Consider the lilies" (Matt. 6:28–30), 56:24
    *Parable of the Prodigal Son (Luke 15:11–32),* 58:44
    Bread for stone (Matt 7:9–12), 1.04:59
10. "Light of the World," 1.05:40
    "You are the light of the world" (Matt. 5:13–16).
    "By whose authority?" (Matt. 21:23–27; 22:16–21, 36–40; 23:1–10), 1.08:00

("This is the beginning.")

11. "Alas for You," 1.10:38

"Alas for you" (Matt. 23:13–15, 33–34, 36)

"Jerusalem, Jerusalem" (Matt. 23:37–39), 1.12:16

12. "By My Side," 1.13:53

Judas Iscariot (Matt. 26:14–16), 1.16:58

13. "Beautiful City," 1.17:51

Back at Bethesda Fountain in Central Park and the junkyard

The Last Supper (Matt. 26:20–29), 1.21:08

14. "On the Willows," 1.25:02

*Psalm 137*

"Stay here" (Matt. 26:36–41, 34, 42), 1.27:14

Temptation in the desert (Matt. 4:3–11), 1.29:09

Betrayal (Matt. 26:47–56), 1.30:12

Crucifixion (Matt. 27:33–55), 1.32:30

15. Finale, 1.32:49

Death, 1.35:00

Easter morning (Matt. 28:1–10), 1.35:52

City alive, 1.38:40

16. End Credits, 1.38:54

# Chapter 11

# Jesus of Nazareth

*Franco Zeffirelli, director. Not rated. 382 minutes. 1977. Artisan Home Entertainment, 2000*

## Plot Summary

The first movement of Zeffirelli's four-part, nearly six-and-a-half-hour-long story of Jesus opens with a leisurely portrayal of first-century Judaism, including Nazareth synagogue services and Torah debates, Joseph and Mary's betrothal and wedding, Jesus' circumcision and bar mitzvah, and Joseph's funeral. Despite two trips to Jerusalem and one to Bethlehem, Zeffirelli's attention is focused on Nazareth, the village of Mary and Joseph. In the opening scene, the village rabbi reads a text about the coming of a future messiah king, which provokes a call to the people for strict Torah observance. For Zeffirelli, authentic Judaism is of a royal messianic type.[1]

After betrothal arrangements are made for the marriage of Joseph and Mary, Mary responds obediently to an unseen, unheard messenger whose revelation she describes to her mother, Anna,[2] as news of Elizabeth's pregnancy. Meanwhile, Herod the Great discusses Jewish religion and politics with his Roman advisors. A messiah is a bad dream, he says, promising that there will be no messiahs while he reigns.[3] After Elizabeth's baby is born, Mary tells Joseph her own news. A stunned Joseph consults the village rabbi, who warns him that if exposed, Mary could be stoned as an adulteress. To avoid this outcome, Joseph decides to put his betrothed away privately. But a heavenly voice intervenes (one that the audience hears), instructing him to take Mary as his wife. After their wedding, Augustus's census[4] forces Mary and Joseph to travel to Bethlehem where the baby is born.[5] The shepherds and the wise men visit separately, and between the visits, Jesus is circumcised in Jerusalem. Warned by the wise men, the holy family flees Herod's slaughter of the innocents.

Zeffirelli constructs a number of childhood scenes to foreshadow Jesus' future ministry. For example, when Herod dies and the holy family returns to Nazareth, a young Jesus—like the Infant of Prague—raises his hand in a silent Christian blessing as the family looks down on the village below them.[6] When Joseph teaches Jesus and other village boys about the relationship between carpentry and theology and describes ladders as possible connecting points between heaven and earth, Zeffirelli shows a blond, strikingly blue-eyed Jesus climbing one.[7] After Jesus' bar mitzvah, when a group of Roman soldiers commandeers food from Nazareth locals and the people cry out for deliverance, Zeffirelli responds with a close-up of the blue-eyed Jesus watching thoughtfully from a distance. And finally, when Jesus is twelve and the holy family visits Jerusalem, Joseph places a sacrificial lamb "without blemish" on Jesus' shoulders.[8] And then when Jesus' parents find him in the Temple, teaching the religious leaders, he argues that "prayer from the heart is more important" than sacrifice.

Years pass, and in the midst of increasing Zealot activities, John the Baptist begins his wilderness ministry. Apparently soon after Joseph's death, Jesus appears at the Jordan—without explanation—to be baptized. John intones, "This is my beloved Son" and "Behold the Lamb of God who takes unto himself the sins of the world," and then tells two of his disciples to follow Jesus. Immediately after this, Herod Antipas arrests John. Curiously, Zeffirelli does not film or mention Jesus' wilderness temptations.[9]

The second movement of the film centers on Jesus' Galilean ministry. Here Zeffirelli opens Jesus' public activity with his sermon in the Nazareth synagogue. After Jesus is rejected there, he turns to Capernaum, where he preaches in a synagogue and in Peter's and Matthew's homes, and where he performs his first miracles.[10] In his preaching, Jesus cites the fulfillment of prophecy, the upcoming internalization of the law, and the end of the people's captivity to sin. His message, of course, corresponds to the hopes of the Nazareth rabbi's sermon in the film's opening scene.

Jesus' Galilean ministry also focuses on the creation of apostolic Christianity and ends with Jesus giving Peter the "keys of the kingdom of heaven" (Matt. 16:16–19). As Jesus gathers and instructs his disciples, vignettes characterize the disciples according to Christian tradition and provide human interest: John is the man of the spirit; Peter is the fiery fisherman; Matthew is the tax collector; Thomas is the doubter; Simon is the Zealot; Mary Magdalene is the transformed prostitute; and Judas is the manipulative intellectual.

Zeffirelli develops the stories of Peter and Judas more than those of any other disciples.[11] Peter is a realist, a fisherman who has no time for prophets until Jesus meets his cynicism with a miraculous catch of fish (described retrospectively). But even then, Peter challenges Jesus' willingness to associate with tax collectors like Matthew. When Jesus goes to eat in Matthew's house, a drunken Peter stands outside with his back to the door. In response to Peter's rejection of Matthew, Jesus tells the parable of the Prodigal Son and reconciles Peter and Matthew. Reluctantly, Peter leaves his fishing business and his family to follow Jesus.

Judas enters the story after the Baptist's execution. At John's graveside, he talks with a group of Zealots about their future plans. Cynical about the prospects of political revolt, Judas decides to follow Jesus and visits Jesus at night to see if he can join Jesus' growing band of disciples. He tells Jesus that he is different from the other disciples (he is a scholar) and asks if Jesus has any need of a man like him. Jesus, clearly anxious for the first time in the film, covers his face with his hands, and then tells Judas ominously that "the tree will be known by its fruit." Yet when Judas meets with the Zealots later on, he has clearly embraced Jesus' message rather than their fantasies of revolt. He claims that, as the Baptist had said, men must change before kingdoms will change. Simon the Zealot, who also desires a "change within," decides to follow Jesus and becomes the twelfth disciple.

Having now chosen the twelve disciples, Jesus sends them out by twos on their own mission. Judas and Simon the Zealot are paired up and are nearly caught up in a botched attempt to kill Herod Antipas. When the disciples return, full of excitement about what they have accomplished, Jesus asks them, "Who do the people *in Galilee* say that I am?"[12] and "Who do you say that I am?" When Peter states that Jesus is the Messiah, the Son of God, Jesus tells Peter that he will be the rock on which the church is to be built.[13] Jesus then says that he is going to Jerusalem, and Judas interrupts him, excitedly saying, "Oh yes, master!" and "The elders of Israel must know and recognize you!" But suddenly and without warning, Jesus rebukes Judas, beginning to speak of his upcoming death in Jerusalem. Then, with a crescendo of music and with outstretched arms prefiguring his ascension, Jesus says that three days after his death he will rise again.[14]

The third movement of Zeffirelli's film opens with the Sermon on the Mount and ends with the Sanhedrin's lengthy debate about the center of Jewish religion and how Jesus' message relates to that.[15] By placing the Sermon on the Mount with its Beatitudes and Lord's Prayer immediately following Jesus' prophecy of his upcoming death, Zeffirelli transforms Jesus' otherly-focused speech into a reflection of his own inner resolve and spiritual purpose. Following the "sermon," Jesus and his disciples are shown traveling to Jerusalem, surrounded by other excited, singing pilgrims. On the way Jesus hears of his friend Lazarus's illness.[16] Jesus then stops in Bethany and raises Lazarus from the dead, promising similar life for all his believers (John 11:25). The scene thus foreshadows the apostolic church's mission and message.

Just before Jesus' triumphal entry into Jerusalem, Judas meets with Zerah (Zeffirelli's invention), who is a young member of the Sanhedrin. Judas tries to convince Zerah to have the Sanhedrin proclaim Jesus the king of Judea because he is the "only one who can bring peace to Israel." Zerah promises Judas that Jesus will have a Sanhedrin hearing. However, Jesus' cleansing of the Temple, his healing of a Roman centurion's servant,[17] and his harangues against the Pharisees alienate every Jewish political faction and dash Judas's best-laid plans. Most importantly, Jesus fails to turn Judas's "head" knowledge into a "heart" knowledge. Finally, Jesus' healing of a blind man in the Temple leads to accusations of blasphemy (John 9:35–40; 10:30). In the climactic confrontation, Barabbas kills a Roman soldier and then accuses Jesus of being a traitor. As Judas watches, aghast, Jesus disappears from the Temple.

Later that day, Nicodemus visits Jesus to warn him about an upcoming meeting of the Sanhedrin, at which Jesus will be the topic of debate. But Jesus changes the subject, telling Nicodemus that he must be born again.[18] Nicodemus leaves and makes it back in time for the Sanhedrin meeting, where he and Joseph of Arimathea try to defend Jesus in the midst of a lengthy debate.[19] Like the Nazareth rabbi in the film's opening scene, Nicodemus describes the coming of the messiah as the heart of Judaism and urges his colleagues to consider the possibility that Jesus might be that messiah. But Caiaphas makes the charge that Jesus is a false prophet due to his blasphemy (Jesus claims to be the Johannine Son of God) and argues that there is an urgent need to do something with Jesus. Zerah then steps forward, saying he has a way.

The final movement of the film dramatizes the church's message of Jesus' passion and opens with Judas meeting with Zerah again. When a confused Judas admits that Jesus is probably right about the heart being more important than politics, a crafty Zerah suggests that Judas no longer believes that Jesus is messiah. He challenges Judas to bring Jesus to the Sanhedrin to be proved either the messiah or a false prophet.[20]

At the Last Supper, Jesus tells Judas to go quickly, and a smiling Judas thinks that Jesus has finally agreed with his Sanhedrin plan. After Judas leaves, Jesus institutes the Eucharist. Then, at Gethsemane, Judas hands Jesus over to Zerah of the Sanhedrin. The disciples wake up, and Peter calls Judas a traitor, but Judas says it is the only way; Jesus needs to speak before Caiaphas. As the confusion becomes a near riot, Jesus saves his disciples from arrest, telling the Temple police that they already have the one they want. Judas then races off in search of Zerah, hoping to be part of the planned meeting with Caiaphas. But when he finds Zerah, Zerah informs him that this is going to be a trial for blasphemy, not a mere inquiry. Taking a bag of money that Zerah thrusts at him, the broken Judas leaves.

Caiaphas, claiming he is not holding a Sanhedrin trial, convicts Jesus of blasphemy and has Jesus taken to Pilate—the only one who has the authority to try Jesus. En route, Jesus looks sadly at Peter, who is about to deny him. After Peter's three denials and near arrest, he runs away in the dark. In one of Zeffirelli's most powerful edits, he segues to Judas who is running off to commit suicide (thus connecting the two chief disciples of the film's second half). Judas's body is then shown hanging from a tree, with the money lying on the ground beneath him.

Pilate arrives in Jerusalem at dawn to Zealot cries of "Free Barabbas" and is immediately confronted with the problem of Jesus. Pilate wishes to have nothing to do with the man, whom he considers a dreamer and a religious problem, but Zerah convinces Pilate to try Jesus anyway. When scourging does not satisfy the Zealot-inspired crowd and when they call for the release of Barabbas rather than Jesus, Pilate turns Jesus over for crucifixion.[21]

Zeffirelli cuts back and forth between the Via Dolorosa[22] and Calvary, and Zerah, who wanders aimlessly about the Temple. Zeffirelli's crucifixion is far more violent than those of his precursors, but the audience knows this primarily from the anguish on Jesus' face, which Zeffirelli shows repeatedly in close-ups, and in Jesus' gasps for breath.[23] Intriguingly, Jesus' cross is a scaffold, not a free-standing cross. Jesus utters all the words from the cross except "I thirst." As Jesus dies, Nicodemus looks at the cross from afar, quoting Isa. 53:3–7 (recalling the messianic Judaism of the film's opening scene) and whispering "born again."[24] After Jesus dies, a gentle rain sweeps the hillside as the deposition and pietà occur. Meanwhile, Zerah convinces the Romans to guard the tomb.

On Easter morning, as three women are led to the tomb by the Roman guards, two men in white tell the women that "Jesus is not here." The Roman guards enter the open tomb and bring out the burial cloths, which the women later find lying on the ground. Mary Magdalene then returns to the disciples and tries to convince them that she has seen the Lord. But only Peter believes, and he launches into his first post-Easter sermon.[25] Suddenly Jesus appears to the disciples, explains Scripture, enjoins them to receive the Holy Spirit, and commissions them. The movie ends with a shot of the empty grave cloths on the tomb ledge.

### Memorable Characters

- Jesus: As befits Zeffirelli's "spiritual" message, Jesus is an iconic, unblinking, otherworldly divine figure. In short, Zeffirelli has returned to the early pattern in Jesus films where stories of conversion and degradation swirl around the flat, undeveloped character of Jesus. Jesus is conceived virginally, raised by loving parents in Nazareth, and trained in the synagogue and in Joseph's carpentry shop. He spends more of his Galilean ministry in synagogues than any other cinematic Jesus does. His announcement of his death in Jerusalem is jarring, because there has been virtually no serious opposition to him in Galilee, and neither a sacrificial nor a martyr's death has been part of his message. However, when he arrives in Jerusalem, his message of heart over head manages to alienate every political faction within Judaism. When he heals a blind man in the Temple and says that he and the Father are one and the same, the charge of blasphemy is leveled against him. Jesus refuses to recant after his arrest when he is brought to Caiaphas, and then before Pilate he claims to be a king. His death and resurrection prove his divinity.
- Zerah: Zeffirelli's invention, like Stevens's invented Sorak (and the Dark Hermit), is a character intended to reduce anti-Semitism in the passion.[26] He is a youthful member of the Sanhedrin and politically astute. He arranges for the Romans to put a guard at Jesus' tomb and enters the tomb Easter morning, where he says, "Now it begins."
- Peter: Zeffirelli invests this central disciple/apostle with a good deal of human interest.[27] Peter is a drunken sailor, quick tempered but generous, offering his Capernaum house for Jesus to use for teaching. When some townsfolk bring a paralytic and ruin part of his courtyard roof, Peter gets upset. Nevertheless, Jesus proclaims Peter to be the "rock" upon which he will build his church, and although Peter does deny Jesus three times, he is the first to believe Mary Magdalene's words "He is risen"—without having seen Jesus.
- Judas: Zeffirelli first introduces him at John the Baptist's funeral, where he speaks of his interest in becoming a follower of Jesus, whom he believes could be the messiah—priest and king. He is a translator of documents and can read and write Hebrew, Greek, and Latin. He is of a higher social class than the other disciples, having never worked with his hands. The Zealots try to incorporate him into their plans to overthrow the Roman occupation, and at first he refuses to get involved. But when he gets to Jerusalem, he meets privately with Zerah, hoping to get Jesus a hearing before the Sanhedrin. Judas is a fully round character, conflicted between his mind and heart; pulled between politics and religion. He hands Jesus over to Zerah thinking he is doing what Jesus wants him to do, and he shakes his head in bewildered denial when Jesus asks him if he betrays his master with a kiss. Still thinking he and Jesus are working together on the same plan, he tries to gain entrance to the Sanhedrin, hoping to support Jesus as he talks with Caiaphas. But when Zerah tells him that Jesus is being tried for blasphemy

and gives Judas a bag of money, Judas goes off and hangs himself. His scheming political ideas have betrayed him, and he dies of a broken heart.

- Joseph of Arimathea: This wise member of the Sanhedrin, a Pharisee, and a lover of Jewish law is often found in Jesus' company in Galilee. He is at Simon's house when Mary Magdalene washes Jesus' feet with her tears, and he debates Jesus about the center of Jewish law. He defends Jesus as best he can before the Sanhedrin, showing in the process that he is a "believer" in Jesus as Messiah.
- Nicodemus: He is the Judean equivalent of Joseph of Arimathea in Galilee: a member of the Sanhedrin who is at Bethany when Jesus raises Lazarus from the dead, who warns Jesus of Sanhedrin opposition, supports Jesus before the Sanhedrin, and quotes part of Isa. 53 as Jesus dies.

### Memorable Visuals

- Various Jewish rituals (reading of Torah, circumcision)
- Annunciation to Mary
- Mary in labor pains on the way to Bethlehem
- The three kings (in red, white, and blue) meeting and discussing the meaning of the star
- Mary's highly eroticized birthing scene
- The child Jesus climbing a (Jacob's?) ladder
- Jesus, with hand lifted in blessing, as miracles occur
- Peter and Matthew as Jesus tells the parable of the Prodigal Son
- Judas asking if he can be one of Jesus' disciples
- Mary Magdalene washing Jesus' feet
- Zerah suggesting to Judas that Judas no longer believes Jesus is the messiah
- Zerah giving Judas a bag of money
- Caiaphas tearing his robes and reciting the Shema when Jesus says, "I am"
- Peter's remorse after denying Jesus, cut to Judas's remorse at betraying Jesus
- Jesus, in red robe and crown of thorns after the scourging, backlit as he enters Pilate's court again and looks (ethereally) skyward
- Roman soldiers at spear point, keeping sympathetic Jewish crowds from getting close to Jesus
- Nicodemus reciting Isa. 53 while watching the crucifixion

### Key Scriptures

Although Zeffirelli draws widely from the canonical Gospels, his Jesus is primarily a prophet of Jer. 31:31–34 in his early Galilean ministry, but increasingly Johannine when he gets to Jerusalem. The story of the founding of the apostolic church is, of course, reminiscent of Matt. 16:17–20 and Acts 1–7.

### Cultural Location/Genre: Religious Drama, Television Miniseries

In 1965, director George Stevens "sued Paramount and NBC . . . when the television station planned to screen [his film] *A Place in the Sun* (1951) with commercial breaks."[28] Stevens eventually lost the battle, and *The New York Times* noted a few months later that Stevens, along with other Hollywood directors, then "launch[ed] a vigorous counterattack in their campaign to reduce or eliminate commercial interruptions from motion pictures shown on television."[29] Stevens went on to argue that "a motion picture should be respected as being more than a tool for selling soap, toothpaste, deodorant, used cars, beer and the whole gamut of products advertised on television."[30]

Zeffirelli apparently did not share the uneasiness of Stevens, for although Zeffirelli's *Jesus of Nazareth* appeared on NBC television without commercial breaks, the film had been cut for future advertising spots. Initially, General Motors was to be the major sponsor of the miniseries, but the company withdrew its support after thousands of fundamentalist Christians wrote to the company, criticizing the as-yet-unseen film. And so Proctor and Gamble[31] came forward to ensure that Zeffirelli's film would appear on television.

Zeffirelli's six-hour, Emmy-nominated film debuted on the two successive Sunday evenings of Holy Week, 1977, and just three months after ABC television's blockbuster twelve-hour miniseries *Roots*. And like *Roots* and Young's miniseries *Jesus* (1999), one could argue that Zeffirelli's film can only properly be viewed when accompanied by commercials.

The television setting, along with its annual rebroadcast, made Zeffirelli's film DeMille's successor as the most popular Jesus movie.[32] Accordingly, it gave a whole new generation their first and most memorable view of Jesus.[33] Clearly, the TV miniseries setting significantly changes the Jesus of film. While the Jesus story obviously grows in length,[34] the TV format also guarantees constant interruptions. Even on DVD, the repeated fades to black remind viewers of the commercials that would have constantly interrupted the miniseries. Further, the miniseries format ensures that the movie will not be seen at one sitting but will be watched over a period of at least two days. As a result, what was said about the counterculture in the films of Jewison and Greene has now become true of the "orthodox film tradition" about Jesus: it (he) has become a commodity within consumer culture.[35] The film tradition with its Jesuses must now compete for an audience and for its viewers' attention in the midst of a multitude of household and commercial distractions. Not even the most reverent portrayal of Jesus is in a religious setting when it is shown on television. Thus, Zeffirelli's Jesus, like Jewison's, becomes just one celebrity among a host of others.

The television setting probably also accounts for several of the underlying motifs in the movie. First, television touts family values in order to attract the widest viewing audience and the most lucrative advertisers. Accordingly, most of the first part of the film sets Jesus in a happy family. Nazareth becomes ancient Galilee's equivalent of Mayberry, with Joseph the replacement for Andy Griffith, and Anna, Aunt Bea.[36] Second, television speaks to audiences that are comfortably ensconced in the status quo from which TV itself profits. Accordingly, in Zeffirelli's film, the appropriate response to political and social troubles is a form of "spirituality" set in opposition to "the mind" (which might interfere with consumer capitalism). Thus, for Zeffirelli's Jesus, it is the "heart," not the "head," that matters. Of course, all of this is appropriate for a U.S. culture of expressive individuals who, in a culture of sameness, distinguish themselves primarily by their consumer choices.

Zeffirelli's appeal to U.S. political values is a bit more subtle. Yet two of his more remarkable myth-making strategies occur in the birth narrative and in the passion narrative—those segments shown most often on TV and those most familiar to Christian audiences. In the birth narrative, Zeffirelli breaks with Jesus-film tradition by choosing to film each of the three kings independently following the mysterious star from their own continents (Asia, Africa, and Europe), until they meet not far from Bethlehem.[37] In Zeffirelli's rendering, when they first meet they pose, facing the camera—one clothed in red, one clothed in blue, and one clothed in white.[38] The colors of the U.S. flag, representing the nations of the world, are thus joined together under one bright star—the other symbol on the U.S. flag—to form a perfect American Christmas story.

In the second segment, set just before the passion narrative, Zeffirelli films an imaginary Sanhedrin debate about what to do with Jesus. There, Joseph of Arimathea speaks of "rights" and of "representing the people." He wonders whether the members of the Sanhedrin might not be "too cut off from [the people] and from their real problems," whereas Jesus speaks with a "new vision which seems to answer all their hopes." Jesus' message is one of "goodness [and] . . . the virtues of humility." Another member of the Sanhedrin chimes in with how "our tradition is kept alive by new ideas." With the U.S. bicentennial (1976) and the inauguration of the peanut farmer Jimmy Carter[39] as the first "born-again" U.S. president still fresh in American memory, Zeffirelli evokes the contemporary American political climate by placing Jesus' conversation with Nicodemus ("You must be born again," John 3:3) immediately before this Sanhedrin debate about representation and "new ideas." Not coincidentally, the conversation reflects Jimmy Carter's 1976 acceptance speech of the Democratic Party presidential nomination more than it does first-century Judean politics.

But Zeffirelli made his movie for Italian TV as well as American TV. In fact, the movie reflects Italian, post-Vatican II Catholicism in many ways, especially in its sympathetic portrayal of Judaism. However, unlike Pasolini's *The Gospel According to St. Matthew* ten years earlier, Zeffirelli's film is canonical, not revolutionary. It is spiritual, not materialist. It is mythic (in the sense of accepting the social status quo), not political. Most importantly, Zeffirelli's film is the story of the apostolic church, not of the little people.

## Director

Zeffirelli's spiritual focus is even more evident in his *Brother Sun, Sister Moon* (1973). This film traces the early career of St. Francis from his call, through his rebuilding of a church in Assisi, to his successful audience with the pope. Most critics panned the film, calling Zeffirelli's Francis a flower child and reviling its lack of substance. Reportedly, Zeffirelli himself said that one should not think too much about the film and that he intended it as a simple experience. Some might say the same about his Jesus film. It reviles intellectuals in favor of experience. The film's spiritual message leaves the world untouched.

Zeffirelli's best-known films are visually ornate dramas based on classical sources (often Shakespeare). His most famous is *Romeo and Juliet* (1968). Olivia Hussey, who plays the Virgin Mary in *Jesus of Nazareth*, was Juliet in that award-winning film. *Hamlet* (1990) is Zeffirelli's most infamous film, leaving critics quite divided; most prefer the versions of Olivier (1948) and Branagh (1996). In addition to their objections to the casting and to the performance of the lead (Mel Gibson), critics disliked Zeffirelli's obvious shortening and reinterpretation of the play. In particular, some critics objected to the invention of an early scene where Hamlet, Gertrude, and Claudius are present at the funeral of King Hamlet, which critics felt revealed crucial motifs of the story too early.

The length of *Jesus of Nazareth* and the inclusion of so much of the canonical Gospels obscures Zeffirelli's similar treatment of the Jesus story. In fact, most of the film's first movement is an invention that reveals Zeffirelli's key motif: spiritual Christianity supersedes messianic Judaism. Of course, it may not be the length that obscures Zeffirelli's obvious interpretation of the Gospels. It may be the fact that most of his audience shares his conception of Christianity as the successor of Judaism, with a message of family values and "spirituality" untouched by, and not touching on, any sociopolitical problems.

## DVD Extras and Technical Features (First DVD)

Trailer (0:37)

Cast and Crew (filmography is updated through 1999)

Historical Information (twenty pages, the only named source of which is Henri Daniel-Rops, *Daily Life in Palestine at the Time of Christ* [1962]).

## DVD Chapters

### First DVD

1. *Jesus of Nazareth*
     Opening scene in Nazareth, 2:15
2. Sermon, 2:20
     Joseph listens to a synagogue sermon about the king, messiah, who will stand on the roof of the Temple and proclaim that the time of deliverance has come. "Those who believe and are faithful to God will rejoice... be careful to observe all things written in the law of Moses..."
3. The Marriage Contract, 4:54
4. Betrothal to Each Other, 7:13
5. Message from God, 9:06
     Also witnessed by Anna, her mother
     The angel's words are not heard, only Mary's responses.
         "How can that be, no man has ever touched me. Behold the handmaiden of the Lord, let it be done to me according..."
     "There's news of Elizabeth, she's going to have a son."
6. King Herod, 13:06
7. "Blessed Mary," 15:37
     Blessed, 16:36
     "My soul doth magnify," 18:08
8. A Special Child, 18:40

"Mary's always been a bit strange, not like the others."
  Naming of John, 19:45
 9. Joseph's Dilemma, 21:50
    Bill of divorce, 24:17
10. Nightmares, 25:51
    Mary being stoned by villagers, 26:11
    Angel's voice is heard, "Joseph, son of David," 26:47
11. Wedding Day, 27:18
12. Discussion of a Census, 30:35
13. Fulfilling the Prophecy, 33:06
    "It is written he himself is pure from sin . . . ," 34:02
    "I must go to Bethlehem," 34:33
        "Thou, O Bethlehem."
14. Traveling to Bethlehem, 36:05
    A laboring Mary, 36:23
    One king and the star, 36:38
    A laboring Mary, 37:05
    Another king and the star, 37:19
    A laboring Mary, 37:44
    Another king and the star, 37:56
    A laboring Mary, 38:24
15. Three Kings, 38:34
16. No Room in the Inn, 42:54
17. A Child is Born, 46:37
    Shepherds see the star, 46:37
    Birthpangs, 47:04
        Is it a child crying, or another bleating lamb like those heard half a minute earlier?
18. The Shepherds Come, 49:40
    Shepherd boy with a lamb around his shoulders, 52:00
19. News of the Birth, 52:15
    News of the wise men, 52:27
    Herod says, "O thou Bethlehem," 52:56
    Herod does not meet the kings.
20. A Seal in Flesh, 54:11
    Simeon, 55:56
21. Gifts from the Wise Men, 57:54
    Names of the newborns (flight to Egypt), 58:49
        Flock of lambs, 59:35
        Three kings, 59:37
    "King of Israel who will take away the sins of the world," 1.00:53
    A word of warning, 1.02:05
    "Kill every male child," 1.03:12
22. Slaughter of the Innocents, 1.04:19
    On the way to Egypt, 1.06:54
23. A Home in Nazareth, 1.07:27
    "Herod is dead."
    Road back to Nazareth, 1.08:29
    Child Jesus blesses Nazareth, 1.09:42
24. Gifts from God, 1.10:28
    Joseph teaches carpentry again, with a bit of theology.
    Joseph's (Jacob's?) ladder, 1.11:18

Lambs being led below
25. Roman Soldiers, 1.12:52
    Jesus' bar mitzvah; he reads Torah in the synagogue; Mary watches
    Zealots introduced, 1.16:16
    "How long must we wait, O Lord?" 1.17:12
        The boy Jesus watches (cf. Young's *Jesus*).
26. Pilgrimage to Jerusalem, 1.17:44
    A lamb on Jesus' shoulders, 1.19:06
    "The prayer from the heart is more important," says Jesus in the Temple.
27. An Unholy Marriage, 1.21:15
    Rabbi reads a collage of messianic Scripture in synagogue.
    John the Baptist, 1.22:38
        An unholy marriage
28. John the Baptist, 1.26:33
    Jesus' future disciples, 1.28:47
    Mass baptisms, 1.28:52
29. Not the Messiah, 1.29:37
    Salome listens—Herodias demands that Herod Antipas arrest John, 1.31:19
    "Who are you?" 1.32:43
30. Returning to God, 1.34:57
    Joseph on his deathbed: "They will run the shop."
    "Into thy hand, I commend my spirit," 1.36:40
    Mary recites the Shema: "The Lord our God is one."
31. The Messiah, 1.37:57
    Andrew and Philip in the background, 1.41:33
    Jesus wanders off into the wilderness, 1.42:05
    John arrested, 1.42:29
32. The Scriptures Are Fulfilled, 1.43:00
    "The Kingdom of God comes not in a way foreseen by men" (Luke 17:20–21), 1.45:54
33. The First Followers, 1.47:18
    "Stone the blasphemer," 1.47:31
    Andrew and Philip are Jesus' first disciples, 1.48:15
    Sent by John whom Herod has just imprisoned, 1.48:44
34. Driving out Satan, 1.49:47
    In the Capernaum synagogue, John watches, 1.50:25
        "Dead stone commandments for . . . unthinking minds"
        "God wants to write the law on your hearts."
        The good news is this: "Your captivity is over."
            "Captivity in sin . . ."
        "God fulfills the promise . . . , and reconciles himself to man."
        "God is coming to you . . . even to the most wretched. Do not shut the door in his face."
35. Fishermen, 1.54:57
    John speaks: "There must be something more for man between birth and death . . . your preach-
    ing gave me hope . . . we want the law to be alive, written in our hearts."
    Great catch of fish, 1.56:46
        No catch; complains about tax gatherers like Matthew
        Jesus does not say, "Drop down your nets," 1.57:56
        It's a miracle. It's not a miracle, 2.00:56
36. Reading the Signs, 2.01:20
    The paralyzed man in Peter's house
    Matthew (not named), 2.02:21

Kingdom of heaven is like a treasure, a pearl, a net, 2.03:05

"It's a time for joy in what God has freely given; but one day God will ask you to account for the gift. . . . Be prepared, the Kingdom of Heaven is at hand."

37. The Tax Collector, 2.05:15

Levi, or Matthew

Paralytic (Mark 2:1–12), 2.06:56

38. The Home of a Sinner, 2.09:56

According to the Pharisees

"I have come to call sinners . . . the heart of the Law is mercy" (Matt. 9:13).

39. A Story of Brothers, 2.14:03

Peter: "Forgive me master, I am just a stupid man."

40. Unfairly Imprisoned, 2.21:16

"Free John the prophet."

"Before kingdoms change, men must change," says John the Baptist.

41. A Difficult Decision, 2.27:43

Peter leaves his fishing boat.

42. Healing the Child, 2.30.00

"I've come not to bring peace, but a sword . . ."

Jairus, 2.31:47

Thomas, Jairus's servant, brings news of the girl's death.

43. Doubting Thomas, 2.35:03

"Can't you believe without seeing, Thomas?"

44. Start of a New Life, 2.37:22

Peter: "I told my wife I'll come back in the spring."

"You'll never go back. We'll never be the same—nor will anyone else in the whole world."

45. The Princess's Dance, 2.39:42

46. The Head of the Baptist, 2.47:07

47. Burying John, 2.49:01

John's disciples (with Zealots?) discuss politics; Judas is there.

"I have seen the kind of power that he has. Could he be the one priest and king, to lead our people . . . could he be the messiah?"

"I believe . . . ," says Judas, "but let him fulfill his mission."

48. Mary Magdalene, 2.53:41

(a prostitute)

49. Entering the Kingdom of Heaven, 2.57:53

Judas watches; Joseph of Arimathea, a leading Pharisee from Jerusalem, is there.

Rich young ruler, 3.02:14

50. The Scholar Judas, 3.03:53

Judas—"I read and write Hebrew, Greek, and Latin; I translate documents."

Judas is a different social class than the other disciples. "Do you need a man like me?"

Jesus covers his face. "The tree is known by its fruit" (Matt. 12:33).

## Second DVD

51. Endless Fish and Bread, 0:00

Mary Magdalene is there, and lots of people with physical ailments.

Jesus, in deep meditation? (John 6), 2:20

"He's a prophet sent from God!" 5:45

52. Plans of Revolt, 5:56

To avenge the death of John and kill Herod

"The kingdom is at hand—well, a kingdom needs a king."

Judas, "your absurd fantasies . . . I'd rather die than see his words manipulated by men like you. What will defeat his enemies? Your madness, or his mission?"

"Wait until the Passover in Jerusalem . . . , you bring Jesus to us, we have our people among
the Temple guards, they will arrest the Sadducees, and we will force them to declare Jesus
king of the Jews."

Simon the Zealot rejects the plan: "Israel will be reborn by change within."

53. A Tainted Woman, 10:15

A friend of tax collectors (Luke 7:13)

The role of the law for the Pharisees

Joseph of Arimathea is there.

"Are you willing to accept *our* laws . . . we hear you heal on the Sabbath" (Matt.
12:10–12).

Mary Magdalene (Luke 7:36–50; John 8:11; Mark 14:8)

54. Blessed among Women, 16:23

Sending out the Twelve (Matt 10:5, 8–16, 19–20)

Mary, the mother of Jesus (Luke 11:27–28), 18:35

"Anyone who obeys our Father in heaven is brother . . ." (Mark 3:31–35).

55. Assassination Attempt, 19:24

"The king is coming."

Herod is almost killed because two of Jesus' disciples were preaching in town.

(The two disciples are later revealed to be Judas and Simon the Zealot.)

Jesus has no interest in the Zealots.

Herod kills Zealots.

Judas and Simon the Zealot talk about the Zealot deaths, 22:12

"They thought they could force God's hand."

"Jesus will go to Jerusalem, and we will deal with the Sanhedrin on his terms and there will
be no need for a bloodbath."

56. Peter Has Spoken the Truth, 23:12

The return of the Twelve

"Who do people say that I am?" (Matt. 16:13–23)

"Peter has spoken the truth, and now you know it. But you must not reveal it to any man; the
time has not yet come."

Time to go to Jerusalem

Judas says, "Oh yes, master, the whole city awaits you!"

"No, Judas, the Son of Man will be rejected . . ."

57. The Lord's Prayer, 28:23

Sermon on the Mount (Matt. 5:1–12; 6:8–13)

58. The Holy City, 31:51

Peter and Jesus talk at night. Peter tells Jesus he can't go to Jerusalem if he is going to die there
(Matt. 16:22–23).

59. Raising Lazarus from the Dead, 37:23

News of Lazarus's illness, 38:10

60. "Proclaim Jesus King in Judea," 43:46

Lambs brought to the Temple and slaughtered

Judas meets Zerah, who speaks of Jesus' miracles, 46:05

"He is the only man who can bring peace to Israel."

"Let Jesus prove himself before the Sanhedrin."

61. Palm Sunday, 48:27

Cleansing the Temple, 51:15

Judas rebukes Jesus.

"Open your heart, Judas—not your mind."

62. Services at the Temple, 55:46

Mary, mother of Jesus, comes to Jerusalem.

"Blessed are the eyes that see what you see" (Luke 10:23), 56:23

"I thank you for hiding these things from the learned" (Matt 11:25; Luke 10:21).

"First must be your slave" (Mark 10:43–45)

"Come to me" (Matt. 11:28), 57:45

"Inherit the kingdom from the foundation" (Matt. 25:34).

"I was hungry" (Matt. 25:35).

63. Religious Zealots, 59:27

Jesus meets Barabbas, 1.01:00

"The day of revenge has come."

"Love your enemies" (Matt. 5:44). (Judas listens.)

"They will perish by the sword." (Matt. 26:52)

"I take on the sins of the world."

64. Out of the Mouth of Babes, 1.04:22

"By what authority?" 1.05:08

"John's authority?"

65. "Seek and Ye Shall Find," 1.07:50

(Barabbas listens.)

66. Adulteress, 1.10:18

(not Mary Magdalene)

Jesus seems to make a fish symbol.

67. Friend to the Romans, 1.13:29

Centurion's slave (Luke 7:1–10)

"So the Zealot orders have changed," says Barabbas.

68. The Blind Man Can See, 1.16:40

69. The High Priests, 1.21:48

"I and my father are one" (John 10:30), 1.26:45

Barabbas kills a Roman guard in the Temple.

Judas is confused, 1.28:26

70. Warning, 1.28:33

Nicodemus (John 3), 1.29:34

71. The Temple Elders, 1.31:52

"If we're not cut off from them and their real problems . . ."

Heart vs. mind; a message of comfort, goodness, purity; virtues of humility

72. Judas's Decision, 1.41:49

"I thought political action could solve everything; thought it was enough to think clearly and act clearly. He doesn't need my ideas—he says the heart is more important."

73. Passover, 1.45:15

Prophecy of betrayal, 1.48:40

74. The First Communion, 1.50:45

75. The Betrayal, 1.56:53

Prayer in garden

Judas comes, 1.58:40

76. An Invaluable Help, 2.01:37

Thirty pieces of silver, 2.02:49

77. The Son of God, 2.04:10

Peter's denials (prelude), 2.04:12

Before the Sanhedrin, 2.04:39

(including John 18:19–23)

78. Three Denials, 2.10:11

Judas hangs himself, 2.12:28

79. Pontius Pilate, 2.12:56

"Free Barabbas!"

Jesus appears, 2.15:19

Pilate washes his hands, 2.15:32

Defilement, 2.16:10

80. Trial, 2.17:45

81. Mockery of a King, 2.23:31

Scourging

Mockery, 2.24:05

"Behold the Man," 2.25:27

Release of a prisoner, 2.28:23

82. The People Shall Decide, 2.29:33

"Free Barabbas!"

Mary Magdalene arrives

Jesus, guilty of treason, sentenced to be crucified, 2.34:20

83. The Crucifixion, 2.35:19

Via Dolorosa, 2.35:51

Veronica, 2.38:25

No Simon of Cyrene

Crucified, 2.39:15

Last words, 2.40:34

84. Two Thieves, 2.40:43

85. A Mother's Sorrow, 2.42:56

The Roman Centurion whose servant Jesus healed

Mary Magdalene—"One of the family"

John, the Beloved Disciple, comes, 2.44:50

Nicodemus quotes Isa. 53, 2.47:38

"Brought as a lamb to the slaughter"

"Father, into thy hands," 2.49:42

86. End of Suffering, 2.50:45

Peter weeping, 2.51:11

Deposition, 2.51:49

(No spear thrust, or "This is the Son of God")

87. An Empty Tomb, 2.53:45

A tomb reserved; a guard needed

Women go to the tomb with Roman guards, 2.56:04

88. He Has Risen, 2.58:49

Mary Magdalene has seen him.

89. A Question among Disciples, 3.04:21

Peter believes without seeing.

90. Appearing to the Disciples, 3.07:30

Roman guards, members of the Sanhedrin return to the tomb—Zerah says his disciples must have taken the body. Zerah enters the tomb, sees the empty cloths: "Now it begins."

91. Closing Credits, 3.10:49

# Chapter 12

# The Jesus Film

*Peter Sykes and John Krisch, directors. Rated G. 117 mins. 1979. Madacy Entertainment, 2003*

## Plot Summary

Sykes and Krisch's[1] rendering of Luke's Gospel opens with a camera shot of deep space, with photographs of the heavens and of earth, and with a scrolling intertitle of John 3:16–17. This beginning—more Johannine than Lukan—jarringly conflicts with the words of its omnipresent narrator, who proclaims that the story to follow comes entirely from Luke. But the opening quotation from the Gospel of John fits well with the film's evangelistic goal—to convert millions.

As the camera pans a pastoral Galilean countryside, the narrator[2] recites part of Luke's preface (1:1–4, leaving out the opening phrase "*many others* have undertaken . . .") and combines Luke 1:5 with Luke 2:1 to emphasize the historicity and "absolute truth" of the Gospel account that will follow.[3] Throughout the film, the authoritative, omniscient narrator will often introduce scenes and summarize narratives, thereby continuing to emphasize the "absolute truth" mentioned in the prologue. For the most part, the characters with speaking roles in the film will be those who also speak in the Gospel itself.

The directors skip entirely the annunciation to Zechariah in the Temple and the subsequent birth of John the Baptist. Instead, the story begins with a shortened version of the angel Gabriel's annunciation to Mary, which comes as a bright light that covers the virgin's face and reveals a human form. Mary's home, where the annunciation takes place, seems improbably large and extravagant.[4] Its plastered walls are painted in two colors, and it has latticed alcoves and nine-foot ceilings. Its size, coupled with the extensive interior furniture, resembles more closely the homes of the wealthy in Jesus' era,[5] but the depiction also suits the middle-class American audience for whom the film was originally intended.[6]

Sykes and Krisch's selections from the infancy narratives highlight the film's evangelical Protestant perspective.[7] Thus the narrator describes the shepherds as the "first evangelists" and summarizes their message as one of "the virgin mother and the savior's birth" (notably, the former is not part of Luke 2:9–17). Setting aside the Lukan stylistic device of paired stories (two annunciations by an angel, two miraculous births), the directors show only the prophecy of Simeon before turning to the story of Jesus in the Temple at twelve years old. A character on-screen wonders whose child Jesus is,[8] and Jesus' words to his parents imply the film's central Christology: Jesus is on earth to take care of his (heavenly) Father's business.

Quite unexpectedly, the words "Inspirational Films presents," then *The Public Life of*, and then *Jesus* appear on-screen, followed by a screen with the words "a documentary taken entirely from the Gospel of Luke." This is the only hint of a title to the film.[9] After a brief historical introduction (Luke 3:1–3), John appears in the desert, preaching and baptizing. But John does not speak apocalyptically of the chaff burning with unquenchable fire, nor does the genealogy of Jesus precede his desert temptation. At Jesus' baptism the narrator recites the words of the heavenly voice (3:22), then Jesus goes off into the desert, where Satan appears as a hissing snake that tempts Jesus. Satan speaks his own words with a supernatural, reverberating voice.

As in the infancy narrative, the directors add messianic motifs to the opening of Jesus' ministry. For example, after Jesus preaches in his hometown of Nazareth, the synagogue crowd rebukes Jesus by saying "*Only the messiah* can fulfill that promise." Similarly, in introducing Jesus' deeds in Capernaum, the narrator adds, "The people *longed for the messiah* to free them from the [Roman] tyranny."

Sykes and Krisch follow the main outlines of the Lukan Jesus' Galilean ministry, but they select and dramatically reorder events and teachings. The changes emphasize Jesus as evangelist and healer along with the faith responses of individuals. Thus, Sykes and Krisch place the parable of the Pharisee and the Tax Collector (18:10–14) just before the call of Peter, who listens to it attentively (5:1–11). After Peter's miraculous catch of fish, Sykes and Krisch show Jesus again preaching in a synagogue. Here he describes his purpose as coming "not to destroy men's lives but to save them" (9:56),[10] and after quoting an obscure text from Isaiah[11] he leaves and raises Jairus's daughter from the dead (8:40–42, 49–56).[12]

Having established Jesus' miraculous powers, his knowledge of Scripture, and the themes of his preaching, Sykes and Krisch return to the substance of Luke 5:27–9:45.[13] However, they omit the pericopes that deal with the opposition of religious and political authorities to Jesus, waiting to introduce this plot element with the story of Herod's (Antipas) imprisonment of John the Baptist (3:18–20), which is placed after the anointing by Mary Magdalene in the house of Simon the Pharisee (7:36–8:3).[14] Notably, there is no mention in the film of John the Baptist's death (9:7–9). Thus Peter's response to Jesus' question "Who do men say that I am?" comes off a bit bizarrely: "Some say you are John the Baptist" (9:19). Moreover, without any reference to Herod's murder of John or to the Pharisees' deep-seated opposition to Jesus (e.g., 5:29–6:11), Jesus' disclosure of his upcoming death (9:22) lacks any historical contextualization. Not insignificantly, Sykes and Krisch's Jesus says nothing of the *elders, chief priests, and scribes* rejecting him.

Sykes and Krisch confirm Jesus' first prophecy of his death and resurrection with the transfiguration (9:28–36), a relatively rare scene in Jesus films. In extremely soft focus, Moses and Elijah stand beside Jesus, now in blindingly white clothing, and tell him that he "will fulfill God's purpose and die in Jerusalem." As a heavenly cloud descends, the narrator, again standing in for God, intones God's heavenly words of affirmation.

After exorcising a demon from a young boy (9:37–43), Jesus, still dressed in dazzling white, wanders about the Galilean countryside teaching his twelve male disciples and the women named in 8:1–3. He recites for them the Lord's Prayer—a prayer that more closely resembles the Matthean version (cf. Matt. 6:9–13)—and using examples from nature, encourages his disciples to trust in God. Not until the parable of the Mustard Seed (13:18–20) does Jesus return to a city (13:22). Notably his audience now includes those who criticize his behavior (5:30). After he heals a crippled woman in a synagogue (13:10–14), Jesus finally publicly confronts a religious leader (the leader of the synagogue), angrily calling him and those with him "hypocrites."

At this point the story shifts to follow what appears to be a group of pilgrims on the way to Passover in Jerusalem—although there is not yet any clear reference to this in the film (cf. 13:22). Sykes and Krisch's "road to Jerusalem" section opens with a rich man's question, "What must I do to inherit eternal life?" (18:18–27; cf. Mark 10:17), and is followed by Jesus' teaching about the kingdom of God (17:21–22). As he and his disciples (Peter and Judas) pass by two crucified victims,[15] Jesus talks about the coming day of the Son of Man and his suffering and rejection (17:22–25).

Then, with Roman soldiers looking on, the pilgrims stop in the desert near Jericho.[16] When someone asks, "Who is my neighbor?" people in the crowd respond with "Not those soldiers!" and "What about Caesar?" But Sykes and Krisch's Jesus ignores the political implications of these responses by telling the parable of the Good Samaritan (10:29–37), which emphasizes showing kindness to those in need. In Sykes and Krisch's rendering, the parable becomes an open invitation for entering the kingdom of God (18:15–17; 9:47–48), an invitation that stands in stark contrast to the exclusive aloofness of the religious leaders. With the healing of the blind man and the story of Zacchaeus, viewers are finally given explicit reference points to Jesus' Jerusalem journey (18:35–19:10), which is followed by Jesus' third prophecy of his death (18:31–33).

Sykes and Krisch introduce Jesus' final days in Jerusalem with the narrator quoting Luke 9:51b, which is immediately followed by the triumphal entry into the city (19:35–37, 39–44).[17] Jesus then goes to the Temple where he overturns the money changers' tables and releases the sacrificial animals (cf. Mark 11:15; John 2:15).[18] The cleansing of the Temple leads directly to a meeting between Pilate and Caiaphas, where Pilate states, "I understand that many have already hailed him as king."[19] Threatened thus by Pilate, Annas and Caiaphas decide to confront Jesus; however, before the confrontations begin, the narrator offers an important caveat: Jesus attacks only *the hypocritical section* of the scribes and Pharisees.[20] Sykes and Krisch use the story of the poor widow's payment of the Temple tax (21:1–4) to frame the priestly challenges to Jesus' authority (20:2–26), and these are the challenges that eventually lead to his arrest and execution.[21]

Sykes and Krisch follow the structure of the Lukan passion narrative much more closely than they did the Lukan structure of Jesus' ministry. However, their Jesus recites the Passover blessings over the wine and bread (which are not mentioned in any Gospel), and they include textually suspect sections of Luke that intensify the sacrificial nature of Jesus' death and the divine plan of salvation. For example, Sykes and Krisch include

Jesus' words at the Last Supper that interpret his death as a death on behalf of his followers (22:19b–20; missing in many ancient manuscripts). And they also include the "sweat like great drops of blood" scene (Luke 22:43–44), which is also missing in most ancient manuscripts. Sykes and Krisch also turn the passion narrative into a clearer conflict between Jesus and Satan by having Peter exclaim, "Then there *is* no traitor!" to which Jesus replies, "*Satan* has desired to test all of you" (22:31–38).[22] Only then, after the Passover meal, are viewers shown the Council's clandestine meeting to "rid themselves of Jesus." And only then is Judas shown leaving the Last Supper, with the narrator's words stating, "Then entered *Satan* into Judas" (22:2–3).

After the betrayal and arrest, Peter denies Jesus three times. But instead of merely weeping (22:62), Sykes and Krisch's Peter, as an example for all later sinners, passionately prays for forgiveness. A brief Jewish trial ensues, and the narrator reintroduces Pilate as "vicious" and "personally responsible for thousands of crosses." However, when the priests accuse Jesus of causing an uproar in the Temple market (not mentioned in Luke 23:1–5) and of perverting the people, the "vicious" Pilate quickly responds, "I see no reason to condemn this man; no reason." The priests then state that Jesus forbids paying taxes to the emperor and claims to be the Messiah—a king. When Pilate discovers that Jesus is from Galilee, he makes the priests take Jesus to Herod. However, Herod fails to pass a sentence on Jesus, and the priests have no recourse but to confront Pilate a second time. Without a word from the priests, Pilate again immediately states that Jesus has done nothing to deserve death. But when voices in the crowd begin clamoring for Jesus' crucifixion,[23] Pilate has Jesus scourged[24] and goes off to write the death sentence.[25]

Sykes and Krisch do not show the release of Barabbas, but instead move directly to the Via Dolorosa. On Jesus' long journey to the cross, people of all races condemn Jesus and try to help him; and finally, a white Simon of Cyrene is compelled to carry the crossbar of Jesus' cross. As befits the Protestant, evangelical underpinnings of the film, no Veronica wipes Jesus' face en route to the cross.

The directors show the nails being driven into Jesus' hands in a close-up and emphasize his agony throughout the crucifixion.[26] However, Jesus finds the strength to speak all the Lukan words from the cross (23:34, 43, 46) while his disciples watch him.[27] Sykes and Krisch add a Roman soldier's sarcastic observation that Jesus' shredded tunic is "no ordinary mystic's garment"—perhaps as an ironic confirmation of Jesus' exalted person and purpose—and the narrator's voice-over reports the supernatural events surrounding Jesus' death.

After the burial, the camera remains in the darkened tomb. When the women arrive on Easter morning, they see a blinding light and the forms of two men who speak in one echoing voice (the scene is reminiscent of the opening annunciation to Mary). The women return to the unbelieving disciples, and Peter rushes to the empty tomb to find the grave cloths still lying there. Finally, two men, fresh from their journey to Emmaus, report that Jesus appeared to them; and suddenly Jesus is in their midst. Jesus then commissions the disciples (Matt. 28:18–20). The camera ascends into space during these last words (Jesus' words become fainter), and the camera looks down upon the earth, providing a visual bookend with the film's opening. In a brief epilogue the narrator reassures viewers that Jesus is alive today and wishes to come into each person's heart, and then Jesus recites John 11:25–26 by way of confirmation.

## Memorable Characters

- Jesus: He is the happy, miracle-working Messiah of the Jewish poor and needy. He is essentially apolitical, demanding little of his followers beyond faith and kindness. He does not refer to himself as "the Son" of "the Father" (cf. 10:17–24), nor does anyone other than the angel Gabriel call him "Son of God" (cf. 4:41; 5:24). Finally, no one ever accuses Jesus of being demon possessed (cf. 11:14–23). Jesus is nearly always smilingly friendly and is a lover of children.[28] He is rarely angry at anyone. After the transfiguration his clothing turns brilliantly white and remains so until shortly after his entry into Jerusalem.
- Peter: This evangelical Christian "converts" immediately after Jesus' opening sermon in Nazareth (4:1–30) and Jesus' parable of the Tax Collector and Sinner (18:10–14). This placement highlights the spiritual nature of sin and the relationship of preaching to conversion. Peter is the spokesman for the disciples, telling Jesus to send the people away before the feeding of the five thousand; he answers Jesus' question "Who do people say that I am?" with "Some say John the Baptist . . ."; and after his threefold denial of Jesus, he prays, asking for God's forgiveness. Peter is at the cross (with other disciples) when Jesus dies, and he runs to the tomb after the women tell the disciples that the tomb was empty.
- Mary Magdalene: The sinner woman of Luke 7:36–50, she is at the feeding of the five thousand and is the one who says, "But all we have are five loaves and two fish." She listens attentively to the recitation of the Lord's Prayer, follows Jesus from Galilee to Jerusalem, where she watches him die, and then visits the empty tomb on Easter morning. Later, she is in the room with the eleven apostles when Jesus appears to them (Luke 24:36–51). ·
- Judas: He has a scruffy beard and always wears a little turban. Jesus touches him often. Judas is the one who tells Jesus that his mother and brothers want to see him (8:19–20); and when Jesus asks the question, "What will it profit a man if he gain the whole earth and lose his own soul?" (9:25), the camera focuses on Judas. He is with Peter when Jesus walks by two crucified victims and prophesies his own upcoming death. Finally, Judas is shown meeting with the "Council of the Elders" (22:3), at which point "Satan entered into him."

## Memorable Visuals

- The heavenly view of earth in the opening and closing
- The dove descending and resting on Jesus (reportedly more than forty takes were needed to get the dove to land on Jesus' shoulder)
- The blinding light with Moses and Elijah at Jesus' transfiguration

- Jesus teaching his disciples to pray the Lord's Prayer—rather than actually *praying* it
- Nighttime, campfire setting of Jesus talking about his upcoming death
- Jesus with Zacchaeus
- The question of paying taxes to Caesar
- Extremely long Via Dolorosa
- The close-up of the nails at the cross

## Key Scriptures

While the film draws primarily from Luke, it emphasizes sections of that Gospel and adds material (either invented or from other Gospels) to portray a hoped-for messiah who comes and dies to save people from their sins and from Satan's power (4:18–19; 5:8; 13:16). The citation of John 3:16–17 in the opening and of John 11:25–26 in the epilogue is indicative of Sykes and Krisch's Johannine interpretation of Luke's Gospel. The camera's descent and ascent also parallels the descending-ascending divine Son of John's Gospel. In keeping with the film's purpose, it touts evangelism in the beginning (the shepherds' message) and at the end (the Great Commission).

## Cultural Location/Genre: Evangelistic Tract

Closely associated with Bill Bright, founder of Campus Crusade for Christ, the film's cultural context is American Protestant evangelicalism. The producers intended the film to fulfill the Great Commission (Matt. 28:16–20), which is quoted at the end of the film. The film continues to be marketed as an evangelistic tool and can be downloaded for free from the Internet. Advocates for the film claim that it has been translated into more languages and has been seen by more people than any other Jesus film. Reportedly, it has been shown to many indigenous people who have never before seen a movie.

American Protestant evangelicalism is also highlighted in the film in three other important ways. First, the film's narrator, Alexander Scourby, is well known for his recorded reading of the King James Bible (1966). Accordingly, for many evangelical Christians, his voice adds an additional "scriptural" element of authority to the film. Second, traditional evangelical conversion stories are emphasized by placing Jesus' parable of the Tax Collector and Sinner (18:10–14) before the call of Peter (5:1–11), with the camera focusing on Peter's reaction and his subsequent confession of sin. Third, near the center of the film, Sykes and Krisch frame Jesus' teaching on discipleship as a nighttime campfire vigil, complete with a woman singing while accompanying herself on a guitar-like stringed instrument.[29] For American high school and college students who have spent summers at Bible camps, the scene is reminiscent of the last night of camp, complete with bonfire testimonials and guitar sing-alongs—only to be surpassed by rousing Sunday morning worship services and subsequent heartrending good-byes.

In the film, Peter's soul-saving testimony ("You are God's messiah") precedes the evangelist's (Jesus') campfire call to discipleship, which is then followed by the mountaintop experience of Jesus' transfiguration (a Sunday morning, camp-closing worship service?). Notably, like many youths, Peter wants to "stay at camp" by building a couple of permanent shelters to keep alive the emotional high of the (summer camp) experience. But sadly, the camper-disciples must leave, come down from the mountain, and face the day-to-day routine of parents, embarrassing siblings, and incompetent church leaders (Luke 9:37–43). Finally, near the end of the film, after Peter "backslides" by denying Jesus three times, he confesses his sin and is restored—thus providing evidence of the "eternal security of the believer"[30] and completing the evangelical journey of faith.

Despite the directors' significant editorial changes to the text of Luke, their film is presented as Jesus' "story taken entirely from the Gospel of Luke." Furthermore, in some DVD formats, the film explicitly touts itself as a documentary, while in others the title and accompanying descriptive genre are entirely missing.[31] Perhaps, like the earliest copies of the Gospels themselves, the film is intended to be "anonymous" and without title. Its narrative style, however, is rather far removed from the neorealist approach of Pasolini's fifteen-year-old *The Gospel According to St. Matthew*. By comparison, Sykes and Krisch's directing style is closer to the episodic structure and stilted literalism of the filmed passion plays of the early twentieth century.

The claims to be the "absolute truth," to be a "documentary," and to be "taken entirely from Luke"—coupled with the film's lack of a recognizable on-screen title—are rhetorical claims intended to convince audiences of the film's "objectivity." In fact, the narrator adds the word "absolute" to Luke's preface (1:4), so that the film's viewers are ostensibly treated to an account of Jesus that is without peer in the movie industry or the church. Not surprisingly, Jesus offers an appropriate, evangelistic rendering of Luke 7:23 that befits the film itself: "Happy are those who have *no doubts* about me" (or this movie).

These rationalistic inflections of the Lukan text are well suited to the directors' evangelistic purpose. However, in addition to making the quite troubling philosophical equation between truth / text and reality, the claim to objectivity is quite simply inaccurate. The plot summary above and the DVD chapters below highlight the directors' rearrangements and interpretative additions to Luke. All these changes are in keeping with the evangelistic theology of the film's directors or are appropriations from Jesus film tradition. What the "absolute truth" claim really does is inflate a particular interpretation to the status of divine authority, simultaneously and ironically undermining whatever truth claims the other canonical Gospels might make. In short, the film is not "the Gospel of Luke," and it is not a "documentary."[32] It is an evangelistic tract.

## Director

John Heyman, producer of this Jesus movie, formed the Genesis Project in 1974 with the goal of rendering the entire Bible on film. But due to financial constraints, the chapter-by-chapter, verse-by-verse project never made it past Gen. 22 in the Old Testament or beyond Luke 2 in the New Testament. By 1978 Heyman had secured additional funding for his project and with Peter Sykes and John Krisch as directors, the decision was made to finish the Gospel of Luke.

The credits of Peter Sykes, the primary director, are mainly B-level horror movies dealing with demon possession and a few early episodes of the British television show

*The Avengers.* Reviewers have savaged his directing skills for being boring, dull, and at times incomprehensible. And while Sykes and Krisch's Jesus film has been praised by some for its attention to first-century costumes and architecture, and for its authentic on-site locations, the directors' editorial additions to Luke's Gospel and their rearrangements of the Gospel's structure are at times bewildering. The acting tends to be amateurish, and the changes in Lukan structure do little to enhance the film's plot.

## DVD Extras and Technical Features

### DVD 1

The Story of Jesus for Children, 1.1:14 minutes long: Excerpts from *Jesus*, cobbled together with a detective-like story where children try to find out who Jesus is.
On the set, 4:40 minutes long

### DVD 2 (25th Anniversary Deluxe Commemorative Edition)

Knowing Jesus personally (closing appendix), 1.54:07–2.00:39
Behind the Scenes, 6:16 minutes long
Tributes, 25:01 minutes long: "Millenial Tribute to Jesus. On the occasion of the two-thousandth anniversary of the birth of Jesus Christ, men and women of influence take the opportunity to honor his life."

## DVD Chapters

The "Event Index" sheet that comes with the DVD indicates there are 63 stops in the film. This is correct. If a viewer clicks "Next" from the "Play" menu, the viewer will be taken to the "next" one of these stops. However, the "Choose a Scene" menu on the DVD "Root Menu" has only 27 chapters. Thus, in the summary below, the 27 DVD chapters are listed first. These are followed by the "Event Index" (paper insert) stop numbers in parentheses. Non-Lukan additions are in italics.

*John 3:16–17* 0:00–0:48
    1. Prologue-annunciation (Luke 1:3a), 0:00
          (2:1a), 00.19
          (lacking 1:1–2, 5b–25)
          (2) Mary Visits Elizabeth (1:39), 1:11
          (lacking 1:49–80)
          (3) The Birth of Jesus (2:1), 1:54
          (4) Shepherds and Angels (2:8–20), 2:48
          (5) Prophecy of Simeon (2:21), 3:33
          (lacking 2:22–24, 36–38, 40)
          (6) Jesus with the Teachers in the Temple (2:41), 4:33
          (John the Baptist appears in the background talking with Jesus, just before his parents arrive.)
          Title 5:44 (In some software media programs the title will appear only when the subtitles menu is activated.)
    2.    (7) Baptism of Jesus (3:1), 6:13
    3.    (8) Temptation in the Wilderness (3:23a), 9:57
          (lacking 3:23b–38)
    4.    (9) Jesus of Nazareth (4:16), 12:10

(lacking 4:25–28)

5.  (10) Jesus at Capernaum (4:31), 15:11
        (lacking 4:32–44)
    *"The Roman occupation of the nation was in evidence everywhere, and the people longed for the
    messiah to free them from the tyranny,"* 15:18
    (11) Pharisee and Tax Collector (Luke 18:9–14), 16:18

6.  (12) Miracle of Catching the Fish (5:1–11), 17:11

7.  (13) Jesus Raises Jairus's Daughter (8:40) 19:04
    *"His arm will be against the Chaldeans"* (Isa. 48:14–15; Luke 9:56. The subtitles quote a dif-
    ferent text: Isa. 55:6–7, 12).
        (lacking 8:42b–48)

8.  (14) Jesus Calls Matthew (5:27), 21:40
        *Matthew Levi, Matt. 9:9; 10:3*
        (lacking 5:12–26; 6:33–11)
    (15) Jesus Chooses the Apostles (6:12), 22:53

9.  (16) Sermon on the Mount (6:17), 24:51
        (lacking 6:43–49)
        Ends with 11:27–28
        (lacking 7:1–10)

10. (17) Simon the Pharisee (7:36), 29:35
        *Mary Magdalene* is the anointing woman, hair uncovered (cf. 32:40)

11. (18) Jesus Teaches (8:1), 32:27
        Now Mary Magdalene has her hair covered.
    (19) John the Baptist in Prison (7:18), 33:03
        (begins with 3:19–20; then moves to 7:11–17)

12. (20) The Parables (8:4), 34:49
    (21) Illustration of the Lamp (8:16), 37:11
    (22) The True Family of Jesus (8:19), 37:45
        Judas gives Jesus the message.

13. (23) Jesus Stills the Storm (8:22), 38:00
    (24) Jesus Heals the Demoniac (8:26), 39:52
        (lacking 9:1–11)

14. (25) Jesus Feeds the Five Thousand (9:12), 42:02
        Mary Magdalene is at feeding of five thousand (and with Jesus as he and the Twelve travel
            throughout Galilee and toward Jerusalem).
        *A young boy* (John 6:9) gives the loaves and fishes to Jesus.
    (26) "Who do you say that I am?" (9:18) 44:33
    (27) Jesus Foretells His Death and Resurrection (9:21), 45:21
    (28) Price of Discipleship (9:23), 45:50
        "What will it profit a man?" (camera is focused on Judas)

15. (29) The Transfiguration (9:28), 47:38
        Elijah and Moses tell Jesus *he will die in Jerusalem.*

16. (30) Jesus Heals the Demoniac Boy (9:37), 49:17
        (lacking 9:43b–50; 9:52–10:22, 38–42)
    (31) The Lord's Prayer (11:1), 51:27
        *Primarily the Matthean version (Matt. 6:9–13; but cf., KJV)*
    (32) Teachings on Prayer (11:9), 52:18
        (lacking 11:14–26; 29–12:21)
    (33) Worry and Faith (12:25), 53:44
        (ends with 17:5–6; lacking 17:7–19)
        (lacking 12:35–13:9)

17. (34) Jesus Teaches on the Kingdom of God (17:1), 54:35

Temptations to sin (17:1–2), 55:08
Mustard seed (13:18–20), 55:22
Not the righteous, but sinners (5:30–32), 55:42
Sell your possessions (12:32–34), 56:08
(35) Jesus Heals a Woman (13:10), 56:25
(lacking 13:20–16:16, 18–31)

18.  (36) Rich Young Ruler (18:18), 57:56
On their way to the Passover in Jerusalem
(37) God's Kingdom Is Within You (17:20), 59:07
Jesus, Peter, and Judas pass by four crosses, 59:32
(lacking 17:26–18:9)
(38) The Great Commandment (10:24), 1.00:08
(Introduced by 16:17)
(39) The Good Samaritan (10:29), 1.00:49
"Suffer the little children" (18:16–17; 9:47–48), 1.01:55

19.  (40) Jesus Heals the Blind Man (18:35), 1.02:32

20.  (41) Zaccheus (19:1), 1.04:08
(lacking 19:11–27)

21.  (42) Triumphal Entry (19:35), 1.06:59
(9:51)
*Palm branches (John 12:13)*
(43) Jesus Weeps over Jerusalem (19:41), 1.08:15
(44) Jesus Cleanses the Temple (19:45), 1.08:56
*Overturning tables and releasing animals (Mark 11:15; John 2:15)*
(45) Political and Religious Leaders Show Opposition (20:20), 1.10:40
*Pilate and Caiaphas talk about the threat of Jesus (an invented scene).*
*The narrator speaks of the "hypocritical section of the scribes and Pharisees.*

22.  (46) Widow's Mite (21:1), 1.11:13
(47) The Authority of Jesus Challenged (20:1), 1.11:58
(48) Parable of the Vineyard (20:9), 1.12:50
(49) Render unto Caesar (20:20), 1.14:33
(lacking 20:27–47; 21:5–38)

23.  (50) The Last Supper (22:1), 1.15:21
(lacking 22:9–13)
(51) The Greatest in God's Kingdom (22:26), 1.18:10
(52) Plot to Kill Jesus (22:2), 1.20:31
(53) Garden of Gethsemane (22:39), 1:20:48
(54) The Arrest (22:47), 1.23:04

24.  (55) Peter's Denial (22:54), 1.24:46
*Peter's prayer of repentance (an invented scene)*
(56) The Trial (22:63), 1:27:54
Before the Sanhedrin
Before Pilate, 1.30:12
The narrator describes *Pilate as "vicious" and "personally responsible for thousands of crosses."*
To Herod, 1.31:11
*Beaten by Herod's men*
Back to Pilate, 1.32:57
Release of Barabbas, 1.33:37
*Scourged by Pilate's men, 1.34:07*

25.  (57) The Crucifixion (23:26), 1.35:27
Simon of Cyrene, 1.36:10
*Inscription over the cross is in three languages (John 19:20).*

(58) Jesus' Death (23:44), 1.44:55
(59) The Burial (23:50), 1.46:31
   *Spices put on the corpse (John 19:39–40)*
26.   (60) The Resurrection (24:1), 1.48:28
(61) On the Road to Emmaus (24:33), 1.51:11
(62) Jesus Appears to the Disciples (24:36), 1.51:28
27.   (63) The Ascension (24:50), 1.52:59
   *Great Commission (Matt. 28:18)*
Appendix, 1.54:06

Chapter 13

# Monty Python's Life of Brian

*Terry Jones, director. 94 mins. Rated R.*
*1979. Criterion, 1999*

### Plot Summary

Like a stereotypical Jesus epic, this film opens with the infancy story and with wise men following a star, traveling from the east to find the Jewish Messiah (Matt. 2). The wise men arrive at a stable (apparently in Bethlehem) and find a mother who has just given birth to a child. They offer gifts to the mother and the baby, and after inquiring as to the newborn's name, they worship the child named Brian. Shortly after leaving this stable, they discover another newborn, lying in a manger not far from the first one. They realize that the second newborn is the real Messiah and rush back to recoup their gifts, leaving a certain amount of chaos in their wake. Thus, the opening scene establishes one of the Python group's major themes: Brian, coincidentally born at the same time and place as Jesus, will in many ways live a life parallel to that of Jesus.

After a comic title sequence, the Jesus epic continues with Jesus and Brian as adults. Brian and his mother happen upon Jesus as he is delivering the Beatitudes from the Sermon on the Mount (Matt. 5), and Brian, his mother, and others at the back of the crowd end up quarreling with those who want to listen to Jesus but cannot hear him clearly. An outrageous argument follows that deals with the interpretation of Jesus' misunderstood words—for example, why should cheesemakers and Greeks be blessed more than other people?

Soon, Brian and his mother leave so that his mother can attend a stoning. To do so, she dons a beard, because Jewish women are not allowed at such events. Like the Sermon on the Mount, the stoning goes awry, and the religious leader who had organized the trial and punishment becomes the victim when he unwittingly speaks the name of Jehovah (thus incurring the charge of and penalty for blasphemy). On the way home to Jerusalem, Brian and his mother pass by crosses with skeletons (perhaps an allusion to Nicholas Ray's opening scenes in *King of Kings*), and Brian speaks to a disgruntled ex-leper, who no longer has a trade because Jesus has healed him. At home, a Roman soldier awaits Brian's mother, who is a prostitute. Brian leaves in anger when his mother tells him that he also is a Roman.

At the children's matinee in the Jerusalem Coliseum, the People's Front of Judea talk aimlessly about Roman oppression, their plans for overthrowing Rome, and their hatred for radical splinter groups. Brian, who sells refreshments at the coliseum, tries to enlist in the PFJ to prove his Jewishness. They give him a job painting anti-Roman graffiti on buildings. The first Roman detachment to catch him corrects his Latin and makes him write "Romans go home" correctly one hundred times on the buildings. A second Roman detachment chases him, and Judith, a member of the PFJ, takes him to PFJ headquarters. The PFJ is pleased with Brian's actions and gives him a new job working with a group planning to kidnap Pilate's wife.[1] Inside the palace, rival resistance groups, all intent on kidnapping Pilate's wife, meet and start fighting each other. Only Brian survives the debacle, but the Romans capture him and imprison him. However, Brian manages to escape at his trial when his guards break into uncontrollable laughter on hearing the name of Pilate's friend (Biggus Dickus).

The Romans pursue Brian but luckily a passing UFO picks him up (perhaps an allusion to the temptation of Jesus, Matt. 4:5–6; Luke 4:9–11). After the UFO is shot down in a space dogfight, it crash lands, leaving Brian back in Jerusalem. The Romans pursue him again, so Brian hides in PFJ headquarters, which the Romans search unsuccessfully several times. Finally, Brian falls from a ramshackle terrace into the Jerusalem marketplace, where he reluctantly takes on the role of a prophet in order to avoid detection and capture. The crowds quarrel with him about his makeshift, confusing teaching, until he walks away, refusing to say anything more.

In a humorous twist on the Markan motif of Jesus' messianic secret, Brian's confused audience pursues him to learn his "secret." Thus, Brian is caught between the pursuing Romans and his pursuing followers, and as he flees, he drops a gourd and a sandal. His followers collect these objects and divide into sects, arguing over which is Brian's definitive symbol. His followers finally catch him in the wilderness when he falls into a hermit's pit. When the crowd learns that Brian has made the hermit speak after eighteen years of silence (Brian had fallen on top of the hermit, causing the hermit to yell in pain—thus breaking his vow of silence), they believe a miracle has occurred. The crowd becomes convinced that Brian is the Messiah when he refuses to acknowledge the miracle or his messianic identity. While the crowd beats and chases off a heretic who doubts that Brian is the Messiah, Brian and Judith go to his mother's home, where they spend an evening together in sexual embrace.

The next morning a naked Brian opens his window to find an adoring crowd awaiting the Messiah's next revelation. Brian's mother tries to send them away but reconsiders when they call her the mother of the Messiah. Brian tries to teach the crowd not to follow him blindly, to think for themselves, and to recognize their unique individuality, but they simply intone mindlessly after him, "We're all individuals."[2]

Roman soldiers soon appear on the scene and arrest Brian, with the result that Pilate decides to add Brian to the 139 crucifixions already scheduled for the day.[3] Brian's girlfriend, Judith, then rushes off to try and rally the PFJ to save him, while Pilate addresses the crowd in preparation for the crucifixions. Judith makes her way back to Pilate and the crowd and convinces the crowd to request Brian's release. However, when Pilate proclaims Brian's freedom, he is already on the Via Dolorosa.

The PFJ finally moves into action and reunites with Brian at Calvary, celebrating Brian's landmark martyrdom by singing, "For He's a Jolly Good Fellow." The centurion arrives to free Brian, but another mistaken identity mishap results in the release of the wrong man.[4] Judith then appears and thanks Brian for his noble death while Brian's mother mocks him. In the finale, the crucified victims sing, "Always Look on the Bright Side of Life (or Death)."[5] And as the camera pans out from the hill of crosses, a narrator states that the record is available in the foyer.

## Memorable Characters

- Brian: His life parallels that of Jesus, but the comic treatment of the central character and the skewed perspective he lends to the story profane the Jesus of epic film. Much like the early Jesus in Scorsese's *The Last Temptation of Christ*, Brian is unsure of himself and rejects the role of Messiah that the crowds foist on him. Brian's first, confused attempt at prophetic teaching is also quite similar to that of the Jesus in *The Last Temptation of Christ*.
- Jesus: Though rarely seen, he is still the Jesus of epic Hollywood films, but the focus here is on Brian, the "other Messiah."
- Other key characters are Brian's mother (played by an obviously male actor), the People's Front of Judea, and Judith. These three characters parody the Virgin Mary, the Zealots (see especially Nicholas Ray's *King of Kings*), and Judas.

## Memorable Visuals

- The wise men fighting with Brian's mother and taking back their gifts
- The misunderstood Sermon on the Mount
- Alms for the ex-leper who complains about the loss of his begging job
- The miracle of the hermit
- The crowd acclaiming the naked Brian as Messiah and repeating the mantra, "We're all individuals"
- The song-and-dance crucifixion finale

## Key Scriptures

The film focuses on other nativities and crucifixions during the Roman oppression of Judea rather than on events unique to Jesus' life. The film also offers alternative explanations for the growth of Jesus sayings and miracle traditions, and for the development of religious sects and religious heresy. Thus, one would be hard pressed to find any one text of Scripture that dominates the film. Perhaps the best choice would be those warnings of Jesus found in his apocalyptic discourse: "Beware that no one leads you astray. Many will come in my name and say, 'I am he!' and they will lead many astray. . . . And if anyone says to you at that time, 'Look! Here is the Messiah! Or 'Look! There he is!'—do not believe it" (Mark 13:5–6, 21).

## Cultural Location / Genre: Comedy, Parody

The Monty Python troupe stands in the antiestablishment tradition of British comedy. And at the time of the film's release, many objected to it, calling it blasphemous. *Life of Brian* was even banned in some countries. The troupe had contributed to this reception by describing their film to the press (while it was still in production) as "Jesus Christ: Lust for Glory." Furthermore, one of the working skit ideas was a scene with Jesus (the carpenter) on the cross, upset at the cross's shoddy workmanship. Nonetheless, most critics defended the film after its release, saying that it was a parody of Jesus epics, not a parody of Jesus' life.[6]

*Life of Brian* thus treats the Jesus epic genre as Mel Brook's *Blazing Saddles* does the western. The setting is appropriate for a Jesus epic (in fact, the troupe used some of Zaffirelli's sets from *Jesus of Nazareth*), but the story and tone are off kilter. In particular, the movie decenters Jesus. He is no longer the absent center around which stories of conversion swirl. Jesus has become a bit player. The story instead focuses on Brian, and Brian does not follow the character type appropriate to the biblical epic. He does not convert to Christianity.

Late in the film, Brian tries to tell the crucifixion squad, "You don't have to take orders," and his line works well as an underlying theme of the film as a whole. Monty Python's humor mocks culture's institutions and society's "common sense." Everything becomes grist for the Python's intellectual and aesthetic anarchy. For the same reason, some viewers might feel that the film has nothing positive—other than its mocking humor—to put in the place of the culture it mocks. This humor, of course, allows the Monty Python troupe and its fans temporary flight from the values of the dominant culture. It is no coincidence that in the finale, the jokester is the only condemned person to escape crucifixion.

Ironically, the audience's "temporary flight" may ultimately support the culture the troupe attacks by allowing people to continue unchanged in that dominant culture. Yet for the troupe, devout, unquestioning belief in anything ought to be challenged. The only good is sitting lightly (comically) in life, as is likewise shown in the troupe's treatment of the legends of King Arthur and the Knights of the Round Table in their more famous *Monty Python and the Holy Grail* (1975).

## Director

*Monty Python's Flying Circus* was a British television comedy sketch show that aired on the BBC from 1968–1974. Over the years the Python troupe produced four feature-length films, two of which Terry Jones directed with Terry Gilliam. In 1996 Jones directed *The Wind in the Willows* (released in the U.S. as *Mr. Toad's Wild Ride*).

The finale of Jones and Gilliam's 1983 Monty Python film, *The Meaning of Life*, is certainly revelatory of the sort of anarchy that is rampant in *Life of Brian*. The film was a series of skits loosely arranged around the question of the meaning of life— frequently mentioned and deferred—and the conceit of an abstract "life" from birth to death. In the concluding skit, one of the troupe members opens an envelope, reads its statement about the meaning of life, and notes that its message of self-preserva-tion, peace, and harmony is rather trite.

To an antiestablishment troupe like Monty Python, nothing is sacred—least of all, institutional religion. Thus, Monty Python's relegation of Jesus to a bit part, to a fig-ure that the modern audience can no longer quite hear, mocks more than just the Jesus of epic films. It also disenfranchises the canonical Jesus Christ (Messiah). Like-wise the film's hillside of crosses profanes the death of Jesus, relegating it to the realm of the ordinary and the commonplace.[7] Moreover, the application of the word "mes-siah" (Christ) to the misfit Brian threatens to drive a wedge between the Jesus of his-tory and the Christ of the Church. "Messiah" becomes a term associated with loony groupies who need a leader because they cannot think for themselves. The term has nothing to do with a divinely granted status.

*Life of Brian* does, however, invite serious reflection on Christian discourse; espe-cially the declaration that Jesus is messiah/Christ. Further, the amusing riffs on the "messiah's" chief symbols (sandal and gourd instead of bread and wine), the develop-ment of miracle traditions, and the persecution of heretics all raise questions about the origin of the canonical (or orthodox) Christian tradition itself. Could the Jesus of the Christian tradition also be the result of mistaken identity? An antiestablish-ment troupe can hardly leave the establishment, canonical Christ alone. In fact, that canonical Christ has vanished not only behind Brian, but also behind the Hollywood, epic Jesus in this story-alongside-the-canon.[8]

## DVD Extras and Technical Features

The title sheet insert includes a two-page history of the film's production, and the DVD title menu adds six additional features. These include three commentaries, deleted scenes, theatrical trailers, and British radio ads. The commentary chapters match the DVD chapters below. They are simply given different names in the two commentaries.

English Subtitles
Commentary One—Terry Gilliam, Eric Idle, and Terry Jones
  1. The Virgin Mandy
  2. Angst and Animation
  3. The Dogsbody of the Group
  4. A Pile of Poo
  5. A Great Leading Man
  6. Keith Moon
  7. Day for Night
  8. The Effluents of Jerusalem
  9. Comedy Rules
10. Exploding Cigars
11. The Art of the Deal
12. *Jesus Christ—Lust for Glory*
        The humor in the film is not about what Jesus said, but the fact that for two thousand years
            people have not been able to agree about what Jesus said in the first place.
13. Hermit in a Hole[9]
14. Nether Regions

15. Cockadoodle-do

    Tunisian Muslim women publicly view the male penis.

    (Many Tunisian Muslims had been extras in Zeffirelli's *Jesus of Nazareth*.)

    George Harrison makes an appearance.

16. Mr. Cheeky

17. Tunisian Comic

18. Troglodytes

19. "I'm Brian"

20. The Wrong Crosses

## Commentary Two—John Cleese and Michael Palin

 1. Human Nature

 2. Terry's Bits

 3. Slips of the Tongue

 4. Baby Oil

 5. A Decent Chap

 6. Judith Iscariot

 7. Schoolboys

 8. The Metronome

 9. Pig Latin

10. "A Load of Old Rubbish"

11. Python Philosophy

12. Lost Laugh

    Looking for messiahs, and the gullibility of people

    The central theme of the movie kicks in.

    "The piece of gourd that passeth all understanding"

13. Hermits

14. "How Shall We Fuck Off?"[10]

15. Doing God a Favor

    Malcolm Muggeridge's critique

16. A Terrible Nice Bloke

17. A Rabble of Rubble

18. An Instrument of Torture

19. Strange New Revolutionaries

20. The World Is Full of Loonies

## Deleted Scenes

Sheep, 4:36

Pilate's Wife, 1:59

Otto, 4:26

"The Sign That Is the Sign," 1:15

Souvenir Shop, 0:42

## Theatrical Trailer, 2:45

## British Radio Ads

Michael Palin

Eric Idle

Terry Gilliam

John Cleese

The Pythons Documentary

1. Prologue: Graham Chapman Rests, 0:00
2. The Phenomenon, 3:34
3. Hail, the Pythons, 5:15
4. Py•thon•esque \pi-the-'nesk\, 17:44
5. Insomniacs, Intellectuals, and Burglars, 20:21
6. Nth-Rate Philosophers with Attitude, 24:47
7. Judea AD 33, 32:00
   "No direct parody of Jesus . . . ," 34:55
   On miracles, 35:28
8. Tunisian Tummy, 35:52
9. Transplants, Teeth, and Tax Evasion, 37:12
10. Python on Python, 40:29
11. Fellow Travelers, 46:59
12. Epilogue: An Orgy with Cherryade, 49:15

## DVD Chapters

1. Logos / Three Wise Men, 0.00
   Star appears, 0:30
2. Opening Titles Animation, 4:20
3. Judea AD 33, 6:54
   Sermon on the Mount, 7:00
   A stoning for blasphemy, 10:40
4. "Alms for an ex-leper," 14:17
   (Matt. 8:1–4; Mark 1:40–45; Luke 5:12–16; John 9:8–12), 14:38
5. "You're one of them," 16:21
   "Your father was a Roman centurion," 17:17
6. The People's Front of Judea, 18:12
   (Zealots)
7. "Romans go home," 23:52
   Judith rescues Brian, 27:38
   Plans to raid Pilate's palace, 27:42
   Roman taxation, 28:24
8. Raid on Pilate's Palace, 31:02
   (Compare with Barabbas's plan to overthrow the Romans in Ray's *King of Kings* [31], 1.45:30)
9. Pilate, 38:19
   "My father was a Roman," 39:41
10. Crash Landing, 42:36
    Extraterrestrial rescue (Matt. 4:5–7; Luke 4:9–12), 43:13
    Apocalyptic prophets, 44:52
11. Haggling, 46:16
    The People's Front of Judea, 48:20
    Crucifixion described, 50:25
12. The shoe and the gourd, 52:27
    Apocalyptic preaching, 52:39
    Sermon on the Mount, 52:50
       "Don't pass judgment on others," 52:50
       "Consider the lilies"
    Parable of the talents, 54:00
       "Blessed are they . . ." 54:39

Secrets of the kingdom, 55:15
Shoe and gourd, 55:35
13. Give Us a Sign, 57:46[11]
Healing the "dumb," 58:26
Miraculous food in the desert, 1.00:10
14. Hail Messiah, 1.00:22
Healing the blind, 1.01:00
Messiah, 1.01:21
Judith, 1.02:50
15. "A very naughty boy," 1.02:56
Brian and his mother, 1.04:00
"You don't need to follow me," 1.06:38
"You are all individuals," 1.07:08
George Harrison's cameo appearance, 1.09:00
Arrest, 1.09:56
"Do we have any crucifixions today?" 1.10:20
16. "One cross each," 1.11:33
The People's Front of Judea plans for the future.
Judith tells them Brian has been arrested, 1.12:18
Awaiting crucifixion, 1.13:20
17. Pilate's Passover Address, 1.14:15
Release of a prisoner, 1.14:29
Awaiting crucifixion, 1.16:54
Brian, 1.17:04
Via Dolorosa, 1.19:32
Release of a prisoner, 1.20:45
"Release Brian!" 1.21:04
Judith shouts—like Mary Magdalene in DeMille's *The King of Kings*.
"I shall welease Bwian!" 1.21:30
Via Dolorosa, 1.21:34
Looking for Brian, 1.21:53
18. The Jewish Section, 1.22:32
The People's Front of Judea
Via Dolorosa, 1.22:41
With a forest of crosses, 1.22:48
Via Dolorosa, 1.23:02
A forest of crosses, 1.23:04
"Penitent thief," 1.24:51
19. The Rescue Committee, 1.25:11
The Judeans People's Front, 1.27:41
Suicide Squad, 1.28:08
Judith, 1.28:33
("Mary Magdalene" the faithful witness)
Brian's mother, 1.29:00
20. Always Look on the Bright Side of Life, 1.29:28
"Cheer up Brian!" 1.29:33

# Chapter 14

# The Last Temptation of Christ

*Martin Scorsese, director. 163 mins. Rated R. 1988. Criterion, 2000*

### Plot Summary

Scorsese's film departs from both the Gospels and the Jesus-film tradition by imagining Jesus as a fully round character who only gradually discovers who he is and what his task in life entails. Scorsese constructs this Jesus character through the Neoplatonic lens of Nikos Kazantzakis's Jesus in his novel *The Last Temptation of Christ*. As the opening credits roll, a disclaimer appears, stating that like that novel, the film depicts the human quest to attain God and portrays life as a battleground between flesh and spirit.

The movie opens with Jesus sprawled on the ground, writhing in pain.[1] A voice-over gives the audience access to Jesus' mind, so the audience hears him reflect on a painful spiritual possession that he has repeatedly attempted to escape.[2] In fact, Jesus the carpenter makes crosses for the Romans so that God will hate him—or so he tells Judas. On another level, Jesus seems to know that somehow his future is tied up with crosses, but he does not yet know that his destiny is to be hung on one.[3] Not coincidentally, in the very next scene Jesus laboriously carries a cross for the crucifixion of Lazarus, an otherwise unknown prophet/messiah.[4] Jesus knows that if the voices in his head are from God, he will not be able to cast out God. But if the voices are from the devil, then he intends to pay his debt (for his sins) in whatever way God requires.

The people around Jesus—particularly Mary Magdalene and Judas—despise Jesus as a weakling. Judas, a Zealot, despises Jesus for his collaboration with the Romans; and Mary Magdalene, a prostitute, loathes Jesus for his rejection of her and his inability to love her as a woman. In Scorsese's film, woman symbolically represents the flesh that the spiritual Jesus must ultimately deny.

After visiting Mary Magdalene and asking for her forgiveness (their conversation suggests that she was once betrothed to Jesus and that he broke the betrothal, a betrayal that has led her to a life of prostitution), Jesus flees to the desert where he has various visions that Scorsese cleverly induces the audience to share.[5] One of Jesus' last visions purifies him of the satanic snakes "inside" him (the snakes speak with the voice of Mary Magdalene) and prepares him for God's mission. At this point, Jesus believes that his message will be one of pity for all humans.

Jesus meets Judas again, who has now been commissioned by the Zealots to kill Jesus for his collaboration with the Romans. But Jesus is able to postpone this fate by telling Judas that he and Judas both have roles to play in God's plans. Even though he is not sure what Jesus intends, Judas decides to follow him but promises to kill Jesus if he strays one inch from a revolutionary path. With Judas, his first disciple, beside him, Jesus stops the stoning of Mary Magdalene and proclaims God's love to the violent crowd. Seeking tangible help for real-world problems, the crowd misunderstands Jesus' message as a call to violent action against the rich. When Judas and Jesus escape the crowd, Judas critiques Jesus for privileging spiritual freedom over political, physical freedom. Angrily, Judas demands that Jesus visit John the Baptist to determine whether or not Jesus is the Messiah.

At the Jordan, John baptizes Jesus but Jesus, in a subsequent night conversation with John, disagrees with John's idea that the kingdom will come through a violent, divine judgment. Jesus argues that God's kingdom will be ushered in through love. Unconvinced, the Baptist sends Jesus into the desert to learn God's will. At the end of a long temptation sequence, Jesus finds the axe of God's judgment (John's message) and returns to civilization. Not coincidentally, the first people he meets on his return are two women, Mary and Martha of Bethany, who nurse him back to health. He then returns to his disciples who would have left his service if not for Judas's leadership. Jesus then "literally" offers his heart to his disciples, declaring that together they will take an axe to the wealthy and to the Jerusalem Temple. In response, Judas (replacing Peter) makes the disciples' confession of faith: "Adonai!" (Lord).

Miracles, conflicts with religious leaders (with Jesus favoring his "heart" over Jewish law), and some fairly confused teaching scenes ensue. The resurrection of Lazarus functions as the climax to Jesus' ministry,[6] and soon thereafter Jesus enters Jerusalem with his disciples and cleanses the Temple. There Jesus declares that God has a new law, that he is divine and the saint of blasphemy, and that God is a spirit freely given to the whole world. "God," Jesus says, "is not an Israelite." After Jesus' disciples save him from the Temple guards, Saul of Tarsus, a Zealot, asks Judas why he has not yet killed Jesus as ordered. Finding Judas's answer unacceptable, Saul finds Lazarus and kills him, for Lazarus's resurrection has drawn large crowds to Jesus.

As tensions mount, Jesus changes his message one more time. Telling Judas that Isaiah had visited him in the night (a vision that the audience sees), Jesus declares that God now wants him to die (Isa. 53:3–5, 7) and then return as an apocalyptic judge. After a triumphal entry into Jerusalem with the disciples expecting a political overthrow of Roman and Jewish priestly power, Jesus enters the Temple for a second cleansing scene. In the violence that ensues, Judas tries to prompt a revolt. But Jesus refuses to take any action, merely praying silently (the audience is privileged to another voice-over of Jesus' thoughts) and hoping that this is (finally) what God wants. Jesus collapses with bleeding stigmata, and Judas is once again forced to save Jesus from the Temple guards.

To Judas's bewilderment, Jesus then tells Judas that he must betray his master by bringing the Temple guards to Gethsemane. Jesus is finally able to convince Judas to do this by reminding Judas that his original commitment was to kill him if he strayed from the path of revolution.[7] The scene then moves to the Last Supper (including the transubstantiation of the wine), where Judas leaves to set in motion the final events of Jesus' life. Jesus then takes a few of his disciples to the garden, where he prays for strength, for he is confused about the relative worth of the flesh and the spirit.

After the betrayal, Jesus stands before Pilate as Pilate curries his horse. Under an informal investigation, Jesus describes his message in images drawn from Dan. 2, with himself as God's stone thrown at Rome. But he then reverts to a message of an otherworldly kingdom. Despite Jesus' evocation of an otherworldly kingdom, Pilate senses the political danger in Jesus' message and condemns Jesus to death.

Roman soldiers brutally beat and whip a naked Jesus and then mock him. After Peter's denial, Scorsese offers a Bosch-like Via Dolorosa, filmed in slow motion and with muted sound, as if it were seen through the beaten Jesus' stupor.[8] At a skull-laden Golgotha, the naked Jesus is crucified. The action moves back and forth between external reality and Jesus' tortured, internal thoughts (with the external sound muted).[9] He asks God to forgive his tormentors and then asks God why he has forsaken him.

At this point, the film suddenly breaks from the canonical crucifixion events and the Jesus film tradition. Jesus looks down from the cross and sees a young girl, sitting at the foot of his cross. She describes herself as Jesus' guardian angel, and she then leads a bewildered, nonmessianic Jesus down from the cross. In the subsequent sequence (which the viewer eventually discovers to be a death-throe fantasy), Jesus marries Mary Magdalene. After she dies in childbirth, he marries Mary of Bethany, has an affair with her sister Martha, and raises a family.

Years later, he meets Saul (Paul) of Tarsus and quarrels with him. Jesus disputes Saul/Paul's claims that Jesus was the Son of God who died for humanity's sins and was resurrected. Finally, Jesus lies dying in his home as Jerusalem burns (70 CE). Judas arrives at Jesus' deathbed, calling Jesus a traitor, and shows him that the girl Jesus thought was his guardian angel was actually Satan. Judas tells Jesus that his place was on the cross, where he was supposed to die as Messiah and save the world. Finally, refusing the temptation to be a mere man, Jesus describes himself as God's prodigal son and returns to the cross, ready to die. He knows now that he is God's true Messiah. Declaring it (salvation?) accomplished, he dies with a smile on his face.[10] Keening, strobe lights, and church bells follow.

## Memorable Characters

- Jesus: Scorsese's Jesus is the first fully round Jesus character in film. He is a tortured, alienated visionary; a carpenter whose specialty is making crosses. One scarcely knows whether he is sane until his climactic, spiritual victory over normal human life when he dies as God's son and Messiah. It is not entirely clear whether Jesus' death is beneficial for others, although he claims he is dying for the sins of the world. Judas and a rather sleazy Saul/Paul declare the same.
- Judas: He is Jesus' "beloved disciple," whom Jesus says is a stronger person than he himself is. Judas represents human political struggles, as he is a Zealot intent on overthrowing Roman power in Judea. Judas is Jesus' primary support in his quest. Without Judas, as Jesus says and the fantasy sequence proves, there is no redemption.

- Mary Magdalene: She represents the pleasures of the flesh; her voice and image are intertwined with that of Satan on more than one occasion. There are hints that Jesus was betrothed as a child to Mary, but when Jesus broke the betrothal, Mary went into a downward spiral that led to her life of prostitution. In the "last temptation" sequence, Jesus comes down from his cross to marry Mary Magdalene, but sadly, she dies in childbirth.

## Memorable Visuals

- Jesus writhing on the ground in the throes of a painful possession
- Jesus making crosses and helping in the crucifixion of a fellow Jew
- Jesus repeatedly alone with Judas at night and asleep on Judas's chest
- Jesus stricken twice with stigmata
- Jesus living an "ordinary" family life with three women
- Jesus' smiling death on the cross as the Messiah

## Key Scriptures

In one sense, Jesus' story is an interpretative conflict over which Scripture will define his life, Isa. 53 (Suffering Servant) or Gen. 22 (obedient but rescued son). In another more important sense, the key Scriptures are the Synoptic Gospel temptation narratives and the stories of the cleansing of the Temple. Those are the Gospel stories that define Scorsese's Jesus. The rest of Jesus' ministry is little more than filler. The temptation is so important that Scorsese offers three different takes on it: Jesus' wilderness call, his wilderness temptation, and the fantasy as he is dying on the cross. Of course, Scorsese (following Kazantzakis) adds the crucial temptation of woman / flesh to the Gospel's versions. The resulting worldview reflects a Neoplatonic twist on the Johannine dichotomy between this world and the world above.

## Cultural Location/Genre: Biopic, Buddy Film

Critics interested in religion in film generally describe the 1960s as a transitional moment in the history of Hollywood film. Supposedly, films treated Christianity respectfully before the 1960s and cynically thereafter. If so, Scorsese's respectful treatment of the Jesus story is an exception to this general rule. He manages to redeem the Jesus story cinematically at a time when Hollywood generally favored vague mysticism in its religion and preferred to debunk Christian tradition. Nonetheless, Scorsese's film was not successful. Conservative religious groups criticized it before it was even finished and boycotted it when it appeared in theaters. Whether the film is orthodox or not, its Jesus was quite far removed from the popular American understanding of a triumphant, self-confident Jesus.

Nonetheless, Scorsese's Jesus reflects the inward turn toward a privatized, expressive individualism that increasingly marked American religion after the 1960s. If the successful biblical epics ending in the 1960s bespoke American civil religion, Jesus films thereafter spoke to a culture of individuals who were intent on expressing themselves "fully" and might choose to do that through an intensely privatized form of religion.[11] Likewise Scorsese's Jesus rejects his (social and political) humanity in order to fulfill his personal destiny as Messiah and Son of God. In the process of choosing God (himself?) instead of Mary Magdalene or Judas's politicized religion, Scorsese's Jesus becomes a virtual icon for this late-twentieth-century American mythology. Scorsese's interest in allowing his audience to share Jesus' thoughts and visionary reality unites the audience in a unique way with a Jesus who *becomes* messianic (and divine) through soul-searching angst.

Various critics have observed that there is a tendency toward Gnosticism in both American religion and in the Jesus-film tradition. Similarly one can read Scorsese's film as a capitulation to this culture or as an attempt to tweak it slightly in an orthodox direction. If one reads the film in the latter way, one would note that Scorsese does not deny the value of the flesh in favor of the spirit (as some say Gnosticism would), but rather affirms the superiority of the spirit to the flesh (as Neoplatonism and Christian orthodoxy do). Thus, like the monk of Jesus' early visions, Jesus does ultimately escape the flesh. But his temptations, however fantastic, are real; the flesh has its appeal. More importantly, Jesus' spiritual triumph rests firmly on the loyal support of Judas's earthbound commitments. On this reading, the film does not ultimately succumb to the incipient Gnosticism in American religion and film but articulates a more orthodox Christian position. However, Scorsese's film does show how close orthodoxy itself stands to Gnosticism.

Scorsese's trademark of alienated, tortured heroes also places a stamp on *The Last Temptation of Christ*. Jesus has become a Scorsese hero like those of *Mean Streets* (1973), *Taxi Driver* (1976), *After Hours* (1985), and *The King of Comedy* (1983). That means Jesus is really human, and like other humans in Scorsese's Neoplatonic world, Jesus is torn by the conflict between the flesh and the spirit. Without a doubt, Scorsese has created the most human Jesus in film.[12] Tortured by God as no previous Jesus of film, the audience knows, for the first time in film, what Jesus thinks and doubts.[13] Initially this Jesus does not know whether God or some other spirit guides him. And when he determines the divine origin of his visions and message, he still does not know for sure what God's plan is. In short, Scorsese's Jesus, like no other Jesus in film, is a fully round character who learns and develops. As a result, Scorsese has pushed the epic Jesus film toward the Hollywood biopic genre.[14]

## Director

Despite its limited budget, *The Last Temptation of Christ* continues the tradition of Jesus films in its setting and style. In particular, Scorsese picks up the long-running cinematic triangle of Jesus, Judas, and Mary Magdalene first made popular in DeMille's *The King of Kings* and employed later in Jewison's *Jesus Christ Superstar*. As in those treatments, Judas's concern is for material reality (either economic or political) and Mary Magdalene the prostitute's concern is for physical love (her love is for Judas in DeMille's film). However, in contrast to DeMille and Jewison, Scorsese is able to draw on his long tradition of making "buddy films" to create far more compelling interactions between the three dominant players.

Scorsese's *Mean Streets* (1973) provides the closest parallel. There, Charlie (Harvey Keitel) plays a mid-level member of the Italian mob, racked by a Catholic sense of guilt. As the opening voice-over (provided by Scorsese himself) remarks, one atones for one's sins on the streets and in the home—not in church. Charlie thus tries to find salvation by maintaining both his place in the mob, and his friendship with Johnny Boy (Robert DeNiro) and his love for Johnny Boy's sister, Teresa.[15] Intriguingly, as in *The Last Temptation of Christ*, (heterosexual) sex is sinful and the homoerotic relationship between the buddies is more important than the hero's relationship with the girl.

Charlie's strategy becomes untenable when Charlie's boss decrees his relationships with Teresa and Johnny Boy illicit, and when the romantic and suicidal Johnny Boy refuses to pay his gambling debts to other mobsters. As in *The Last Temptation of Christ*, Charlie, like Judas, tries unsuccessfully to save his too-other-worldly friend. Not surprisingly, the demise of the friend effectively marks the end of both movies, and the buddy's world (Keitel's in both movies) is left undone. In short, *The Last Temptation of Christ*, like *Mean Streets*, becomes the ultimate buddy movie.

## DVD Extras and Technical Features

The title sheet insert includes a four-page summary of some Christian (conservative Catholic and Protestant fundamentalist) reactions to the film prior to its release in 1988. Special DVD features are titled: Commentary; Scorsese's visual research; Costume designs; Production and publicity stills; On location in Morocco; and Peter Gabriel.

English Subtitles

Commentary

Recorded in 1997 exclusively for the Criterion Collection. Martin Scorsese, Willem Dafoe, Paul Schrader, and Jay Cocks. The commentary chapters match the DVD chapters below. They simply are given different names in the commentary.

1. Scorsese introduction
2. "God as a headache"
3. An ancient controversy
4. Plagued by God
5. Barbara Hershey
6. Fully human, fully divine
7. The language of Christian times
8. Telling stories
9. Casting Jesus
10. A wild revivalist meeting
11. A sense of humor
12. The natural and the supernatural
13. The Jesus curse
14. "We left Hollywood behind"
15. Jesus' power
16. An existentialist book
17. "Judas plays everyman"
18. Peter Gabriel
19. A Roger Corman technique

20. A blood cult
21. An unplayable scene
22. David Bowie
23. Time limits
24. Camera positions
25. The last temptation
26. Controversy
27. The great democratic equalizer
28. Death Muppet
29. Humiliation
30. "Why do you want me to do it?"
Scorsese's visual research (bibliographic resources)
  1. *The Biblical Archeology Review*
  2. *National Geographic*
  3. Paintings
  4. Books and films
Costume designs
Production and publicity stills
On location in Morocco
  From the original VHS Video master (16 minutes)
    Tomb of Lazarus
    Baptism of Jesus, 0:55
    Wedding at Cana, 7:55
    End of crucifixion, 9:57
Peter Gabriel (interview conducted August 29, 1996)
    Introduction
    Video interview (12 minutes)
    Photo gallery

## DVD Chapters

1. Logos, 0:00
2. The Feeling Begins, 0:29
    A flock of sheep pass by in the background (seen through an open door) as Judas asks Jesus, "How will you ever pay for your sins?" 5:46
3. Condemned to Die, 7:03
    Mary, mother of Jesus, first appears, 8:55
    Mary Magdalene first appears, 9:06
4. Magdalene, 12:25
    Mary, mother of Jesus, asks Jesus if it is God or the devil in Jesus, 12:31
    Jesus visits Mary Magdalene in her house of prostitution, 14:59
5. "I need you to forgive me," 17:28
    "I remember when we were children," 22:20
6. The Master, 23:00
7. Purified, 28:17
    Judas, the first disciple, 30:13
    The prostitute (Magdalene) ready to be stoned for working on the Sabbath, 33:46
8. The Sermon on the Mount, 37:27
    "Nothing good from Nazareth" (John 1:46), 37:29
    Parable of the Sower (Matt. 13:1–23; Mark 4:1–20; Luke 8:4–15), 37:33
    "Love one another" (John 13:34), 38:52

Beatitudes and Woes (Matt. 5:1–7:28; Luke 6:12–49), 39:45

Sons of Zebedee follow Jesus, 41:12

9. The Foundation, 42:07

A fishing scene, with the call of James, Andrew, and other disciples

"Turn the other cheek," 44:22

"We'll go see John the Baptist," 46:45

10. John the Baptist, 48:12

Baptism of Jesus, 50:42

John the Baptist and Jesus talk about "an axe laid to the roots," 51:42

John the Baptist tells Jesus to go to the desert, 53:09

11. "Speak to me in human words," 53:46

"Why are you trying to save the world? Aren't your own sins enough for you? What arrogance to think you can save the world! The world doesn't have to be saved," 56:26

"Any country you want," 58:40

12. Return from the Desert, 1.01:40

Mary and Martha (of Bethany) take Jesus in

John the Baptist's death, 1.03:54

Peter, the "rock," 1.06:20, 1.06:38

Sacred heart of Jesus, 1.07:59

"I believed in love, now I believe in this," 1.08:58

13. Casting Out Devils and Working Cures (Luke 13:32), 1.09:13

Exorcisms, 1.09:26

Healing a blind man with spittle, 1.10:30

Wedding at Cana, 1.11:30

Mary Magdalene is there.

14. Rejected at Nazareth, 1.14:56

"It's me the prophets preached about."

"He's insane, he has a demon," 1.17:13

Mary Magdalene is beside him, 1.17:57

Rejection of his mother, 1.18:10

15. Lazarus, 1.19:20

16. The Saint of Blasphemy, 1.23:33

The moneychangers in the Temple, 1.24:42

"This is my Father's house," 1.26:00

"I am the end of the old law" (Matt. 5:17–18), 1.27:00

"When I say 'I,' rabbi, I'm saying God" (John 10:30), 1.27:06

"I came to bring a sword" (Matt. 10:34; Luke 12:51), 1.27:24

"This temple will be torn down."

"God is not an Israelite," 1.27:54

Saul (later Paul) talks with Judas, 1.28:44

17. The Shadow of the Cross, 1.29:05

Lazarus killed by Saul (later Paul)

Jesus tells Judas the secret of his upcoming death, 1.31:00

Isaiah's prophecy, "He was wounded for our transgressions. . . .I am the lamb" (John 1:29, 36), 1.31:36

"Now I finally understand. . . . All my life I've been followed," 1.32:59

"And do you know what the shadow is? The cross," 1.33:13

18. "King of the Jews," 1.33:53

"We're setting up a new government" (Matt 20:20–28; Mark 10:35–45; Luke 22:24–27), 1.34:17

Thomas (John 11:16), 1.34:43

Triumphal entry into Jerusalem, 1.35:50

Cleansing the Temple a second time, 1.37:12

Waiting, 1.37:35

19. Waiting for the Sign, 1.37:45

"I'm going to baptize everybody with fire!" (Matt. 3:11; Luke 3:16), 1.38:04

Stigmata, 1.39:24

"Judas, help me!"

The plan is made, 1.40:36

"That's why God gave me the easier job," 1.42:40

20. Passover/Last Supper, 1.43:41

Lambs, blood, and purification

Last Supper, 1.44:50

Mary, mother of Jesus, serves; Mary Magdalene is there.

Peter's stigmata, 1.47:36

Judas leaves, 1.48:00

21. "Do I have to die?" 1.48:16

Jesus prays in the garden, 1.48:35

A cup is handed to Jesus, 1.51:36

Judas's "betrayal," 1.52:37

A sliced ear, 1.53:07

Jesus heals it and looks at Judas.

22. Pontius Pilate, 1.53:49

Daniel's prophecy (Dan. 2:31–46), 1.55:35

Description of crucifixion, 1.57:02

23. Golgotha, 1.58:18

Peter's denials, 1.58:48

Via Dolorosa, 1.59:15

Golgotha, 2.00:54

24. "Why have you forsaken me?" 2.05.00

Guardian angel, 2.07:08

"If he saved Abraham's son . . . ," 2.07:35

"You are not the messiah," 2.09:11

25. The World of God, 2.09:39

"Who's getting married? You are" (to Mary Magdalene), 2.10:35

Mary Magdalene dies, 2.14:50

"There's only one woman in the world," 2.17:21

26. "There's only one woman in the world," 2.17:56

Mary and Martha, 2.18:19

27. Paul, 2.21:57

Paul preaches the resurrection of Jesus, 2.22:15

28. Moving On, 2.28:25

Jerusalem burns, Judas returns, 2.32:27

Satan revealed, 2.35:40

29. "It is accomplished," 2.36:55

On the cross, 2.38:10

Death, 2.39:26

30. Credits, 2.39:28

Chapter 15

# Jesus of Montreal

*Denys Arcand, director. 120 mins. Rated R.*
*1989. Koch Lorber, 2004*

### Plot Summary

Arcand's award-winning film opens with the camera focused on a person preparing to hang himself—a scene that appears to be part of the film's plot. However, when applause erupts, viewers realize that the suicide is actually the end of a play—in fact, a play adapted from Dostoyevsky's *Brothers Karamazov*. In the play, the character hangs himself because he has acted on his brother's death-of-God, no-hope-of-resurrection philosophy. Afterwards, the actor, named Pascal, deflects critics' praise of him by pointing John-the-Baptist-like to another actor standing in the background. The actor's name is Daniel Coulombe, and Pascal says of him, "There's a good actor." To the initiated viewer, this is only one of many clues to the fact that there are multiple Jesus figures in the film.

Father Leclerc, a Roman Catholic priest and the rector of St. Joseph's Oratory of Mount Royal in Montreal, enlists Daniel to modernize the priest's long-running passion play, which has been performed every summer on the oratory grounds. As playwright and producer, Daniel collects the troupe of actors with whom he wishes to work: Constance, the priest's secret lover; Martin, an actor reduced to dubbing porno flicks; Mireille, a young model tired of being treated as a sex object; and René, who narrates science films and who agrees to join the troupe only when they agree to let him add Hamlet's soliloquy to the play.[1] Apparently, Daniel wants his play to be historically accurate, so he researches the historical Jesus by delving into scholarly books in a library. There he receives a piece of unsolicited, evangelistic advice.[2] Daniel also investigates church art, looking for an accurate image of Jesus, and he meets a "Deep Throat" theology professor in a parking garage[3] who secretly offers Daniel the latest historical information on who Jesus "really was." The professor is afraid to be publicly associated with this controversial information because his theology department is funded by the church. In short, Daniel becomes an amateur, albeit subversive, historical critic.

The resulting rehearsals and performances of Daniel's play present a Jewish Jesus who is the illegitimate son of a Roman soldier, a magician who may have learned some of his skills in Egypt, and a historical person who is known to us largely from Gospels written much later by his disciples (who may, in fact, have embellished or lied). Daniel makes a point of emphasizing that Jesus comes from a world whose magical worldview is much different from our own—one that moderns can no longer understand.

Loosely based on the Stations of the Cross, Daniel's play begins with Jesus' trial before Pilate, followed by a scene at an archaeology dig where "professors" talk about what moderns know of Jesus. From there the scenes shift to focus on Jesus' miracles and teaching, ending with a return to the passion narrative where Jesus is whipped, crucified[4] (with a running commentary about the horrors of crucifixion),[5] and proclaimed as resurrected—some five to ten years after his death.

Although the play relegates Jesus to the past with all his talk of the end of the world and his trust in magic, the disciples' message (and Jesus' sermon) asserts a humanistic message for moderns: Seek salvation within yourself and love one another.[6] As the play ends, Jesus/Daniel walks down underground stairs to the crowd's applause.

Furious with the scandalous production and worried about losing his comfortable religious position, Father Leclerc informs Daniel that the board members of the oratory will decide whether the play should continue or not. Until the final decision is made, however, the troupe continues to perform Daniel's play each summer evening on the oratory grounds, and the play grows in popularity. Apparently unaware of the effect that playing Jesus has had on him—and almost imperceptibly to the viewer—Daniel's mundane, daytime behavior begins to emulate certain characteristics of his nighttime Jesus character.[7] For example, when he visits Mireille's audition for a new beer commercial, he becomes incensed by the depersonalization to which the director subjects her and "cleanses" the set, destroying expensive cameras and computers. As a result, police arrest Daniel during the next performance of the passion play while he is "dying" on the cross. Thus, Daniel is a no-show in the final, underground resurrection scene of the evening's production. Daniel is then forced to appear in court, and after the court-appointed psychiatrist attests to Daniel's sanity, a date is set for his trial. After he is released on his own recognizance, a smooth-talking lawyer invites Daniel to a skyscraper-topping restaurant for lunch. Over a meal of virgin marys and Magdalen lobster,[8] the lawyer offers to represent him in endorsement ventures that will capitalize on his growing fame. "The world is yours," the lawyer intones. But Daniel turns down the offer.

With Daniel temporarily out of the production, Father Leclerc tries to interest the remaining members of the troupe in performing his old, original passion play. In mockery, Daniel's troupe plays out various dramatic methods of representing Jesus. The scene, like others in the film, calls attention to the importance of interpretation in any presentation of the Jesus story. When Daniel subsequently confronts Father Leclerc in the oratory, the priest admits that Daniel's Jesus may be more historically accurate than the church's Jesus; yet he insists that the desperate masses need the church's more comforting, narcotic Gospel. Father Leclerc is also afraid that Daniel's Jesus will offend the powers-that-be and that he will lose his comfortable position.

Undeterred by the priest's refusal to allow the play to continue on church property, the troupe puts on one last, unauthorized performance. Security guards stop the performance and accidentally knock over Jesus/Daniel's cross, seriously injuring him.[9] Constance and Mireille accompany Daniel to St. Mark's Hospital, where Daniel regains consciousness and leaves with the women. In the subway, in front of a billboard featuring Pascal's head[10] in an advertisement for cologne, Daniel delivers an apocalyptic discourse that echoes Mark 13—but without its references to the supernatural and salvation. Daniel collapses again, and the women hold him pietà-like. He is rushed once more to a hospital—this time to a Jewish hospital, where an English-speaking doctor (in white) tells the two women that Daniel is brain dead. The doctor then asks Constance to give them Daniel's body.[11] As Daniel lies in a cruciform pose, doctors harvest and dispense his organs. Arcand cuts back and forth between the organ recipients and Daniel's followers who, except for Mireille, decide to establish a theater in Daniel's memory (with the help of the smooth-talking lawyer). The closing shot shows two women singing *Stabat Mater* in the subway for spare change—the same women who had appeared at the beginning of the film singing in St. Joseph's Oratory and later at the audition for the television beer commercial.[12]

## Memorable Characters

- Daniel / Jesus: The Jesus of Daniel's play is a figure from antiquity that held a supernatural worldview foreign to moderns and prophetically challenged the religious status quo. But in his ordinary daily life, Daniel (either consciously or unconsciously) also becomes "Jesus." These two Jesuses, along with other Jesuses in the film (one thinks of the Jesus of the church and of the priest's original play), call attention to the implicit acts of interpretation involved in any construct of Jesus.
- Father Leclerc: The chief antagonist. He represents the compromises that religion and art often make with consumer (comfortable) society, and in that role reflects the Gospels' high priest Caiaphas. But Arcand sensitively nuances the priest's compromises, refusing to present him simply as a spineless or evil character.
- Daniel's troupe: Constance represents the woman caught in adultery; Mireille represents Mary Magdalene; Martin represents Peter; and René represents Doubting Thomas.
- Judas: Notably missing from Daniel's play and from Daniel's life outside the play. Arcand refuses to demonize any character—except perhaps for the lawyer who betrays not Daniel but the play itself (the Jesus tradition), by talking Constance, Martin, and René into continuing the play after Daniel's death.

## Memorable Visuals

- Daniel as "Jesus" falling with the toppled cross
- Daniel "clearing the Temple" at the audition for the beer commercial
- Daniel's apocalyptic preaching in the subway
- Daniel's "resurrection" as an organ donor

## Key Scriptures

The story of death in a world where God is absent resembles Mark 15:34; however, while that text states, "My God, my God, why have you forsaken me?" Daniel's Jesus simply says, "Forsaken," when he dies. Daniel's use of a demythologized Mark 13 (i.e., without references to the Gospel, the Son of Man, or God) as an apocalyptic, subway rant further illustrates the differences between Arcand/Daniel's world and that of Mark's Gospel.

## Cultural Location / Genre: Passion Play

This French-Canadian film is sharply critical of the encroachment of Hollywood and the United States on Canadian art and society. Arcand is able to exploit this social criticism by rejecting the epic Jesus tradition of Hollywood for a simpler passion play that is set within a story that abuts on modernity.[13] The story line of the play[14] and of the film critiques commercial and consumptive society. Everything—Mireille's body, the Jesus story, Daniel's artistic integrity—is capable of becoming a commodity for sale. Moreover, the film's realistic end (everyone but Mireille sells out) offers little hope that art or religion can avoid capitalist co-opting. Uncompromising figures, like Jesus and Daniel, have little chance in the modern society of commercial and political compromise.

Arcand's film also displays the metaphysical anxiety that marks postmodern culture. First, characters in the film have difficulty distinguishing story and reality. For example, during one performance of the passion play, a Pentecostal-type believer cannot distinguish Daniel from her Lord and savior and rushes toward him, shouting, "Jesus." Later, of course, the dramatic role of Jesus does take over Daniel's life outside the play. Second, the film calls attention to the importance of interpretation with respect to the Jesus story. It does this simply through the wide range of Jesuses reproduced in the film, including the Jesus of church art, of the traditional passion play, of radical historical scholarship, of evangelistic and ritual devotion, of Daniel's revised play, and of the different methods of acting, as well as the Jesus incarnate in Daniel. In this film and in its world, Jesus is an endlessly manipulated sign.

## Director

While sharing certain things in common with Jewison's *Jesus Christ Superstar*, which is also a passion play set within a movie, *Jesus of Montreal* is more like Griffith's *Intolerance*. Both Arcand and Griffith pair the Jesus story with a modern story to provide an interpretive perspective for the modern story and a vantage point for criticizing their respective societies. However, Arcand's demythologized, apocalyptic vision of life is rather far removed from Griffith's love of epic spectacles that end in supernatural fantasy.

Arcand's earlier film *The Decline of the American Empire* (1986) typifies his interests. In that film, eight middle-aged people, who work in a university history department or are affiliated with those who do, leave town for a weekend retreat. This story line, however, is merely a setting for a number of conversations about sex. A young, robust man visiting one of the women revealingly remarks that after listening to their conversations all day he expected an orgy, but all he received was fish pie. Mere words have replaced action and experience. Therein lies a key to the word "decline" in the film's title; but there is more. A taped interview of one of the historians discussing her new publication begins and ends the movie. In her interview, she contends that societies decline to the extent that notions of personal happiness permeate culture. The film's endless conversations about sex reflect such a declining culture. Little is left but despair in the face of the apocalypse, as romantic love fails to be a stopgap.[15] Arcand's *Jesus of Montreal*, unlike the Gospel of Mark, is perhaps not much more hopeful. Is the life Daniel finally offers to the world given only passively—inadvertently, the result of his youthful body (harvested for its strong heart and corneas)? Or is Daniel also able to pass on to Mireille something that is more than physical? Something deeper and longer lasting?

## DVD Extras and Technical Features

English and Spanish subtitles, English dubbed track. Cast bios and trailer. Thirty unnumbered chapters.

## DVD Chapters

Important contemporary recontextualizations of the Jesus story are in italics.
   1. A Good Actor, 0:00
         *Death of John the Baptist* (Mark 6:24), 2.02
         *Preaching of John the Baptist* (Mark 1:7), 2:50
   2. Inspiration, 3:19
         Title, 3:20
         Singing Pergolesi's *Stabat Mater*, 3:50
   3. Constance, 7:05
         *The Call of the First Disciples*, 7:25
         The crucifix hanging on the wall behind Constance is a subtle allusion that connects Daniel's
            words to Constance and the Jesus story.
         *Peter*, 8:12
   4. Looking for Jesus, 11:09
         *Crucifixions*, 12:05
   5. A Way Out, 13:47
         *Woman caught in adultery,* 14:37
   6. René, 17:59
         *Thomas*
   7. Mireille, 21:49
         *Mary Magdalene (She walks on water and advertises perfume.)*
   8. Que Sera, 24:07
         A new infancy narrative, 24:07
         *Tax collectors and sinners,* 25:31
         *Thomas* (John 11:16), 25:39
            "Doing tragedy is dangerous."
         *Little children,* 26:36

Practice, 27:50
  *Gospel Preface,* 28:22
  Trial before Pilate, 29:20
9. First Station, 29:35
  Second Station of the Cross, 34:12
10. Yeshu Ben Panthera, 34:29
  Historical Jesus, 34:35
    Birth, 35:25
11. A Magician, 36:05
  A strange world, 36:14
  Third Station of the Cross, 37:07
    Miracles, 37:21
  Interruption ("Speak to me, sweet Jesus"), 39:16
12. Son of Man, 39:48
  Sermon on the Mount, 40:00
    "Invite the poor, the maimed" (Luke 14:7–14), 41:31
    "Who do people say that I am?" 41:55
      "I am the son of man," 42:19
      "By whose authority" (Matt. 21:27; Mark 11:33; Luke 20:8)
    Arrest, 42:45
  Fourth Station of the Cross, 42:58
13. Crucifixion, 43:03
  Scourging, 43:08
  History of crucifixion, 43:10
  Via Dolorosa, 44:25
  Last Station of the Cross, 47:45
  *John baptizing* (John 3:28, 30), 48:05
14. Last Station of the Cross, 48:10
  In the grave, 48:20
  Appearances after death, 50:40
  Actors' reflections, 52:50
15. Bravo, 54:13
  Raelians, 56:19
16. Didn't Like It, 57:57
  Daniel and Fr. Leclerc, 58:05
17. A Must See, 1.1:04
  Fame spreads, 1.01:07
    *Where is he from?* (John 7:40–43), 1.01:20
  *Anointing woman,* 1.02:36
  *Cleansing the Temple, 1.03:40*
18. Audition, 1.05:07
19. Woe to You, 1.10:30
  Sermon on the Mount, 1.10:32
  Woes against the Pharisees and scribes, 1.10:47
  Little children, 1.11:23
    "Whoever would be greatest"
  "Do not be called rabbi," 1.11:36
  Daniel's arrest, 1.11:55
  Daniel's absence, 1.13:53
  *Trial before Pilate,* 1.14:07
  Judgment, 1.14:09
20. *Barabbas,* 1.15:45

*Jesus and Herod,* 1.15:54

*Trial before Pilate,* 1.17:45

21. Richard, 1.18:21

   *Temptations*

22. Restrictions, 1.22:30

   A return to the original script

23. There must be more, 1.26:03

   *Sanhedrin meeting,* 1.26:08

      "Institutions live longer than individuals" (John 11:50), 1.28:58

24. Precious, 1.31:08

   *Last Supper,* 1.31:14

25. Security Reasons, 1.34:40

   *Betrayal and arrest,* 1.33:35

   Crucifixion, 1.34:39

      The cross falls (the third cross scene), 1.36:40

26. Emergency, 1.38:31

   "Doing tragedy is dangerous," 1.38:21

   St. Mark's Hospital, 1.38:30

   *Resurrection appearances,* 1.40:09

   *Darkness,* 1.40:34

      "I was forsaken by my father," 1.41:24

   *Apocalyptic discourse* (Mark 13:2, 14–33), 1.41:38

   *Descent into Hell* (1 Pet. 3:19), 1.41:52

27. False Prophets, 1.41:57

   *Death of John the Baptist* (Mark 6:27–28), 1.42:13

   *Deposition,* 1.44:49

28. Too Late, 1.45:35

   The Jewish Hospital

   *Death,* 1.46:42

   "Give us his body," 1.48:17

29. Miracles, 1.48:47

   Burial, 1.50:30

   *Resurrection,* 1.51:35

   *Great Commission* (see also Matt. 16:13–23), 1.51:52

      "Mary Magdalene" leaves, 1.52:33

   New heart, 1.52:35

   New eyes, 1.52:39

   Singing on faith, 1.53:50

      (Pergolesi's *Stabat Mater*)

30. Credits, 1.55:21

# Chapter 16

# Jesus

*Roger Young, director. Not rated. 174 mins. 1999. Trimark, 2000*

### Plot Summary

Roger Young's story of Jesus opens with a montage of violent events conducted in the name of Jesus Christ—the Crusades, a heretic being burned at the stake, and a dying soldier screaming the name "Jesus!" in a nameless World War I battle. Suddenly, Jesus awakens from the nightmare. In an overhead view reminiscent of Scorsese's opening shot in *The Last Temptation of Christ*, Jesus is shown lying on the ground in the desert. But in Young's film, Jesus is not alone. He is accompanied by Joseph, his out-of-work father.

Young cuts rapidly from this story to several other subplots establishing the characters of Pilate; Livio, Caesar's historian and spy;[1] Mary, the mother of Jesus; Herod Antipas; Mary Magdalene, a prostitute; and Caiaphas. Livio, functioning as the film's interpreter of Jewish customs and politics,[2] introduces Caiaphas to Pilate. He calls Caiaphas the Jewish high priest who "has to appear to be on the side of his own people," even though he "owes his position to Rome—a very narrow path to tread." When Pilate, newly arrived in Jerusalem, demands that Roman symbols be set up in the Temple, he faces his first confrontation with Caiaphas. Caiaphas wins this first round when he offers his neck to Pilate's sword rather than allow a Roman to desecrate the Temple. But Caiaphas will lose the final round when Pilate pins on him the death of Jesus.

Joseph and Jesus stop in Bethany at the house of their friends and "blood relatives," Lazarus, Martha, and Mary. Mary is obviously in love with Jesus, but Jesus finds it impossible to return her love and leaves her heartbroken when Joseph and he leave to return to Nazareth. When they get home, they find that a tax collector and his accomplices have ransacked their house and taken their only goat as payment for back taxes. Angrily, Joseph wonders how long his people will suffer and looks inquisitively at his son. Jesus responds, "Are you asking me . . . or telling me?" After Jesus angrily rushes out, an exasperated Joseph asks Mary,[3] "When will he act?" Mary goes outside to sit with Jesus, and Jesus tells her of a man he saw recently who lost everything to taxes. Mary tells him that that will not happen to them—for God will provide. She ends by saying his father (his Father?) thinks he should do what his heart tells him to do. When the two of them go back inside, Joseph is lying on the floor, dying. Joseph's last words to Jesus are "I have loved you as my own. . . ."

After Joseph's funeral, Jesus enters the tomb and tearfully demands that God give Joseph back to him. But Jesus' prayers have no magical effect. In language that foreshadows his own passion, he prays, "Father, this is too heavy. Now, when I am in the most need, you take him from me. You want me to step out, but you leave me alone. How can you ask this of me? . . . Alone? I cannot walk this road alone."

In the next scene Jesus is back in the carpentry shop, frustrated at not being able to make things as well as Joseph could. Mary interrupts him to recount ("once again") the story of her annunciation.[4] She then tells him that it is time for him to go and find the answers he needs. Leaving his own mother at home alone and forsaking Lazarus's sister Mary, who loves him, Jesus goes off into the desert.[5]

Jesus finds his "relative" John at the Jordan, preaching a message of national freedom in the midst of political corruption. John and Andrew, two of Jesus' future disciples sit by, listening, and when John offers an invitation to be baptized, John the future Beloved Disciple is the first one in the water. Later that night, Jesus meets the Baptist at a campfire, and in a flashback, John recounts their visit to Jerusalem when Jesus was twelve. He recalls how they had passed crucified victims on the road back to Nazareth. When he asks Jesus if he remembers that, Jesus does not answer.[6] Instead, he asks John to baptize him. John agrees but only if Jesus confesses his sins and dedicates his life to God.

Jesus' baptism is accompanied by thunder and a flash of light from heaven, and as John kneels and whispers, "Behold the Lamb of God," the watching crowds also kneel in homage. Jesus then wanders off into the desert where Satan appears as a woman in a red dress. The woman says that Jesus must agree to give up "every privilege," "his shield," and "protection" in order for the testing[7] to be authentic; therefore, Jesus "empties himself of his divinity" with a shriek of pain.[8] The woman then "welcomes" him "to life" and disappears. When Satan appears again, he is a man dressed in a modern black suit. Jesus rejects Satan's challenges to solve all the world's problems, to break the laws of nature, and to be "Number One."[9] Instead, Jesus names himself the Lamb of God and says that he will bring God's word to humans—without crushing them with divine power. Satan then departs with the foreboding words "I'll see you again, Jesus" and "It's only just begun."

Jesus returns from the desert to his home in Nazareth, where Andrew and John wait for him. Jesus is a bit befuddled by their interest in him, but after a few days' rest at home, Mary tells Jesus more about his childhood, reminding him of the magi's gifts and his own miraculous powers. Mary tells Jesus that his cousin Benjamin is getting married, so Jesus invites his "followers" along to the wedding.[10] When the wine runs out, Mary pushes Jesus into action. At her insistence he turns the water into wine, for she is sure that a miracle will convince Andrew and John (and the world) that her son is the Messiah. It does the trick.[11] Similarly, Peter and James follow Jesus only after the miraculous catch of fish; and Thomas, with doubts, follows Jesus only after he sees Jesus heal a lame boy.

Jesus faces his first serious opposition in the film not from Pharisees or priests but from the Zealots. In a crucial scene following the imprisonment of John, Barabbas and his band of Zealots attack and kill some Roman guards accompanying Matthew, a tax collector, as he is making his rounds. When Jesus tries to stop the violence, Barabbas strikes Jesus twice in the face (cf. Matt. 5:39). Nevertheless, Jesus tries to teach a recalcitrant Barabbas that he will be free only when he learns to love. After Barabbas leaves, Jesus calls Matthew and Judas to follow him. Judas had been lurking fearfully in the shadows while Barabbas did his dirty work. But like Barabbas, he also hates the Romans, and he is disgusted when Jesus weeps over a dead Roman soldier.[12] However, when Jesus miraculously calls his name, he follows—despite the fact that Jesus' message for all his followers is to love their enemies.

After John's beheading, Caiaphas sends the woman taken in adultery to "Joseph of Nazareth" to expose Jesus as a fraud (cf. DeMille, *The King of Kings*).[13] Jesus is officially "teaching" for the first time in the film, but ironically he is interrupted before he finishes his second sentence.[14] Escaping Caiaphas's trap, Jesus saves the woman, makes the mark of the fish on the ground (cf. Zeffirelli, *Jesus of Nazareth*), and invites Mary Magdalene (not the woman taken in adultery), who has been watching him, to follow. Although Mary Magdalene refuses for the moment, she will eventually become one of Jesus' closest disciples. Jesus then enters the Temple and cleanses it of the money changers, declaring that he has come to renew Israel and denouncing the religious establishment as caring more for Caesar than for God.[15]

The second half of the film opens ominously—but humorously—with Livio putting on an impromptu play for Pilate that deals with Jesus' Temple cleansing and his answer to the question about Roman taxes. It is perhaps one of Young's most effective scenes, and it foreshadows how Livio and Pilate will treat Jesus' subsequent passion. To them it will be nothing more than a game, a farce, with the high priest Caiaphas as the tragic buffoon caught in the middle.

Meanwhile, Jesus has returned to Galilee, where he teaches the crowds beside the lake.[16] Mary becomes Mary Magdalene's mentor, and Jesus selects twelve disciples as his apostles. Then, when Jesus meets his disciples at night on a stormy sea and comes walking on the water to save them from drowning, one of them declares that Jesus is the Son of God.

After telling Herod about Jesus' popularity and his miraculous feeding of the five thousand, Livio suggests that Jesus is John returned from the dead and that Herod should crush him. Jesus, now apparently on his way to Jerusalem for Passover, encounters a distraught Gentile woman who teaches him that his message is for Gentiles as well as Jews.[17] Predictably (for Jesus films), here Judas is the one who challenges Jesus about the extension of the mission beyond Israel. After Mary brings Mary Magdalene to Jesus because "she wishes to join us," Judas excitedly brings to Jesus thirty pieces of silver that he has raised to fund Jesus' ministry. However, Jesus rejects the money and angrily shouts at Judas to give it to the poor. Mary, Jesus' mother, looks at Jesus apprehensively and disapprovingly, as Judas stomps off and throws the money at a group of beggars. But the next morning everyone is happy again, with Jesus laughing and playing "catch-me-if-you-can" among the crowd of pilgrims traveling to Jerusalem. Suddenly, a desperate horseman rides into the crowd, shouting that Lazarus is near death. The raising of Lazarus—whom Jesus says

died that people might believe—will be the climax of Jesus' ministry and will ultimately lead to his own death.[18]

The miracle makes the Sanhedrin worry that Jesus' popularity could cause a revolt
that would incite the Romans to take over the Temple. Then ominously, during the
triumphal entry to Jerusalem, Judas promises Barabbas's band of Zealots that Jesus
will lead a revolt soon. Livio, sensing the impending crisis as he watches Jesus' triumphal entry, tries unsuccessfully to spur Pilate to arrest Jesus, but Pilate prefers to
manipulate the Sanhedrin into handling Jesus themselves. Judas then tries to convince Jesus to revolt, even asserting that Jesus has no other choice; but Jesus
announces instead his upcoming death and says that he has come to bring freedom
from the tyranny of sin, not freedom from the Romans. Judas then declares Jesus a
traitor.[19] Neither he nor Peter can make sense out of Jesus' words, and they leave
Jesus alone with his mother—whom he comforts by saying that he dies in order to
prove God's love. However, Livio's anticipated Zealot revolt in the Temple brings
Caiaphas and Pilate to an agreement about Jesus: Caiaphas needs to find a way to
bring Jesus to Pilate.

During the Last Supper, Judas arranges the betrayal of Jesus with Seth,[20]
because Jesus is not the man Judas thought he was. As Jesus prays in the garden,
Satan returns to tell Jesus that his upcoming death will be in vain: God does not
care for humans; Jesus will not prove God's love; humans do not have the capacity to love like Jesus wants them to; and humans will kill in his name (here Young
replays Jesus' opening dream montage). Jesus responds that he dies to show
humans the love of God, a love so great that it allows them free will.[21] Jesus' God
is thus no dictator.

After Judas's betrayal, Jesus' arrest and Sanhedrin trial, and Peter's betrayal,[22]
Caiaphas brings Jesus to Pilate. Finding little evidence against Jesus, Pilate sends
Jesus to Herod, not to avoid the case but simply in order to have some fun.[23] Later,
after Livio incites the crowd to demand crucifixion, Pilate releases Barabbas, has
Jesus whipped, washes his hands as a taunt to Caiaphas that he has beaten him at
his own game, and orders Jesus crucified.

As Mary, John, and Mary Magdalene watch Jesus on the Via Dolorosa, Peter and
Judas quarrel in a doorway about whose betrayal of Jesus was the worst. At Golgotha, the soldiers nail Jesus to the cross.[24] From the cross, Jesus asks God to forgive
the people,[25] asks God why he has been forsaken, and commits his spirit to God.[26]
An earthquake follows his death, and the aqueduct that takes water to the Temple
is shattered, pouring torrents down upon the place of crucifixion.

After the deposition, Mary, Mary Magdalene, John, and others take the body to
the tomb. On Easter morning, Mary Magdalene finds an empty tomb and tells the
disciples that Jesus' body has been stolen. Peter, John, and Mary Magdalene then
visit the tomb. John believes without seeing Jesus and runs away with Peter to
announce the resurrection to the other disciples. But Mary Magdalene lingers and
sees the risen Jesus. Jesus then visits the disciples who are with Mary and Mary Magdalene in the Upper Room. Having satisfied doubting Thomas, Jesus says that those
who believe without seeing are blessed, and then commissions the disciples. After
Jesus disappears into a bright light, Mary gathers the disciples for prayer.

## Memorable Characters

- Jesus: Jeremy Sisto, recognizable for his previous roles in the films *Grand Canyon* (1991), *Clueless* (1995), and *Suicide Kings* (1997), plays a thirty-something, California-slacker Jesus. Although he is clearly the divine Christ of Phil. 2:5–8, Jesus foregoes that privilege at the outset of his desert experience in order to be fully tested. This "emptying" allows Young to imagine Jesus as a modern, subjective (American) individual struggling to understand his role in the world—a characterization the Gospels and the epic Jesus films of the past do not provide (except, of course, for *The Last Temptation of Christ*). Thus, Young's Jesus is playful and loves life with a childlike innocence. To Peter's remark "I'm trying to love him [Matthew], I really am," Jesus simply laughs and says, "Keep trying, Peter! Keep trying." To Andrew's rejoinder "I'll dance when Israel is free and men are honest," Jesus laughs and responds, "That will be a very slow dance!" Jesus does not preach in synagogues, "break the Sabbath," or get into trouble with Pharisees. His opposition comes first from the Zealots and ultimately from the Jerusalem priesthood alone.

- Joseph, father of Jesus: Like Zeffirelli, Young emphasizes Jesus' relationship with his father. Mary says once, "Your father would be proud," to which Jesus responds, "Which one?" The death of Jesus' earthly father teaches him how to deal with pain and loss as he dies on the cross.

- Mary, the mother of Jesus: She is the most important character other than Jesus. There is no clear evidence of a virginal conception—only of an angel's visit, but apparently Mary and Joseph have no other children. Mary is always dressed in reds and blues, and she pushes Jesus "out of the nest" and into his public ministry. Although she mentors both Jesus and his followers (especially Mary Magdalene), she seems to have little inkling of his impending death.

- Livio: Constructed out of precursors like earlier directors' Lucius, Sorak, Zerah, and the Dark Hermit, Livio manipulates the plot to its traditional end. He also provides narrative commentary and comic relief. He treats Jewish religion and politics as a game and a joke.

- Judas: Along with the Satan figure, he is the film's antagonist because he (along with Satan) denies freedom of choice to others, while Jesus dies to provide it. Judas is a cowardly Zealot; with Peter, he helps to cleanse the Temple; he collects money for Jesus' ministry; he betrays Jesus because Jesus is not who he thought he was; and he fights with Peter (more than once). Surprisingly, the film does not show or allude to his suicide.

## Memorable Visuals

- Montage of violence in Jesus' name at opening and in Gethsemane
- Jesus working with Joseph and then grieving at Joseph's grave
- Jesus in the Temple at twelve years old, reading Scripture and praying in Hebrew

- The wilderness testing
- The great catch of fish
- Jesus getting slapped twice by Barabbas
- Jesus dancing and having a water fight with his disciples
- Jesus learning from the Canaanite woman
- Livio's "play" about Jesus
- Mary Magdalene becoming the "faithful disciple" after Peter's denials
- Judas and Peter fighting while Jesus is on the Via Dolorosa
- Mary watching Jesus die and saying, "They're giving him a place to stand"
- The flash of light at Jesus' baptism and at his disappearance (ascension)
- Mary Magdalene hugging Jesus when he appears to her after the resurrection

## Key Scriptures

Jesus' acceptance of his mission in the desert depends on ideas like those found in Phil. 2:5–11; nonetheless, Jesus' miracles dominate the movie. The miracles climax with the resurrection appearance to the disciples where doubting Thomas sees the nail prints in Jesus' hands (John 20:28–29). The characterization of Jesus depends most on Luke 7:34: "'a glutton and a drunkard, a friend of tax collectors and sinners.'" The extended interpretation of the death of Jesus as a demonstration of God's love is relatively rare in film, but it does rely on John 3:16 (to which the film alludes on numerous occasions).

## Cultural Location/Genre: Television Miniseries, Religious Drama

Even though Young's *Jesus* appeared two decades after Zeffirelli's *Jesus of Nazareth*, Young's film shares a similar cultural situation with that movie. Like Zeffirelli's miniseries, Young's *Jesus* is a commodity[27] shaped for family consumption and pitched to the widest possible viewing audience. And like Zeffirelli's film, one could argue that it can only properly be viewed when watched on television at home, accompanied by and interrupted by commercials. Not surprisingly, the film opens by evoking a number of the crises that middle-class American families faced in the late 1990s: a parent looking for a job; a son, confused about his future and not knowing what to do about the woman who loves him;[28] and a pushy, recently widowed, empty-nester mother.

But Young seems to recognize the role of his commercial Jesus more fully than Zeffirelli did, for in Jesus' desert testings, Satan is portrayed as a businessman-like character who challenges Jesus to be "Number One." Moreover, like Stevens's rendering of Jesus' temptations thirty-five years earlier, Young's emphases reflect the post–Cold War challenge of the United States: Is it the calling of the United States to solve the social problems of the world? Is it the calling of the United States to demonstrate its explosive power?[29] Is it the calling of the United States to be "Number One"? Young's Jesus rejects these three choices, but, unlike Stevens's Jesus, he does not choose to follow a "hard path."[30] Young's Jesus empties himself of divine power, thereby becoming a joyously carefree individual—one who invites all kinds of people to follow him on a directionless journey that somehow finds him in Jerusalem at Passover, a pawn in someone else's trivial game. Young's Jesus—and by extension, Young's twenty-first-century America—is a man-nation without clear direction, one that is bewildered by the role thrust upon him/it, and learning as the journey progresses.

Another important change in the cultural situations between the two made-for-television movies can be seen in the attitude toward institutional religion. Young has replaced Zeffirelli's affirmation of the apostolic church with reflections on the violence done in Jesus' name. Furthermore, Young has replaced Zeffirelli's emphasis on inward spirituality with an emphasis on personal freedom. Put concisely, Jesus is "for" personal freedom, and Judas (and Andrew at the wedding at Cana) and Satan are "against" such freedom, trying to load Jesus down with heavy responsibilities.[31] In short, American individualism has become more radical and more entrenched in the era between Zeffirelli and Young.

Finally, authentic religion is not only a matter of individual expression; it is also something that "feels good," as evidenced by Young's smiling, chuckling, dancing Jesus. On the other hand, the disciples who are most committed to causes (Judas and Peter) are those who betray Jesus and end up fighting against each other. Although reality TV shows like *American Idol* and *America's Next Top Model* were still a few years in the future, Young's portrayal of Jesus choosing his twelve disciples is played out like a made-for-television competition: "It's all about 'me'; I've made it to 'the top.'"

## Director

Roger Young's directing career has focused largely on television miniseries. His 1996 *Moses* was nominated for an Emmy for best television miniseries, and he followed that up with a number of made-for-television comedies and docudramas. More recently Young has directed the television miniseries *Augustus* (2003) and *Hercules* (2005).

With the film *Jesus,* Young recreates Jesus as a model for how authentic North American individuals mature. And he did the same thing with the apostle Paul in his *San Paolo* (2000). While basing it on the book of Acts, Young modernized the story by providing Paul with an understandable, modern psychological dilemma. Where Young's Jesus moves from one (dead) father to another (heavenly) father, Young's Paul must choose between two living father figures, representing different kinds of Judaism: the tolerant Pharisaism of Gamaliel and the violent ethnocentrism of Reuben, a character invented by Young. Despite Paul's friendship with Reuben and his temporary flirtation with Reuben's persecution of Christians, Paul gradually moves toward a "spiritual" path like that of Young's Jesus. That path is characterized by a liberal message of love and tolerance and, of course, freedom of choice. Young demonstrates the superiority of that message through Paul's repeated escapes from Reuben's murderous traps, Reuben's death, and Paul's arrival in Rome (although in chains), in order to promote a message of universal love and tolerance.

## DVD Extras and Technical Features

Music Video
    Leann Rimes, "I Need You" (from the *Jesus* soundtrack)

Soundtrack Presentation (7:30 minutes long)
>       Leann Rimes
>       98 Degrees
>       Steven Curtis Chapman
>       Yolanda Adams
>       Lonestar
>       DC Talk
>       Jaci Velasquez
>       Edwin McCain
>       Hootie and the Blowfish
>       Avalon
>       Sarah Brightman
>       Patrick Williams

Letter from the Pope: November 25, 1999
Subtitles: English, French, Spanish

## DVD Chapters

1. Main Credits
   Title, 1.30
2. Mary, 3:04
   Livio introduced, 3:07
   Mary, mother of Jesus, introduced, 3:52
   Mary Magdalene introduced, 6:34
3. Corruption, 7.26
4. Carpenter, 11:24
   Mary, Martha, and Lazarus, "blood relatives"
5. Suffering, 16:25
   Mary "pays" Roman taxes.
   Joseph dies, 19:22
6. Angel, 20:04
   Annunciation, 23:02
   Jesus visits Mary and Martha, 25:21
7. John the Baptist, 25:24
   John and Andrew listen, 28:16
   John is baptized, 29:00
8. Jerusalem, 31:22
   At twelve, in the Temple
   A forest of crosses, 37:02
9. The Lamb, 37:20
   Jesus asks to be baptized—John consents—if Jesus will confess his sins, 37:46
   Jesus is baptized amidst a flash of light and a clap of thunder.
   Tempted in the desert, 38:52
      "You must be like them in every way—empty yourself" (Phil. 2:5–8)
10. Morning Star, 41:10
    Tested by a modern-day Satan
    Jesus can be Number One
11. Messiah, 46:40
    John and Andrew wait in Nazareth for Jesus to return from the desert (John 1:35–40).
    Miracle of the bird (cf. *Infancy Gospel of Thomas* 2:1), 49:00
       Just after Jesus had been talking about Joseph

The gifts of the kings (magi), 51:04

Wedding at Cana, 52:05

12. Water into Wine, 52:35

Mary tells Jesus, "It is time!"

Mary says, "He is the One, Andrew."

13. Sinner, 56:38

John the Baptist's preaching against Herod

Great catch of fish / call of Peter, 58:25

Can anything good come from Nazareth? (John 1:46)

14. The Word, 1.02:20

Heals a lame man (perhaps Mark 2:1–12), 1.03:16

"Doubting Thomas" watches, 1.06:35

John in prison, 1.06:55

15. Zealots, 1.07:38

Levi (Matthew) is shown but not introduced (Mark 2:14), 1.07:48

Judas is shown but not introduced, 1.07:57

Barabbas is introduced—slaps Jesus (who turns the other cheek, Matt. 5:39), 1.10:38

"I am the way" (John 14:6), 1.12:25

"If a man is your enemy, show him love" (Matt. 5:43–44), 1.13:44

16. Forgiveness, 1.13:58

In Matthew's house (Mark 2:13–16)

Salome's dance (Mark 6:17–28), 1.15:38

Livio is there.

Mary Magdalene, 1.19:33

17. Celebration, 1.19:53

Jesus dances with children and Judas; gets in a water fight.

Woman caught in adultery, 1.21:00

Mary Magdalene looks on.

Mary Magdalene meets Jesus, 1.24:52

"I'm free."

"The kingdom of heaven is like a treasure," 1.22:03

Jesus is interrupted.

Jesus makes the sign of the fish (cf. Zeffirelli, *Jesus of Nazareth*).

18. House of Prayer, 1.25:40

"My Father's house" (John 2:13–16), 1.26:02

Livio watches, asks about payment of Roman taxes.

Jesus overturns money changers' tables only.

Caiaphas watches; Peter and Judas get involved.

Doves fly away (cf. DeMille, *The King of Kings*).

19. Deliverer, 1.27:35

A satirical skit about "rendering unto Caesar," put on by Livio; watched by Pilate, to which

Pilate responds, "I won't crucify him for that!"

"What does the word *messiah* mean?"

20. Ownership, 1.30:50

Sermon on the Mount (Luke 6:12)

Jesus off by himself; Judas says he needs food and water.

Mary, his mother, is in the crowd, as is Mary Magdalene.

Who owns the world? What can they buy with all that money?

"Blessed is the womb" (cf. Sykes and Krisch's *The Jesus Film*), 1.34:33

21. Apostles, 1.34:56

Mary Magdalene meets Mary, mother of Jesus.

"He scares me" (cf. Jewison, *Jesus Christ Superstar*).

Choosing the twelve apostles, 1.36:12
>Judas is picked fifth; Simon (the Zealot?) last.
22. Faith, 1.40:09
>Walking on water (Matt. 14:28–36)
>Livio and Herod talking about the report of feeding the five thousand (cf. Ray, *King of Kings*), 1.43:56
>Daughter of the Canaanite woman, 1.44:45
23. Friend, 1.46:38
>Mary, mother of Jesus, brings Mary Magdalene to Jesus (cf. Ray, *King of Kings*).
>Judas and thirty pieces of silver; "give it to the poor," Jesus yells at Judas
>On the road to Jerusalem? 1.48:48
>>Lazarus is dying, 1.48:56
24. Resurrection, 1.51:24
>Raising of Lazarus
25. Peacekeeper, 1.55:20
>Caiaphas and the Sanhedrin
>Jared (Young's invented Pharisee, based on a combination of Nicodemus and perhaps Joseph of Arimathea) says he was there to see Lazarus come out of the tomb.
>Triumphal entry, 1.57:55
>>Barabbas's men talk to Judas—"Barabbas has been arrested—your Messiah could rally Barabbas's followers."
>>Livio watches.
26. God's Will, 1.59:09
>Livio tells Pilate that Jesus must be arrested.
>Judas talks to Jesus about striking against Roman power, 2.00:27
>"Get behind me, Satan," 2.02:26
>>Judas leaves.
>>Jesus talks to Mary, his mother, alone.
>>"I must die to prove God's love," 2.03:15
27. Sacrifice, 2.03:47
>Zealots in the Temple object to buying sacrificial animals, riot, and are killed (cf. Stevens, *The Greatest Story Ever Told*).
>Caiaphas says Romans now rule the Temple too—Jesus is at fault, 2.04:26
>Jared resigns from the Sanhedrin.
>"Better for one man to die" (John 11:50)
>Pilate calls in Caiaphas to get control of Jesus.
>Pilate: "You want me to do your dirty work for you?"
>"Bring him to me, I will eliminate him."
>Livio comes in clapping; he and Pilate laugh.
28. Last Supper, 2.07:57
>Prophecy of resurrection, 2.11:49
>Judas's betrayal, 2.12:01
29. Judas, 2.13:19
>Peter's betrayals prophesied
>>Prayer in the garden, 2.15:06
>Judas: "He's at the Mount of Olives," 2.15:25
>Satan, 2.16:11
>>Describes death by crucifixion
30. Betrayal, 2.17:58
>Satan shows Jesus the future—all the killing that will be done "in Jesus' name."
>Judas's betrayal, 2.20:16, 2.21:13
>To Caiaphas, 2.22:00

Peter's betrayals

Blasphemer and false prophet

31. Believe, 2.24:40

To Pilate—Mary Magdalene sees him, goes to see Mary his mother

Caiaphas brings Jesus to Pilate (John 18:28–38), 2.25:38

"I find no case against this man."

"Stop worrying Caiaphas—it's a game, just a game," 2.29:22

32. Kings, 2.29:30

Herod (with Livio)

Herodias enters.

"He touches the unclean?"

Back to Pilate, 2.32:52

Pilate shouts out the charges.

"And now we'll let the people speak."

"I have found him not guilty of any of the charges" (John 19:4; 18:39–40).

Pilate proceeds with a half-smile, smirk

Mixed crowd reactions, but loudest are for crucifixion

Livio encourages the Zealots in the crowd to shout "Release Barabbas."

Jesus flogged—crowd control

Judas watches.

33. Sentenced, 2.35:55

Crown of thorns

Pilate and Livio: "Hail the king of the Jews," 2.36:30

Barabbas released, 2.36:31

Jesus and Barabbas talk, 2.36:49

Pilate washes his hands, 2.37:11

(He has thought of the final blow.)

Via Dolorosa, 2.37:50

Judas and Peter fight, 2.38:55

"I was ready to die for him. He was the revolution."

"You killed him."

"You abandoned him."

34. Crucifixion, 2.39:51

No Simon of Cyrene carrying the cross

Earthquake, aqueduct breaks, 2.43:25

(The water for cleansing the Temple? cf. John 19:34–35)

Deposition, 2.43:48

Burial, 2.44:17

Mary cleans his face.

Mary Magdalene goes to the tomb, 2.45:18

35. Ascension, 2.45:21

Mary Magdalene alone

Peter and John run to the tomb.

John says, "He is risen." Peter repeats it to Mary Magdalene, but they have not seen.

"Woman, why are you weeping?" 2.47:22

Mary hugs Jesus. "You must let me go now."

Thomas, 2.49:08

Great Commission, 2.51:35

Ascension, 2.52:13

Mary, the mother, says, "Come" to Mary Magdalene.

Chapter 17

# The Miracle Maker:
# The Story of Jesus

*Derek Hayes, director. 87 minutes. Not
rated. 1999. Family Home Entertainment,
2000*

## Plot Summary

This stop-frame puppet-animated film of Jesus' public ministry intends to tell the story
of Jesus from a child's point of view, while attempting to stay true to the historical and
cultural setting of first-century Palestine. In fact, its story line and scenes are largely a
collage of earlier Jesus films, updated with recent archaeological finds and historical
insights. For example, the film opens with an external view of a walled city and the title
"Sepphoris, Upper Galilee; Year 90 of the Roman occupation." The excavation of this
ancient capital of Galilee began in 1985.

Inside Sepphoris, the camera follows a man named Jairus (Mark 5:22) and his
daughter Tamar, who appears to be about ten years old. The father and daughter are
looking for a doctor who can heal Tamar of her chronic illness. Along the way to the
doctor's house, they meet an old friend, Cleopas (Luke 24:18); a rude Roman soldier
shoves them aside; a crazy woman, Mary Magdalene, wanders by; and Jesus (unidentified) works on a synagogue. As Tamar waits for her father, Jesus (still unidentified) stops
an overseer from whipping Mary Magdalene. The Sepphoris doctor tells Jairus that he
cannot cure Tamar, and as Jairus and Tamar leave the city, so does Jesus, returning to
his home in the nearby village of Nazareth.

In conversation with his mother, Jesus apparently tells her that he has quit his
job, because he "has other work." Then, in a flashback (represented by animation
instead of stop-frame puppetry), Mary tells the story of the twelve-year-old Jesus in
the Temple and recalls his birth in Bethlehem. Clearly, Jesus' "work" is connected
with his divine origins.

Jesus leaves the next morning for the Jordan to be baptized by his cousin John, who
at first resists baptizing him. Then Jesus wanders off into the desert. The temptations
are depicted through animation, which the director elsewhere says he reserves for flashbacks and inner states of mind.

The film then cuts sharply to a surprise meeting between Jesus and his old friend Lazarus, who says that his sisters, Mary and Martha, had recently seen Jesus at the Jordan. Jesus visits Lazarus and his sisters and introduces them to his "new work," which has to do with the "kingdom of God." The scene is reminiscent of scenes in Stevens's *The Greatest Story Ever Told* and Scorsese's *The Last Temptation of Christ,* where Jesus also meets Mary and Martha shortly after his temptations in the desert.

Jesus is next shown teaching in the countryside (with elements drawn from the Sermon on the Mount), where Cleopas, some of Jesus' future disciples, and Tamar and Rachel, Tamar's mother, listen. Tamar faints and is carried away by Rachel, and Judas and a group of Zealots are seen in a nearby cave, arguing over whether Jesus would be useful to their plans for overthrowing Roman tyranny (cf. Ray, *King of Kings*). Judas believes Jesus could help them, because he has unusual powers (cf. Zeffirelli, *Jesus of Nazareth*) and because Rome fears the populace when they all follow one man. So Judas leaves his Zealot conspirators and goes off to follow Jesus.

The next series of scenes center on Capernaum, a city beside the Sea of Galilee (cf. Stevens, *The Greatest Story Ever Told*; Zeffirelli, *Jesus of Nazareth*). Roman imperial power and Jewish priestly authority are evident in the tax booth of Matthew, in the Roman soldiers milling about, in Mary Magdalene's delusions (which occur when soldiers are nearby), and in the invented figure of Asher ben Azarah, a priest from Jerusalem who believes Jesus is dangerous and who has been ordered to report about Jesus to his superiors (cf. Stevens's invented character Sorak in *The Greatest Story Ever Told*).[1]

Jesus calls Simon Peter as the first of his disciples (Luke 5:1–11), heals a paralytic at Simon Peter's house (while Tamar, her mother Rachel, and Asher ben Azarah watch), expels the demons from Mary Magdalene, and then chooses his twelve disciples. Rachel, who by now has seen and heard much about Jesus, finally decides that she needs to convince Jairus to take Tamar to Jesus. Jairus still has his doubts, but he agrees to join his friend Cleopas for a meal to which Jesus has been invited (Luke 7:36–50). When Mary Magdalene bursts into the house, disrupting the meal and washing Jesus' feet, Asher ben Azarah and other men condemn Jesus, saying he is in league with the devil. Jairus, confused, hurries home to find his daughter at the point of death.

Jarius rushes off to find Jesus, but when Jesus stops to talk with the hemorrhaging woman who has just been healed by touching Jesus, Jairus receives word that his daughter has died. Jesus, nevertheless, continues on to Jairus's house, where he raises Tamar from the dead.

The plot of the film takes an ominous turn when Jesus hears that Herod has killed John the Baptist.[2] Jesus cries out in lament to God over John's death, and unbeknownst to Jesus, the political powers of Jerusalem now clearly begin to work against him as the priests hint to Herod that Jesus is more dangerous than John was.[3] Shortly after John's death, Jesus decides to go to Jerusalem for Passover, announcing, "The hour has come" (John 12:23); Judas is convinced that Jesus' language means that Jesus is about to bring the kingdom of heaven on earth through violent means (cf. Zeffirelli, *Jesus of Nazareth*); and the unsuspecting family of Jairus, along with Mary Magdalene, Cleopas, and others, travel alongside Jesus to Jerusalem.

Meanwhile, in Jerusalem, Pilate introduces the Roman centurion under his supervision to the history of Passover and to the arts of crowd control.[4] Pilate's plan is to crucify Barabbas on the day Jews celebrate their freedom (Passover). Oblivious to Pilate's or the priests' scheming, the disciples ask Jesus what roles they will have in the upcoming kingdom, and a rich man asks what one must do to be saved (cf. Sykes and Krisch, *The Jesus Film*). When Jesus and his disciples get close to Jerusalem, Jesus hears of Lazarus's illness. But Jesus refuses to immediately help him, and the scene quickly switches to Jerusalem, where Asher ben Azarah tells Caiaphas that Jesus recently raised Lazarus from the dead.[5]

Jesus enters Jerusalem with crowds shouting, "Blessed be the king who comes in the name of the Lord!" and Judas imagines an upcoming battle for the city.[6] As nervous Roman soldiers watch, Caiaphas, the high priest, is told of the Galileans' arrival. While the priests debate what to do with Jesus, Jesus enters the Temple and overturns the moneychangers' tables and releases sacrificial animals.[7] Roman soldiers rush in to restore order, but their actions are interrupted when someone in the crowd asks Jesus if it is right to pay taxes to Caesar. Viewers are then privileged to be inside Judas's mind as he struggles with conflicting images of the messiah. Would a true messiah say, "Render to Caesar"? Would a real messiah speak of "giving up his life"? Judas decides the answer to these questions is "No," so he leaves to talk to the priests about a price for leading them to Jesus.

Judas returns to the disciples and Jesus as they, along with Jairus's family, Cleopas, and Mary Magdalene, celebrate the Passover together.[8] During the meal, Judas leaves again,[9] and afterwards Jesus and the disciples go to the garden to pray. Along the way they meet Cleopas and Jairus's family, who ask Jesus to stay with them; but Jesus refuses, saying that he will come to talk to them after a short time (John 14:18, 28).

Jesus' garden prayer is visualized through animation, with Satan returning to tempt Jesus to run away from the cross. But Jesus finally resists the satanic lure, and when Judas appears to betray him, a blinding light, the healing of a man's ear, and a strong "No"[10] from Jesus lead to his arrest. Jesus is then taken to Caiaphas and the Sanhedrin, where Nicodemus (not identified by name) objects to the nighttime procedure. But after having condemned himself by his own words, Jesus is delivered to Pilate. There the priests accuse Jesus of refusing to pay taxes to Caesar, of "stirring up the people," and of claiming to be the king of the Jews. Finding no case against Jesus, Pilate sends him to Herod, who mocks him and returns him to Pilate. Pilate, a second time, finds Jesus innocent and asks the priests what he should do. Asher ben Azarah provokes from the crowds a cry for crucifixion and a demand for Barabbas's release. Pilate then washes his hands of "all of this—of all of you," and tells his guards to "deal with their king according to Roman law." There is no release of Barabbas, nor does Simon of Cyrene arrive to carry Jesus' cross.

As Jesus walks the Via Dolorosa, Jairus, Rachel, Tamar, and Cleopas awake and run toward the procession. Tamar manages to get through the crowds to touch Jesus' hand, and as he is crucified, the skies darken. The high priest's taunting, "Come down from the cross," turns into a final temptation of haunting voices in Jesus' head (cf. Scorsese, *The Last Temptation of Christ*). The wind, complete darkness, and Jesus' last words, "It is finished," lead to the ripping of the Temple veil and to the centurion's confession. When he is dead, Jesus' body is taken down from the cross by Jairus's family, who then watch him being buried.

On Easter morning Jesus appears to Mary Magdalene at the tomb, who then runs to tell the disbelieving disciples. After the Emmaus road travelers[11] and Peter relate their experiences, Jesus appears to them all, including doubting Thomas. The closing scene is the Great Commission (Matt. 28:16–20), with Tamar repeating John 14:1–2 to a bewildered little girl as the camera slowly looks up to an empty blue sky.

## Memorable Characters

- Jesus: He is God's son whose unusual healing powers help the weak and infirm. Jesus does not address issues of poverty in his teaching; he does not walk on water or feed five thousand people with a few loaves and fish. Ironically, and despite being a puppet, he is one of the more believable on-screen Jesus figures. He is friendly, has a sense of humor, grieves, is seriously tempted, and is a teacher who uses vivid images. Jesus' anger is reserved for the abuse of the Temple; he is much more patient with those who see him as a sinner due to the questionable source of his power. Thus, Jesus' primary opponents are political rulers and religious authorities (priests) rather than the Pharisees.[12] On a number of occasions viewers are privy to the inner states of Jesus' mind and heart.

- Tamar: Intended to be the twelve-year-old girl of Luke 8:40–56 (Mark 5:21–43), she seems closer to ten years old and apparently is not yet betrothed. She and her parents follow Jesus to Jerusalem, participate in the last Passover meal, follow on the Via Dolorosa, and take Jesus' body down from the cross, preparing it for burial. Tamar and her parents are witnesses of the resurrected Jesus.

- Jairus: There is no hint that he is a ruler of a synagogue (Luke 8:41), but he is a good Jewish man who loves his daughter and loves God. He is somewhat fearful of putting his daughter's life in the hands of an unauthorized miracle worker like Jesus, but he finally does, and Jesus raises his daughter from death. He is the unnamed disciple with Cleopas on the road to Emmaus (Luke 24:13–18) and announces to the eleven that he has seen the Lord.

- Rachel: Jairus's wife, she takes the initiative in getting her husband to go to Jesus to help Tamar.

- Mary Magdalene: Hayes's Magdalene is perhaps the most fully round Magdalene character to be found in a Jesus film. She is not a prostitute but is a "mad woman," demon possessed (Luke 8:2)—perhaps as a result of Roman oppression, as she seems to go into delusional fits whenever she sees Roman soldiers. After Jesus casts the demons out of her, she anoints Jesus' feet with her tears (Luke 7:37–38). She follows Jesus to Jerusalem and laments at his grave after he is buried. She is the first witness to the resurrection.

- Judas: He is a former Zealot attempting to dislodge Roman power in Palestine. He follows Jesus because of his "powers" and goes to Jerusalem hoping that Jesus will violently overthrow the Roman oppressors with his "kingdom of heaven" (cf. DeMille, *The King of Kings*). He stands beside Jesus when Jesus is confronted by Roman and priestly authorities in the Temple. As a result of Jesus' "Render to Caesar" statement, Judas decides Jesus is a false messiah and decides to lead the priestly authorities to Jesus. During the Passover meal, Jesus has to tell Judas a number of times, "Do what you have to do." Judas objects but finally leaves. Viewers are given privileged access to Judas's mental and emotional states during the passion by a number of animated cuts. After the betrayal, Judas is remorseful, saying he has betrayed an innocent man. There is no account of what happens to him after this.

- Herod Antipas: A cold, conniving, treacherous ruler, he understands the tenuousness of his power in Galilee and will do anything to hold on to what little power he has.

## Memorable Visuals

- Jesus building a synagogue in Sepphoris
- Mary Magdalene's demons
- Peter telling Jesus how fishing should be done
- Jesus' lament in response to John's death
- Pilate and the Roman centurion planning crucifixions for Passover
- Judas's mental state before betraying Jesus
- Jesus' prayer in the Garden of Gethsemane
- Mary Magdalene weeping at Jesus' tomb
- Jesus' shadow in the shape of a cross as he talks to the disciples on the road to Emmaus (cf. the resurrection appearance in Ray's *King of Kings*)

## Key Scriptures

The director states that the story of the raising of Jairus's daughter in Luke 8:40–56 was the starting point of his children's Gospel film, but in fact Mark's rendering of the story (Mark 5:21–43) more accurately represents the film's portrayal. The images of trusting like a child and "receiving the kingdom of God as a child" (Mark 10:14–15) are central to the film's focus on the little girl Tamar. These images are then contrasted with Pilate's, Herod's, and the disciples' understanding of kingly power.

## Cultural Location / Genre: Children's Bible Drama

*The Miracle Maker* was released in British theaters in January 2000, but it did not appear in the United States until four months later at Easter time, when it was shown first on network television. Using the stop-frame puppetry of a Russian film company, the film not only reflects the post–Cold War, globalized economic cooperation between Eastern and Western business enterprises, but it also reflects a certain rapprochement between Eastern and Western forms of Christianity. This is particularly evident in the iconic quality of the puppets themselves, for the British scriptwriter believes "model animation distills the essence of the human being" in much the same way as icons do.[13] While Western churches and artists are accustomed to a very naturalistic tradition that depicts

Jesus like one of them, Eastern churches and artists concentrate on revealing the eternal, superhuman, risen Christ within. *The Miracle Maker* Jesus thus ends up being a compromise between the two Christian traditions.[14] The basic, naturalistic face of Jesus was molded in Wales, but it was modified by the Orthodox craftsmen of Russia.

The scriptwriter also describes the film as "a fifth gospel—a gospel from a child's eye view,"[15] but it is unlike the Sunday school, Bible story approach to Jesus found in the Genesis Project's *The Story of Jesus for Children* (an unauthorized adaptation using segments of Sykes and Krisch's *The Jesus Film*). *The Miracle Maker*'s animated visualizations of Mary Magdalene's, Judas's, and Jesus' inner emotions are powerful and troubling, and are probably more terrifying for small children than any cinematic Jesus hanging on a cross. Nonetheless, as the they-lived-happily-ever-after fairy-tale ending dissolves into a bright blue sky, no child—or parent, for that matter—will be wondering what might be going on in the tormented soul of Judas, whether the demons will come back to haunt Mary Magdalene, or whether Jesus has really abandoned those he loves. Tamar may not be able to see Jesus anymore, but she knows that he is still powerful and is still with her, for she shares Jesus' comforting words with a girl younger than she.

## Director

Derek Hayes, a British animator since 1973, formed Animation City in 1979 with Phil Austin to produce promotionals for pop singers Madonna, Rod Stewart, Tom Jones, and others. He directed a number of short children's shows for British television before taking on the feature-length *The Miracle Maker*, which was produced by the Welsh group Cartwn Cymru/Christmas. In 2002 Derek Hayes directed the Cartwn Cymru/Christmas–produced *Otherworld*, another stop-frame puppet film that is a collection of medieval Welsh legends about brotherhood, adolescence, acts of brutal violence, and magic. Unlike *The Miracle Maker, Otherworld* is geared for older children and adults.

Hayes's *The Miracle Maker* won Best Children's Film at the Bradford Animation Festival in 2000 and the John Templeton Foundation Epiphany Prize in 2000.[16]

## DVD Extras and Technical Features

"Making of" Documentary (29:09)
    "A fifth gospel, from a child's eye-view," 3:45
    Orthodox iconography and the image of Jesus, 7:34
    Making the puppets, 11:01
    Historical accuracy, 11:53
    Animation for flashbacks, parables, inner thoughts of characters, 15:04
    Bringing the puppets to Russia, 17:33
Trailer
Cast and Crew
Production Notes
The Script
Animation
Audio Features: English, Spanish

## DVD Chapters

1. The Miracle Maker
   Sepphoris, Upper Galilee; year 90 of the Roman occupation, 1:26
2. Building a new synagogue, 1:30
   Rude Roman soldiers are present.
   Jesus (unidentified) works on a Sepphoris synagogue, 2:30
   A crazy Mary Magdalene wanders by, 2:53, 3:45
3. His Father's Work, 4:49
   Jesus leaves the city and walks home (still unidentified), 5:19
   Flashback to Jesus in the Temple at twelve years old, 6:14
   Flashback to Bethlehem, 7:36
4. John the Baptist, 8:18
   Peter is baptized, 9:12
   Jesus first shown, 8:43; baptized, 9:25
5. Tests, 10:45
   (animation)
6. Build a Strong Foundation, 13:06
   Lazarus, Mary, and Martha are introduced; Lazarus says his sisters saw Jesus at the Jordan.
      Martha serves (Luke 10:38)
      "On earth as it is in heaven" (Matt. 6:10), 14:39
      "Ask and it will be given" (Matt. 7:7), 14:47
   People oppose Jesus, but there is no idea who they are.
      "Whoever the Father sends to me" (John 10:28–29)
   Judas, a zealot, is introduced, 17:25
7. An Abundant Catch, 18:34
   Roman taxation, 18:53
      Mary Magdalene (with Matthew in the background)
      Simon (Peter), with James and John, refuses to pay.
      Mary Magdalene (with Roman soldiers), 19:17
   "Push the boat out," 20:15
      The Mustard Seed, 20:53
      "Don't build up treasure on earth" (Matt. 6:19), 21:34
   "Push the boat farther out," 21:47
8. Healing the Sick, 23:40
   Preparing a report on Jesus to take back to Jerusalem, 24:28
   The paralytic at Peter's house, 24:38
   A log in your own eye (Matt. 7:3; Luke 6:41), 25:14
9. Expelling the Demons from Mary, 28:04
   Choosing the twelve, 29:38
10. Invitation to a Feast, 32:37
    "Those who are well don't need a doctor" (Mark 2:17).
    Mary Magdalene washes Jesus' feet.
    "In league with the devil" (Matt. 12:24; Mark 3:22, 30; Luke 11:15), 34:31
11. Raised from the Dead, 34:40
    Jairus's daughter and the hemorrhaging woman
12. King Herod's Wrath, 39:55
    Herod has killed John (Jesus weeps).
    Herod hears of Jesus, 40:30
       Different kinds of power: Herod, Jesus, Caesar
    "The hour has come" (John 12:27), 41:45
       (Leaving for Jerusalem)

Judas speaks of winning a victory over the Romans
13. The Good Samaritan, 43:04
   Pilate briefs a centurion about Passover
      A public execution of rebels on the day of freedom . . .
   Who will be the greatest? 44:46
   The Good Samaritan, 45:51
14. Lazarus Is Risen, 48:01
   Caiaphas hears of the raising of Lazarus, 49:12
15. A Den of Thieves, 51:31
   Triumphal entry
   "If we let him go on, everyone will believe in him" (John 11:45–50).
   Cleansing the Temple, 53:36
      Judas again, 56:24
16. Judas's Torment, 57:15
   Son of Man came to give his life, to seek and save (Mark 10:45), 57:18
17. The Last Supper, 58:17
18. "Your will be done," 1.01:19
   "You can't come with me now" (John 13:31–14:2).
   Inside the mind of Jesus (the last temptation)
19. Betrayed with a Kiss, 1.04:06
   Sanhedrin trial, 1.06:10
      Nicodemus (John 7:50–52), 1.07:08
20. Denied Three Times, 1.07:42
21. The King of the Jews, 1.08:46
   "This man is the enemy of Rome."
      Opposes paying taxes to Caesar
   Take him to Herod, 1.10:09
22. A Passover Tradition, 1.10:58
   Pilate's second declaration of innocence, 1.11:22
23. The Crucifixion, 1.12:57
   Via Dolorosa
      "Come down now" (temptation), 1.15:05
24. "I've seen the Lord," 1.16:36
   Deposition (Tamar is there)
   Burial (Mary Magdalene laments), 1.17:14
   Easter morning, 1.17:52
      Mary Magdalene enters the empty tomb and laments.
25. Jesus Appears on the Road, 1.20:08
   Jesus appears to Peter.
   Cleopas and Jairus, 1.21:10
      Told retrospectively
26. Doubting Thomas, 1.24:18
   The Great Commission (Matt. 28:18–20), 1.25:33
   "The Spirit will come upon you soon" (Acts 1:8).
      Tamar says, "In my Father's house are many rooms" (John 14:2), 1.26:13
27. "The kingdom of God has come," 1.26:20
28. End credits, 1.26:57

# Chapter 18

# The Gospel of John

*Philip Saville, director. Rated PG-13. 180 minutes. Visual Bible International, 2003*

### Plot Summary

Saville took upon himself the challenging task of directing a film that would not use any words outside of the Gospel of John (Today's English Version) and would not deviate in any way from its narrative structure. Saville's additional, and more-difficult, goal was to end up with a film that people would actually watch. Given the literalistic constraints of his task, Saville's film is reasonably successful.

Limited to the text of the Gospel, Saville must find creative ways for the camera to express his interpretive point of view. And the camera's point of view surprises the knowledgeable Bible reader at the very outset of the film. Here, the film's narrator speaks the cosmic, Genesis-evoking language of the Johannine prologue (John 1:1–5) against the backdrop of a sunrise at the seashore. It is the beginning of a normal day in the world and not what a modern-day Bible reader might expect to see—a telescopic shot of stars and galaxies in deep space. Visually beginning with the dawn of a new day seems to challenge the narrator's voice-over of a Word that "already existed," one that "from the very beginning was with God." Rather than a preexistent Wisdom Christology, the film's opening camera shot seems already to imply an incarnational Christology—prefiguring the "Word became a human being" language of John 1:14.[1] As the rising sun dissolves into a second (but actually the same) sun, the narrator's voice-over intones, "The Word was with God," thus prefiguring the last lines of the prologue where a doubled view of Jesus is shown on-screen just before the narrator's concluding voice-over: "The only Son [sun?], who is the same as God, and is at the Father's side—he has made him known" (1:18).

The important role of the Gospel's narrator is given to Christopher Plummer,[2] who has a major share of the film's speaking parts and who actually delivers comments that could have been entrusted to other characters (e.g., 3:16–21, 31–36).[3] Even when God (12:28) or angels (20:13) speak, the narrator stands in for them.[4] The narrator's omniscient, omnipresent voice thus creates another "word of God" effect that opens and closes the book-film.[5]

When the narrator speaks the words about darkness in 1:5, the screen fades to black. Then, for the remainder of the prologue, the setting seems to be near where John was baptizing. At John 1:9, Saville presents the viewer with Jesus' shadow, and then after a brilliant flash of sunlight, Jesus' feet are shown. His shadowy profile continues to appear sporadically until the narrator gets to John 1:14, when the audience finally sees Jesus directly; however, Saville offers the first close-up of Jesus' face only at John 1:17–18. In this way, the opening camera work announces the theme of the film: the revelation of Jesus' identity as incarnate deity. The camera-eye view of Jesus continues up to 1:29, so that when the Baptist points at the Lamb of God, the audience sees Jesus first—again with a bright ray of sunlight behind him.

After the narrator, Jesus is the most important character in the film. The disciples, the crowds, and Jesus' opponents speak rather infrequently, even though they are all on-screen much more often than the text of John's Gospel requires. Saville depicts the religious authorities primarily through two invented characters—a leading Pharisee and a leading member of the Temple guard—and the Johannine high priest, Caiaphas.[6]

Saville treats with respect the opening questions of the Jewish authorities (1:19–28) who will eventually become Jesus' opponents. While their voices and postures are brusque and somewhat challenging, they leave more bewildered than suspicious. After the Beloved Disciple[7] and Andrew follow Jesus, the scene shifts to the Sea of Galilee,[8] where Andrew brings his brother, Simon (Peter), to Jesus. The film thus clarifies the mysterious identity of the Beloved Disciple at the very beginning; furthermore, his role as an eyewitness (19:34–37; 21:24–25) increases significantly beyond that of the Gospel because he is on camera for many of the scenes between John 2 and 12. As in the Gospel of John itself, revelatory scenes dominate the film, especially its opening (John 1–4) and closing (John 20–21), where the camera tends to linger over awed faces and epiphanies. These revelatory moments thus function as an interpretive frame to the authorities' growing opposition to Jesus.[9]

Like the other three Gospels, the plot of the Gospel of John is episodic. Most of its characters are flat, most are not identified by name, and most are not found in more than one Gospel episode. Saville, however, creates cohesiveness by focusing the camera on recurring characters. Further, as the Gospel reading/viewing progresses, many of these characters' attitudes toward Jesus change, creating incipient plot development. A prime example can be seen in the role Saville gives to Mary Magdalene. Although Mary Magdalene does not appear in the Gospel text until John 19:25, Saville introduces her in the film at John 6:22—first in ornate jewelry and dramatic red clothing.[10] She then follows Jesus into the Capernaum synagogue (6:25), where she is dressed in more subdued clothing and where she listens attentively to his words. She returns in the farewell discourse (13–18), where, dressed in earth tones, she is often seated or standing beside Jesus. Clearly, she has become one of his most devoted followers.

The invented character, "the leading Pharisee," also reveals Saville's plot development through characterization. The leading Pharisee first appears in Jerusalem shortly after Jesus has healed the lame man by the pool (5:15). Jesus addresses most of John 5:28–47 to him, and he walks away only to have Jesus confront him again and again. At the end of Jesus' monologue he seems barely able to contain his anger and disdain for Jesus. Nevertheless, he does not force a bloody confrontation in the Temple when given the opportunity (7:30), waiting until after the raising of Lazarus to make his move (11:47–48; 12:19; cf. 18:30ff.). The leader of the Temple police, on the other hand, represents the changing attitudes of the crowds. He starts out somewhat open to Jesus (John 7:45–46), gradually becomes the one waiting for Judas to hand over Jesus (13:30), and ultimately is the one who slaps Jesus (18:22). Thus, without adding words to the Gospel itself, Saville's camera turns Johannine flat character types into round characters whose changing responses to Jesus reflect a forward-moving plot.

Saville keeps the audience's attention during lengthy segments of narration and monologue by having the camera follow the comings and goings of various characters and by focusing on their menial tasks. Saville also frequently elects to show characters before introducing them by name and before making them part of the film's action. Thus, Saville shows Nicodemus in the Temple destruction scene (John 2:13–22) before introducing him in his nighttime discussion with Jesus (3:1–15). And after John the Baptist says Jesus "must become more important" (3:31), Saville shows Jesus' group of disciples grow from five to twelve—including, of course, Judas the betrayer. Thus, when Jesus feeds the five thousand (6:3), the twelve disciples are already with him, and the viewer is well prepared for the narrator's remarks about Judas and "the twelve" (6:67).

Much as Pasolini did in filming the Sermon on the Mount in *The Gospel According to St. Matthew*, Saville also attempts to keep his viewing audience's interest in the lengthy Johannine monologues by simply changing scenes. Thus, Jesus speaks his farewell discourse (John 13–17) in a room, on a terrace, walking through a vineyard, descending into a cavern and a grotto, and walking to the garden. In standard Jesus-film tradition, Saville also cuts from Jesus' farewell discourse to Judas arranging his betrayal of Jesus with the Temple police and bringing them to the garden.[11] More innovatively, Saville also cuts from Jesus' long speeches to black-and-white flashbacks[12] appropriate to the occasion: for example, John the Baptist's preaching at 5:33; the call of the disciples at 15:16; attempted stonings at 15:18, 20; the woman taken in adultery (not Mary Magdalene) at 15:20; the blind man healed at 15:24; walking on the water at 17:2; Lazarus raised, the lame man healed, the call of the disciples, and turning water into wine (in rich red) at 17:4–9; and Jesus' shadow from the beginning of the film at 17:18. In fact, the numerous flashbacks replay almost the entire ministry of Jesus during the discourse of John 13–17. At one point, Saville even introduces a color flash-forward to the trial before Pilate (at 16:11).

Jesus' statement about the "ruler of this world" (14:30) is centered on the plotting of Judas, the Temple police, and Caiaphas, the high priest. And later on, when Pilate asks the rhetorical question "What is truth?" (18:38), the camera gives its silent response by first turning to a Roman statue, then Roman soldiers, and then Roman emblems. The point is that truth is of little importance when confronted with Roman power. But unlike the Pilates of most Jesus films, the motivations and interests of Saville's Pilate are difficult to decipher. He seems unable to fathom the Jewish authorities' interests in condemning Jesus, especially when the priests, Pharisees, and crowds speak with one voice to have Jesus crucified.

Finally, the facial expressions and body language of Saville's Jesus during his conversations and long monologues are an important interpretative plot device. Jesus is always happy with the common people and always angry with the religious leaders. Yet Jesus can deliver the potentially damning words in 2:4 and 7:6–8 with a smile and a sense of humor. When Philip and Andrew bring news that the Greeks want to see Jesus, Jesus wears a blue robe for the first time, and he sits down heavily, marking the ominous onset of the passion.

Saville's rendering of the great catch of fish on the Sea of Galilee (21:1–14) recalls the prologue's opening camera shot of sunrise and the narrator's voice-over, "In the beginning." Saville seems to be suggesting that here is another beginning— now, however, the images of Jesus focus on close-ups of his face during Peter's three- fold confession (John 21:15–19). The camera's eye presents the scene as one of Jesus' forgiveness and Peter's commissioning (cf. the effect of addressing Jesus' words in 14:1 directly to Peter). It is the end of the Gospel—but clearly not the end of Saville's story.

## Memorable Characters

- Jesus: In contrast to the uncertainty of Scorsese's Jesus (*The Last Temptation of Christ*) or the development of consciousness in Young's Jesus (*Jesus*), Sav- ille's Jesus has a sense of divine purpose from the beginning. He is the divine revelation and the truth, yet without the angry edge that his words often have in the Gospel of John. Even his harshest language is usually spoken with the hint of a smile on his face (see especially John 8:39–59). Further- more, Jesus' revelations of his divine glory are portrayed more subtly in the film than they are in the Gospel of John. For example, Saville chooses to interpret Jesus' escapes from death in terms of natural crowd behavior (7:30; 8:59; 10:39; cf. 18:6) rather than as miracles. The Gospel of John itself is ambivalent at these points, but Saville opts for reticence.
- The narrator: Arguably more important than even Jesus, the narrator pro- vides a divine-eye's view and voice for the story. He has more lines than even the narrator in the Gospel itself, as many of the lines spoken by Jesus' oppo- nents are given to the narrator. He is neither the author of the book nor the retrospective witness, the Beloved Disciple.
- The leading Pharisee: He has a dark-brown beard and long curly hair and wears a black, tight-fitting turban that is flat on top. He is first identified as a Phar- isee at John 7:32, but he appears earlier, just after the healing of the lame man in Jerusalem (5:1–16). He takes on much of the dialogue of otherwise- unidentified opponents (e.g., 7:35–36, 45) and is the Pharisee who most often confronts Jesus (5:39–47). He is the primary accuser of the blind man (9:13–16) and the primary accuser of Jesus before Pilate.
- Mary Magdalene: Philip Saville calls her the first female disciple, and as such she is "absolutely iconic."[13] She is a former prostitute[14] and represents the true convert who becomes the model evangelical believer. She first appears in the story after the stilling of the storm, clothed in red and decked in jew- elry (6:22). Jesus speaks John 6:37–39 (51:39) directly to her; she is in the Capernaum synagogue in more subdued clothing and without jewelry

(6:54, 58 [54:50; 55:34]); and when she follows Jesus outside, he speaks, "And you?" (John 6:67 [56:46]) directly to her, and she nods in assent. She is there with Jesus when he washes the disciples' feet and stands next to Jesus when he says, "Where I am going you cannot come" (13:33). She leaves the supper with the other disciples and is thereafter either standing or sitting next to Jesus, with the Beloved Disciple often on the opposite side of Jesus. The camera focuses specifically on her when Jesus uses the metaphor of childbirth (16:21–22). Beyond the scenes where she is explicitly mentioned in John 19 and 20, she is on the Via Dolorosa, where she gasps when Jesus falls.

- The Beloved Disciple: He is the unnamed "other" disciple of John the Baptist (1:35–40) and usually wears a tight-fitting, beige skullcap. John Goldsmith, the screenwriter, calls him John, which is how he is identified as a member of the cast. He is the ultimate true witness, but he is not the retrospective narrator of the story.[15]
- The leader of the Temple police: When he first appears at John 7:32, he seems almost to believe in Jesus; however, as the film progresses, his opposition to Jesus increases, culminating in his arrest of Jesus (with Judas's help) and in his slapping of Jesus (before Annas).

## Memorable Visuals

- Daybreak at the sea in John 1:1; 21:4
- Jesus' first appearance as shadow, then with rays of bright sunlight
- Jesus in an orant praying position before the miracles
- Jesus teaching in the Temple among the people, with the Temple still under construction
- The disciples and others protecting Jesus from being arrested and from being stoned (7:30; 8:59)
- Jesus with children (10:1–15)
- Mary Magdalene's look of shock as Jesus strips to wash the disciples' feet
- Leaving the "Last Supper" room at John 14:15
- Various flashbacks during the farewell discourse
- Jesus praying for those whom the Father gave him (John 17:19)
- The leader of the Temple police slapping Jesus after Jesus' answer to Annas
- Smashing the legs of those crucified with Jesus
- Joseph of Arimathea and Nicodemus preparing Jesus' body for burial

## Key Scripture

The Gospel of John is the script for this film, with John 3:16 quoted before the film starts. John 1:11–12 is also particularly important, and Saville places a great deal of stress on Jesus' "I am he" and "What I'm telling you is true" pronouncements. These add to the revelatory quality of the story.

## Cultural Location / Genre: Audiovisual Bible

John Goldsmith, the screenwriter of *The Gospel of John*, states that this film has much in common with the silent-film era,[16] apparently thinking of how photographers during that period had to depend so much on the facial expressions of characters and teeming action scenes to carry the drama of a story that could not be heard. Although the connection to the silent-film era may be an appropriate connection visually, the structure of Saville's film has more in common with the recorded Bibles made popular by Alexander Scourby in the 1950s–1960s.

In the late 1940s, the American Foundation for the Blind commissioned Scourby, a radio personality and Shakespearean actor, to read books for phonograph recordings. His readings were so well received that by the 1950s he had recorded the entire Bible, and his 1966 reading of the King James Version of the Bible has been entered into the prestigious National Recording Registry.

With the advent of cassette tapes in the 1970s, the audio Bible became a cheaper and more-convenient way for Christians to connect with the Bible—either while commuting to work or as background meditative words while working around the home. But toward the end of the twentieth century, cable television, music videos, and video games became increasingly popular with adults and youth, changing the way Americans related to stories—including the Bible. People born since 1980 are part of what some now refer to as "broadband culture." This culture—its politics, education, entertainment, and religion—is overwhelmingly visual. On one hand, the transformation of the text of a Gospel into a movie accompanied by visuals fits this culture nicely. On the other hand, the fact that a Gospel does not translate into a very good movie script also makes a filmed Gospel something of an anomaly for this broadband culture.

The Visual Bible project (part of Visual Bible International, which is solely distributed by Thomas Nelson, one of the largest retailers of Bibles in the world) is now in bankruptcy; nevertheless, it managed to produce three Bible films before folding: *The Gospel of Matthew* (1997), *The Book of Acts* (1994), and now, most recently, *The Gospel of John*. *The Gospel of Mark* was in production when it was cancelled for financial reasons. It is highly unlikely that any more Visual Bible films will be produced.

For some, the film's devotion to the exact words of the Gospel of John seems almost Luddite in a broadband culture. The claim of Miroslaw Baszak, the director of photography, that "we are not interpreting the Bible, we are filming the Bible"[17] reveals how far removed he is from understanding the interpretive implications of a "*visual* Bible"—especially when both he and Saville can repeatedly note the iconic nature of the filmed Gospel. One cannot "film the Bible" apart from "interpretation," as Baszak might hope. Nor could Alexander Scourby, a scant generation earlier, simply "read the Bible" without interpreting it through his dramatic pauses and changes in voice inflection.

Despite the fact that Saville's *The Gospel of John* was produced for the MTV generation, like Sykes and Krisch's *The Jesus Film* twenty-five years earlier, Saville's film clearly belongs to American evangelical Protestantism. Accordingly, both disks in the DVD version of the film begin with Christopher Plummer's narration of John 3:16. Saville's *The Gospel of John* does not belong to the art-house theater setting of Pasolini's similarly "literal" rendering of the Gospel of Matthew (*The Gospel According to St. Matthew*); but it does fit nicely into church libraries as an audiovisual Bible, and it is easily adaptable for "postmodern," multimedia sermons.

## Director

Philip Saville began his directing career in 1955, and he has spent almost all his career in the television industry. Before the Visual Bible filed for bankruptcy, he was slated to direct the film version of *The Gospel of Mark*. Saville's *The Gospel of John* belongs to the niche in Jesus films that are purportedly based on one Gospel: the films of Pasolini (*The Gospel According to St. Matthew*), Greene (*Godspell*), and Sykes and Krisch (*The Jesus Film*). Of those films, Saville's devotion to the literal text of one Gospel is closest to Pasolini's adherence to Matthew; however, Pasolini, like Sykes and Krisch, created an original script by editing and rearranging his foundational text. Saville, on the other hand, follows by mandate the text of the Gospel much more literally. The absence of a recognizable movie script between John and the film highlights the difficulties of basing a movie on the Gospel(s). To most moderns, the Gospel without additions and revisions is barely recognizable as a movie.

Notwithstanding Saville's commitment to the text of John's Gospel, his work still belongs to the larger Jesus-film tradition. The film's portrayals of Mary Magdalene, Judas, and the Beloved Disciple—all of which go beyond the text of John—bespeak this tradition, as do the film's location, sets, costumes, and the persona of Jesus. Moreover, it resembles in many ways the early efforts in Jesus films; efforts antedating the plot, character, and epic devices bequeathed to the tradition by DeMille. However, Saville's use of modern visual techniques makes for something more than just a celluloid illustrated Bible.

## DVD Extras and Technical Features

Setup
    Spoken Language: English
    Subtitles
        Spanish
        French
    Special Features: Enhanced Viewing
        An interactive icon that can be turned on or off, giving access to historical and geographical information pertinent to particular scenes.
Two-hour version of the film (The following features are on the two-hour DVD only.)
Historical Background (*Note: the forward arrow within sections is not active.*)
    Jesus, Son of God, 7:20 minutes
        In order of appearance: Peter Richardson, Bruce Waltke, Charles Hedrick, Alan Segal, Stephen Breck Reid, Patricia Dutcher-Walls
    The World of Jesus, 7:48 minutes
        In order of appearance: Patricia Dutcher-Walls, Peter Richardson, Alan Segal
    Glossary of Terms
    Bibliography and Filmography
Production Design: The Making of *The Gospel of John*
    Director: Philip Saville, 7:45 minutes

Screenwriter: John Goldsmith, 11:48 minutes
>    The summing up of the Farewell Discourse, 4:22
>    The leading Pharisee, 6:32
>    Anti-Semitism vs. anti-clericalism, 6:50
>    Like a silent movie, 8:40
>    John, the beloved disciple, 9:12

Director of Photography: Miroslaw Baszak, 6:45 minutes
Production Designer: Don Taylor, 10:19 minutes
>    Filmed in the Sierra Nevada of Spain

Costume Designer: Debra Hanson, 10:08 minutes
Musical Score: Jeff Danna, 10:21 minutes
Hair and Make Up Design: Trefor Proud, 5:35 minutes

About the Cast (Only Henry Ian Cusick [Jesus] and Christopher Plummer [narrator] have video segments related to their characters.)
Jesus, 5:40 minutes
Narrator, 6:05 minutes

About the Filmmakers
Academic Advisory Committee
Interactive Map of the Holy Land: The Miracles of Jesus
The Miracles of Jesus
Trailer
Production Credits for DVD and Special Features

# DVD Chapters

Non-Johannine elements are in italics.
1. Prologue and the Word of Life (1:1–28)
2. Lamb of God, the First Disciples (1:29–50), 6:04
>    *Jesus calling his first disciples from fishing beside the lakeshore (8:57; cf. Mark 1:16)*
>    *The "other disciple" as the Beloved Disciple (Is he John, as stated on the DVD blurb?)*
3. The Cana Wedding; Jesus Goes to the Temple (2:1–22), 12:51
4. Jesus and Nicodemus; Jesus and John (2:23–4:2), 19:37
5. Jesus and the Samaritan Woman (4:3–44), 25:35
6. Healing the Official's Son; Healing the Lame Man (4:45–5:14), 31:35
>    The "royal official" *appears to be Roman* (cf. Matt. 8:5, Luke 7:2) although the note attached to the scene states that the official could be Jewish, Roman, or a mercenary.
>    The leading Pharisee appears, 37:48
7. Authority of the Son; Witness to Jesus (5:15–6:1), 37:55
8. Feeding the Five Thousand; Walking on Water (6:2–24), 43:05
>    *The twelve disciples distribute the loaves and fishes instead of Jesus (Mark 6:41).*
>    *Mary Magdalene appears after the stilling of the storm (John 6:22 [49:25]) then in Jerusalem, where she appears at the last supper (John 13).*
9. Bread of Life; Words of Eternal Life (6:25–70), 49:52
>    *Mary Magdalene follows Jesus to the synagogue in Capernaum.*
10. Festival of Shelters; the Attempted Arrest (7:1–44), 57:57
>    *Jesus working as a carpenter in Galilee (Mark 6:3)*
11. *The Adulterous Woman*; the Light of the World (7:45–8:30), 1.04:10
>    Mary Magdalene is not the woman caught in adultery.
12. Truth Will Set You Free; Jesus and Abraham (8:31–59), 1.11:23
13. Jesus Heals a Man Born Blind (9:1–12), 1.16:06
14. Pharisees Question the Blind Man (9:13–34), 1.19:38

15. Spiritual Blindness; Jesus the Good Shepherd (9:35–10:21), 1.23:01
    *Jesus with children* (10:11), 1.25:32
16. Jesus Is Rejected (10:22–40), 1.27:01
17. Jesus Is the Resurrection and the Life (11:1–27), 1.30:31
18. Lazarus Brought to Life (11:28–45), 1.34:17
19. The Plot against Jesus (11:46–57), 1.38:50
20. Jesus Anointed at Bethany (12:1–11), 1.40:51
21. The Triumphal Entry into Jerusalem (12:12–50), 1.43:15
22. Jesus Washes His Disciples' Feet (13:1–20), 1.51:12
23. Jesus Predicts His Betrayal and Denial; the Way to the Father (13:21–14:14), 1.56:00
    Mary Magdalene reaches for Jesus (13:33–34), 1.59:10
24. The Promise of the Holy Spirit; the Real Vine (14:15–15:6), 2.02:23
    Jesus is now on a rooftop with his disciples.
    "The ruler of this world" (14:30), 2.04:35
        Judas and the Temple police meet the high priest.
    Jesus and the disciples leave the house (14:31).
25. Love One Another (15:7–16:11), 2.05:58
    First flashback (15:16), 2.07:03
    *The woman caught in adultery* (15:22), 2.08:22
26. Victory over the World (16:12–17:9), 2.10:54
27. Jesus Prays for His Disciples (17:10–26), 2.15:55
    "For those who believe through them" (17:20; cf. 12:20)
        Also the royal official, and multiple ethnicities are represented
28. The Arrest of Jesus; Peter's Denial (18:1–27), 2.18:58
    "Another disciple" is the Beloved Disciple, 2:22.00
29. Jesus before Pilate (18:28–19:12), 2.24:31
    "What is truth?" (18:38), 2.26:48
        Camera focuses on a Roman statue, soldiers, emblems.
    "Give us Barabbas!" (18:40)
        The entire crowd says it, there are no dissenting voices.
30. Jesus Is Crucified (19:13–37), 2.31:25
    The sponge of sour wine is not on hyssop, but on *a long stick* (Mark 15:36).
31. The Burial; the Empty Tomb (19:38–20:18), 2.39:41
32. Jesus Appears to his Disciples (20:19–30), 2.43:57
33. Jesus and Peter; Conclusion (21:1–25), 2.47:33
34. Credits

# Chapter 19

# The Passion of the Christ

*Mel Gibson, director. 126 minutes. Rated R. 2004. Newmarket Films, 2004*

### Plot Summary

Gibson's passion-play film has three basic parts: 1) arrest and trial before Caiaphas; 2) trial before Pilate (including beatings); 3) road to the cross and crucifixion. The film opens with two important subtexts that present the passion narrative as the vicarious, victorious suffering of Jesus. The opening Scripture citation from Isa. 53 (the quote is from v. 5, although the intertitle does not specify the verse) is the first subtext. Isaiah 53:5 reads, "He was wounded for our transgressions, crushed for our iniquities . . . by His wounds we are healed" (ESV). The opening Garden of Gethsemane scene evokes the second subtext more subtly as Jesus struggles with an androgynous Satan. As Jesus lies prone on the ground,[1] a snake crawls out of Satan and onto Jesus (the snake's tail can be seen protruding from Satan's nostril at one point). Jesus then rises and heroically crushes the snake's head with his foot, establishing a messianic reading of Gen. 3:15. Meanwhile, Judas makes his deal with Caiaphas[2] and leads the Temple police to the garden.

The savage beating of Jesus, which was the reason for the film's "R" rating, begins in the garden. En route to his Jewish trial, the Temple police pull Jesus by a chain and hang him upside down from a bridge. There, he comes face to face with Judas, who is cowering under the bridge, waiting for the Temple police to pass by. Judas has already begun to lose his grip on reality, and from here on, Gibson portrays Judas's demonic demise in gruesome detail, ending with his suicidal hanging. Gibson also cuts away from Jesus' suffering for scenes showing Mary's symbolic connection with Jesus as co-redeemer, following the Roman Catholic theological perspective that Mary participates in the salvation of humankind.

Finding Jesus guilty of blasphemy, Caiaphas and other leaders take Jesus to Pilate.[3] Pilate, the most human character in the film, tries unsuccessfully to avoid Caiaphas's plot to kill Jesus by pronouncing Jesus innocent on three different occasions. After his first pronouncement of Jesus' innocence, Pilate turns Jesus over to Herod Antipas. But Herod, having established no serious charges against Jesus, sends him back to Pilate.

Pilate again pronounces Jesus innocent. This time, seeing that the Jewish crowd will not be won over by his attempt to release Jesus (they choose Barabbas instead of Jesus), Pilate has Jesus scourged. The scourging, which is the film's most memorable and horrific scene (it lasts nearly eight minutes), is Pilate's attempt to appease the Jews without crucifying Jesus. After being beaten with rods thirty-eight times, Jesus catches his mother's eye and rises victoriously—only to bear a second, and even more sadistic, scourging with cats-o'-nine-tails. The beating begins again with the soldiers starting to recount from one, and it leaves the pavement bathed in Jesus' blood. Mary and the Magdalene lovingly wipe the precious blood of Jesus from the pavement with white linens provided by Claudia, Pilate's wife. Finally, Pilate pronounces Jesus innocent a third and final time in the *ecce homo* scene, and Pilate turns Jesus over to the Jewish leaders' murderous wishes.

On the Via Dolorosa, Gibson's Jesus falls and rises repeatedly, following the Roman Catholic tradition of the Stations of the Cross. At one touching point, the audience sees Jesus' suffering mother try to help him stand as she had helped him once when he was a toddler. Later, Veronica offers her "veil" to Jesus and receives it back—with a bloody imprint of his face, creating a relic that resembles the famous Shroud of Turin. Although conscripted reluctantly, Simon of Cyrene carries Jesus' cross and comes to Jesus' defense in the face of the soldiers' continued abuse of Jesus. Just outside the city gates, Simon encourages Jesus by saying that it is almost over.[4]

When Jesus is nailed to the cross, Gibson focuses the viewer's attention on Jesus' flowing blood. The visuals emphasize the crucifixion's brutality at every opportunity. Yet Gibson also provides several flashbacks to the Last Supper/Eucharist while Jesus is on the cross, joining the historical and the myth-ritual sacrifice of Christ. Gibson's Jesus speaks all seven last words from the cross. And perhaps most important, Jesus twice asks God to forgive "them." The spear thrust brings forth a shower of blood, bathing Mary and John (the Beloved Disciple) in its flow, as they stand beside the cross.

Just before Jesus dies, nature/God speaks vengefully on behalf of his chosen one. After a providential bird pecks at the unrepentant thief's eye, Gibson abandons the human perspective, and in a dramatic visual break, provides a camera view from heaven, looking down at the cross. The camera follows a single raindrop (a divine tear?) to the ground that turns into an earthquake and splits the Temple (not merely the Temple veil) in half. Presumably this destruction signifies the end of Temple ritual and may also be a vengeful reference to the destruction of the Temple in 70 CE. In the aftermath of Jesus' death, Caiaphas grieves in the Temple while Satan writhes upon a desert landscape.

The deposition leads quickly to the pietà. After a fade to black, the stone rolls away from the tomb, and the grave clothes mysteriously collapse. Jesus, bathed in soft light, rises. The film's last shot focuses on the nail hole in his right hand.

Despite flashbacks to Jesus' ministry, Gibson's passion play focuses on a visceral and ritual experience of the cross. Gibson's decision to use an "original language"[5] soundtrack rather than a modern language one has the added effect of requiring audiences to watch the screen intently at all times—even during the most violent scenes—if they want to make sense of the action. Not surprisingly, critics complained about the film's mind-dulling violence and anti-Semitism. Gibson's action-hero Christ is one who conquers through suffering. And while Gibson does not emphasize the resurrection, his Jesus rises triumphantly numerous times from the bloody earth: in Gethsemane, in the scourging, repeatedly on the Via Dolorosa, at Calvary, and finally in the tomb. One expects his unhappy, vengeful return. In fact, the vengeance had already begun at the cross with God's crow pecking at the eye of the unrepentant thief.

Gibson's film was a surprising success and returned Jesus to epic prominence. That return now seems part and parcel of an ongoing revival of religiously themed films.

## Memorable Characters

- Jesus: The bloodiest, most brutalized Jesus ever seen on the silver screen. He is Isaiah's prophesied Suffering Servant, whose tortured, sacrificial body survives horrific beatings on and off screen to carry the largest cross ever seen on the silver screen. Jesus is most human in flashbacks to his childhood and public ministry, where he can open his eyes and smile. Jesus can speak Latin as well as his native language, Aramaic. Curiously, there is no hint of his miraculous birth.
- Mary, the mother of Jesus: She is arguably the most important character other than Jesus. She plays her Roman Catholic role of coredeemer, suffering with her son and willing him forward to his ultimate goal of dying on the cross. She is a loving mother, but there is no hint that she conceived virginally.
- Judas: His motivations for betraying Jesus are unclear. Gibson delights, however, in displaying his demonic torments and death.
- Pilate: Unlike the coldly ambitious Pilate of much of the Jesus-film tradition, Gibson's Pilate is the most human character in the film. He is, however, completely ineffectual in the face of Caiaphas's and Satan's manipulation of the judicial process.
- Claudia, Pilate's wife: She provides support for Jesus' women and is the first Gentile believer.
- Simon of Cyrene: Reluctant to help Jesus at first, he finally becomes the only one standing with Jesus in his sufferings when he tries to bring a halt to the soldiers' harassment of Jesus.
- Caiaphas: Although he is not motivated by greed, this Caiaphas bears a strong resemblance to DeMille's Caiaphas in *The King of Kings.* He is the film's prime villain.
- Temple police and Roman soldiers: These characters achieve a sadistic brutality never before seen in Jesus films.
- Satan: This ethereal, androgynous figure haunts the edges of the story in a fashion similar to Stevens's Dark Hermit (*The Greatest Story Ever Told*). Jesus' conflict with Satan in the garden seals his fate while it recalls the story of Eden lost. However that fate is not revealed until Jesus' death on the cross.

## Memorable Visuals

- Jesus crushing the snake in the garden[6]
- Judas's death
- Jesus' triumphant rise midway through the sadistic, inhuman scourging
- The flashbacks with Jesus and his mother
- Nature/God's vindictive responses: Judas beset by demonic children; the scavenging bird; the teardrop from heaven; the toppled Temple

## Key Scriptures

Gibson's film is overwhelmingly Johannine in its depiction of Jesus' triumphant passion and is like the book of Hebrews (9:11–14, 26–28; 10:12) in its view of Jesus' sacrificial death and in its supersessionism. Some of Gibson's key Scriptures are also Hebrew Bible texts, interpreted from a Christian perspective: e.g., Isa. 53; Gen. 3:15.

## Cultural Location / Genre: Passion Play / Horror

According to the conventional wisdom, the biblical epic died in the 1960s with Ray's *King of Kings* and Stevens's *The Greatest Story Ever Told*. Jesus movies moved to smaller venues in the 1970s. However, the Hollywood epic did not die; it simply moved to outer space and to urban settings. Recently, the epic has made a comeback in other genres like fantasy (*The Lord of the Rings* [2001–03], *Harry Potter* [2001–07]) and history (*Titanic* [1997], *Gladiator* [2000], *Pearl Harbor* [2001]). But no one in Hollywood believed that biblical epics—much less Jesus epics—could make a comeback. However, the financial success of Gibson's film was astounding, and its success ensures that a spate of copycat biblical epics will follow in its wake.

Gibson's film feeds on the fundamentalist religious revivals that began in the last decades of the twentieth century. These revivals themselves were part of a return to right-wing politics and an increasingly unabashed capitalistic form of Christianity. And the vengeance at the heart of Gibson's film fits the religious politics of post-9/11 U.S. imperialism quite well. Both film and political spin doctors of that imperialism have majored in *exporting* suffering. Both justify the righteous violence that establishes/defends the (American) viewing audience's innocence.[7] As with Stevens's *The Greatest Story Ever Told* and Young's *Jesus*, Gibson's depiction of Jesus' temptation is as much about American ideals as it is about Jesus. Gibson's Satan tempts Jesus with the thought that no "one man can bear the full burden of sin" and "no one man can carry this burden. . . . It is far too heavy. Saving their souls is far too costly."[8] In the post-9/11 marriage of U.S. global politics and Christianity, where it has become the "destiny" of the United States to bear the burden for democracy and order in the world, the Neocon temptation is to give up that responsibility and to share it with others in the community of nations. But Gibson's battered and bloody Jesus must accept God's call and bear the brunt of the world's evil and hatred if the world is to be a better place. So also the United States, battered and bloody after 9/11, must continue to be firm in its resolve to bring salvation to the world. It is no surprise that violence and horror are hugely successful film genres in post-9/11 Hollywood.[9]

## Director

*The Passion of the Christ* resembles Gibson's 1995 film, *Braveheart*. Both are epic biopics. However, *Braveheart*'s hero, William Wallace, is far more like the typical action/epic hero than is Gibson's Jesus. In particular Wallace is a reluctant hero, and thus Gibson must carefully establish the need for the hero in *Braveheart*. Like other biopics—and like the Gospels to a certain extent—*Braveheart* does this in the form of the hero's youth and call. Wallace responds to the murderous betrayals and oppressions of the evil Edward Longshanks and his henchmen. The victims include Scottish nobles, William's father and brother, and William's wife, whom he has married in secret. Her death "calls" Wallace to his mission—the freedom of Scotland. By way of contrast, nothing in Gibson's *The Passion of the Christ* provides a similar backdrop for Jesus' struggle with evil. Further, after Wallace's call, *Braveheart* offers several action sequences detailing his cunning, successful opposition to English tyranny. Only betrayal—by Robert the Bruce, who refers to himself as "Judas"—undoes Wallace. In contrast, Gibson's Jesus has no obvious political agenda, and Gibson's Judas lacks any clear motivation.

In other respects, however, *Braveheart* was a dress rehearsal for Gibson's *The Passion of the Christ*. Like Jesus' kingdom, which is "not of this world" and therefore denies Roman sovereignty, Wallace denies Longshanks's sovereignty when accused of treason. Despite temptations to compromise, Wallace steadfastly refuses to compromise his mission for freedom despite the prospect of a torturous death. While he has not prayed previously, Wallace prays in prison to be given the strength to die well (cf. Jesus in Gethsemane). During the terrible tortures that precede his death, Wallace rises from the ground to affirm his mission and accept more suffering (cf. Jesus' rise during the scourging). As in *The Passion of the Christ*, much of the passion in *Braveheart* is filmed in slow motion. Further, Gibson cuts frequently in both films between the suffering hero and the anguish of followers. Gibson's presentation of Wallace's torture is, however, much more subdued than his presentation of Jesus' suffering. What he suggests in *Braveheart*, he concentrates on without wavering in *The Passion of the Christ*.

While both heroes triumph through suffering, Wallace's triumph—and his cause—is clearer. Thus, as Wallace screams "freedom," Gibson shows us Longshanks dying (cf. the toppled Temple?).[10] Further, the mob that has called for Wallace's torture converts to his cause because of his heroism. Finally, the Bruce himself converts and leads the Scots to freedom after Wallace's noble death.[11] By contrast, Gibson's Christ has no such succession. His passion itself is his victory.

## DVD Extras and Technical Features[12]

Widescreen. English and Spanish subtitles. English (audio) commentary for the visually impaired, English (additional text) for the hearing impaired. Thirty-two numbered, untitled chapters.

## DVD Chapters

Chapters simply have numbers on the DVD. The chapter titles below are thus the authors'. Flashbacks are in italics.

1. Prayer in the Garden, 1:00
2. Thirty Pieces of Silver, 3:19
3. Satan, 4:38
   Satan appears, 5:53
4. Betrayal, 9:14
   Judas turns to run, 9:56
   The kiss, 10:31
   Judas runs, 11:44
   Healing the slave's ear, 12:30
   John runs to tell Mary the mother and Mary Magdalene, 14:09
   "Why is this night different . . ." (the beginning of the Passover Haggadah), 14:29
5. Arrest, 14:51
   Judas under the bridge, 15:35
   Sanhedrin called, 16:14
   Judas in high priest's courtyard, 16:59
6. The High Priest's Courtyard, 16:38
   Mary his mother arrives, 18:06
7. Table Maker, 19:39
   *Jesus makes a table,* 19:55
   Pilate hears of Jesus' arrest (Claudia is there), 22:20
8. Before Caiaphas, 23:12
   "He casts out devils with the help of devils" (Matt. 12:24; Mark 3: 22; Luke 11:15).
   "The bread of life" (John 6:35–56), 25:52
   Judas bites himself.
9. Peter's Denials, 28:30
   *"You will deny me three times"* (Luke 22:31–34), 30:01
   Confesses his sin to Mary
10. Judas repents, 31:42
    Child bites Judas (cf. DeMille, *The King of Kings*), 33:30
    (and turns into a demon—a eucharistic reversal?)
    Mother Mary's ear to the ground, 34:54
11. Judas's death, 35:35
    (cf. Pasolini, *The Gospel according to St. Matthew,* and Jewison, *Jesus Christ Superstar*)
12. Pilate and Claudia, 38:02
    Jesus before Pilate, 39:29
    Pilate speaks Aramaic; Jesus speaks Latin.
    "What is truth?" 42:58
13. Herod Antipas, 44:10
    (cf. Jewison, *Jesus Christ Superstar*)
14. Pilate and Claudia Again, 46:20
    "What is truth?" 46:47
15. Pilate Refuses to Condemn Jesus a Second Time, 48:07
    Release of Barabbas, 49:17
    "Crucify him," 51:18
    Claudia, 51:34
    "No, I will chastise him then set him free!" 51:38
16. Roman Guards Whip Jesus, 52:05

(cf. Jewison, *Jesus Christ Superstar*, where Pilate counts the whip lashes)

Mary looks at Jesus; he stands again, 55:29

    (cf. Mary on the Via Dolorosa in DeMille, *The King of Kings*)

Claudia brings cloth to Mary, 59:54

Satan's child, 1.01:26

    Smiles, 1.01:53

*Washing the disciples' feet* (John 13:3–17), 1.02:10

Mary wipes up Jesus' blood, 1.04:23

17. A Crown of Thorns, 1.05:06
18. Mary and Mary Magdalene Wipe Up Jesus' Blood, 1.05:37

    *The woman caught in adultery (Mary Magdalene)*, 1.06:11

19. Pilate Refuses to Condemn Jesus a Third Time, 1.08:09

    "Behold the man," 1.08:52

    High priest says, "Crucify him," a second time, 1.08:58

    "Therefore, it is he who delivered me to you who has the greater sin," 1.10:00

    Pilate washes his hands, 1.11:00

    *The Last Supper*, 1.11:11

    "I am innocent of this man's blood," 1.11:59

    "Do as they wish," 1.12:27

20. Led Away to Be Crucified, 1.12:29

    *Triumphal entry into Jerusalem*, 1.14:07

    *Little boy Jesus falls; Mary runs to help*, 1.17:42

        Mary as coredeemer

    Veronica, (see below), 1.20:03

21. Simon of Cyrene, 1.20:34

    Simon steps forward, 1.21:25

22. Veronica, 1.23:13

    Veronica's veil, 1.23:42

23. Simon of Cyrene yells "Stop," 1.24:44

    "Stop!" 1.25:26

    Veronica's veil, 1.26:59, 1.27:10

        (looks down at her veil, 1.27:21)

24. Golgotha—"We're nearly there," 1.27:54

    Opening the city gates to look at Golgotha (cf. Stevens, *The Greatest Story Ever Told*)

25. Climbing Golgotha, 1.29:30

    *Sermon on the Mount* (Matt. 5:43–46; Luke 6:27–28, 32), 1.29:32

    *"I am the good shepherd"* (John 10:11, 15, 18), 1.31:00

26. Simon of Cyrene Completes His Task, 1.31:24

    Jesus tells Simon he is free to go, 1.32:06

    *The Last Supper*, 1.34:09

27. Nailed to the Cross, 1.35:06

    *The Last Supper*, 1.35:06

        *"You are my friends; greater love has no man"* (John 15:14).

        *"I cannot be with you much longer"* (John 13:33), 1.36:15

        *"You believe in me"* (John 14:1, 6), 1.37:00

        *"This is my body"* (Matt. 26:26; Mark 14:22; Luke 22:19), 1.40:48

28. Lifting Up the Cross, 1.40:57

    Camera shot from above the cross (cf. Jewison, *Jesus Christ Superstar*; Scorsese, *The Last Temptation of Christ*)

    *"Take this and drink"* (Matt. 26:27; Mark 14:24; Luke 22:20), 1.42:34

    Two thieves, 1.43:29

        (cf. DeMille, *The King of Kings*)

29. The Sky Darkens, 1.46:33
    Mary the mother kisses Jesus' feet, 1.48:56
        (cf. Scorcese, *The Last Temptation of Christ*)
    Death, 1.52:18
30. Teardrop of God, 1.52:21
    Pilate, 1.53:01
    Devil, 1.55:14
    Deposition, 1.55:40
31. Resurrection, 1.57:17
32. Credits, 1.58:46

# Chapter 20

# Teaching Jesus Films

Probably the most common way Jesus films are used in classrooms is in piecemeal fashion, where teachers collect film clips to illustrate Gospel incidents or possible interpretations of Jesus and the Gospels. But Jesus films also deserve to be studied for their revelations about culture and for their own structure and narrative unity. Thus, we have structured this chapter (and our book as a whole) to facilitate these two uses of Jesus films. For those uncertain about which particular film clips to use (or for student research papers) we offer for consideration the following "favorites"—including quite diverse interpretations of the Gospel stories in question.[1]

For those who may wish to teach Jesus films as narrative wholes, we conclude this chapter by offering some organizational issues around which courses might be structured. These issues include Gospel sources in Jesus films, religion and theology in Jesus films, contemporizing Jesus, the interpretative tradition of Jesus films, and Christ-figure films. Films are listed by directors only (see p. 175).

## Teaching Particular Film Clips

### Prologue

While several films (notably Sykes and Krisch) use John 3:16 as an introduction to the Jesus story, Stevens visualizes part of John's prologue dramatically, opening with a church icon, segueing to a starry night, and moving finally to a lamp being carried in the Bethlehem stable. All the while, a narrator is reciting part of John's prologue. Saville offers an even more-impressive symbolic interpretation of that prologue, with a visual assertion that Jesus is the incarnate Word. However, most Jesus films invent their own prologues—running the gamut from Scorsese's disclaimers, through Jones's extremely precise notation that the Sermon on the Mount happened "about teatime," to Olcott's travelogue map of the Holy Land.

### The Infancy

The early Jesus films typically present Jesus' infancy—if not the entire Jesus story—as a Christmas pageant. In his silent, black-and-white film, Zecca uses color and superimposed angels strikingly to depict the providential design and angelic protection of the divine infant. Pasolini sets Jesus' infancy in a peasant context. But Zeffirelli devotes by far the most attention to Jesus' Jewish background, lavishly detailing Jewish culture and ritual. However, Zeffirelli also evokes the foundational American myth through his treatment of the three wise men's journeys to Bethlehem. They travel separately from three different continents, and when they join together to face the Bethlehem star, they are wearing red, white, and blue. Jones parodies the infancy narrative by having the wise men initially visit and worship the wrong baby (Brian).

### Jesus' Youth

Many directors use stories of Jesus' youth to foreshadow his future (cf. Luke 2:41–51). For example, Olcott shows Jesus working with his father at carpentry and allows a cruciform shadow to fall over him, frightening his mother. Zeffirelli also shows Jesus working with his father at carpentry, and later his youthful Jesus climbs an unsupported ladder "toward heaven," where he looks down on a shepherd herding sheep. Young includes the miracle of the bird from the apocryphal Gospels, showing Jesus' life-giving powers.

### The Beginning of Jesus' Public Ministry

Saville offers a flashback of Jesus' self-baptism,[2] while Pasolini's and Young's baptism scenes conclude with the crowds worshiping Jesus. Greene's frolicking, Bethesda-Fountain, communal baptism is a unique dramatization of the transformation of Jesus and his community.[3]

The Jesuses of Stevens, Zeffirelli, and Saville know from the beginning who they are and what their ministry will be about. They do not struggle or face meaningful temptations. By contrast, Scorsese and Young depict Jesuses who have to learn their purpose by trial and error. Scorsese's Jesus does so in a tormented, anguished way; Young's Jesus does so as he "matures" after his (earthly) father's death. Their Jesuses are the modern Western everyman.

Ray, Stevens, Pasolini, Sykes and Krisch, Young, and Hayes all place the temptation of Jesus in its Gospel "wilderness" setting. Ray's "test" entices Jesus—and others—to "force" God's hand. Sykes and Krisch offer a satanic snake as the tempter. Young's temptation offers a "modernly" dressed Satan both in the early wilderness setting and in the garden. Here, the test is to override the freedom of other humans. Hayes offers the temptation in animation as something that transpires within Jesus' mind.

DeMille, Stevens, Young, Gibson, and Hayes also depict the tempter returning to Jesus during his final days in Jerusalem. DeMille postpones Jesus' messianic temptation until Jesus arrives in the Temple near the end of his life, and the Garden of Gethsemane (Gen. 3) is the significant place of Jesus' temptation for Jewison, Young, and Gibson. Jesus' temptation is strikingly absent from Zeffirelli's film.

Scorsese uses multiple temptations—two in the wilderness, one in Gethsemane, and the last temptation on the cross—as the generative center of his film. The last of these is, of course, the climactic one. Intriguingly, Hayes, too, depicts a final (though not sexual) temptation on the cross. If the Jesuses of the American films represent the United

States (DeMille, Ray, Stevens, Jewison, Young, Gibson[4]), how might these temptations reflect American anxieties and hopes at various historical moments?

## Jesus' Teaching

Zecca, Olcott, and Griffith offer little or none of Jesus' teaching, in part because they are silent films. At the opposite extreme is Saville's film, based on John, which is primarily a teaching film, with Jesus revealing his identity through his words. Except for one flashback to the Sermon on the Mount, Gibson centers Jesus' teaching on his identity and his words at the Last Supper.

Ray presents a spectacular, dialogical Sermon on the Mount in which Jesus teaches peace, love, and the brotherhood of man—a spiritual kingdom. Stevens's philosopher-Jesus calls all to seek the kingdom of God within (Luke 17:21), not material wealth or well-being (cf. the teaching of the Jesus character in Arcand's passion play). Zeffirelli's Jesus also speaks of matters of the heart, not of intellectual or political matters (rejecting ritual matters on several occasions). The teaching of Sykes and Krisch's Jesus is, in effect, an evangelistic sermon, calling for individual conversions. Young's Jesus offers a message of love, tolerance, and (individual) freedom of choice.

In striking contrast to the religious Jesuses of the film tradition, Pasolini's political revolutionary brings a sword, not an antiseptically "religious" message (cf. Matt. 10:34). Greene's communal performance of Jesus' teaching differs from the tradition in another way, rejecting the soliloquies of the tradition's master-Jesus. The teaching of Greene's Jesus community dominates Greene's film as in no other.

Scorsese's Jesus repeatedly changes his message—from pity, to judgment, and finally to his own sacrificial death. His teaching is dialogical and often halting and confused.

Jones's Brian makes up his apocalyptic message as he goes, providing a humorous twist to the Jesus sayings tradition. Otherwise, Brian's teaching is quite modern: "Just be yourself." Jones's "real" Jesus stands too far away from his audience to be understood clearly, and thus his misunderstood words are the subject of heated debate.

## The Miracles

Zecca offers the most dramatic miracles, including deus ex machina and a closing shot of Jesus at God's heavenly right hand. Zecca also includes by far the most angels in the Jesus-film tradition. Pasolini also offers dramatic versions of the miracles, but in a three-shot technique: the problem, Jesus, the problem resolved. By contrast, and more like the approach of Zecca, Zeffirelli and Sykes and Krisch show dramatic transformations on screen (i.e., they do not cut away from the healed to Jesus for an offscreen transformation). The miracles are, however, most important for Young and Hayes. In Young, the miracles are the primary cause of faith. In Hayes, the plight and resurrection of Tamar provides the perspective for understanding the entire story of Jesus.

While Olcott focuses on people's awed responses to the miracles, Ray is most reticent about showing miracles on-screen, often reducing them to reports by Lucius or the narrator. Stevens favors psychosomatic miracles and the effort it take Jesus to work them. Although Jesus declares that the lame man's faith is what has cured him, Stevens's camera shot lingers on Jesus fingering his prayer shawl. Greene strikingly avoids Jesus' miracles except for one which is, in fact, the result of a disciple's mistaken interpretation of events. Jones follows the mistaken interpretation ploy as well (the silent hermit), but he also offers a scene in which a leper healed by Jesus complains that he is now out of his begging job.

While the passion play in Arcand's film features miracles, the voice-over indicates the huge gap between modernity and the ancient, magical world of Jesus. Young and Hayes seem happily unaware of this gap.

## Gethsemane

Following artistic traditions, Zecca films an angel holding out the cup of suffering to Jesus. Jewison follows art even more obviously by offering, as Jesus struggles at Gethsemane, a montage of crucifixion paintings. Forsaking art, Young offers, as the final satanic test of Jesus, a montage of future violence done in his name. Young's Satan does, however, gleefully recount the upcoming horrors of the crucifixion as well.

If Jewison's Jesus struggles in Gethsemane, Scorsese's Jesus is wracked once more in the garden by doubts about the relative value of the flesh and the spirit. Young's garden scene—with its distinctive flashforwards to violence done in Jesus' name—is no struggle; for Young, the early wilderness test settled the issue. Gibson's garden is a heroic, physical contest between Jesus and Satan, following a Christian interpretation of Gen. 3:15.

## The Jewish Trial

Zecca's Jews are the villains. His Romans prevent even worse Jewish miscarriages of justice against Jesus (contrast Gibson's brutal Roman soldiers). Although Olcott has no Jewish trial, he clearly makes the Jewish priesthood culpable for Jesus' death, for they point accusingly at Jesus from the background as Pilate questions Jesus. Pasolini offers Matthew's anti-Semitic 27:25 and adds a fade to black at the cross with a narrator intoning Isa. 6:9–10. Jewison's black-robed, vulture-like religious leaders are also clearly responsible for Jesus' death. Gibson offers a similar treatment of the Jewish leaders, although he does demarcate Caiaphas and Satan as the chief villains. DeMille is clearer, making Caiaphas the lone culprit. Following the lead of Griffith, Sykes and Krisch try to restrict Jesus' confrontation to the hypocrites among the Jewish leaders.

Stevens offers an extensive Jewish trial, perhaps the longest in film. Using John 9 and a Nicodemus who quibbles about the legality of the proceedings, he suggests a division among the Sanhedrin and the Judean elite over what to do with Jesus. Zeffirelli also provides a Sanhedrin troubled by and divided by Jesus, but shows this through a Sanhedrin meeting *prior* to Jesus' arrest.

Barely mentioning the Jewish trial, Ray foists responsibility onto Pilate, as does Jones. While Jesus repeatedly clashes with the religious leaders in Scorsese's film and is accused of blasphemy, Scorsese likewise presents no Jewish trial.

Greene also rejects the traditional opponents of Jesus in favor of a robot and Judas, who alone hangs Jesus on the "cross." While a priest prompts the Pilate of the passion play in Arcand's film, the film's real antagonist is Father Leclerc, which makes religious institutions or corrupt religious figures, rather than a particular people, the enemy of the good.

### The Roman Trial

Zecca's Romans seem to care for justice, at least for law and order. Lucius's defense of Jesus before Pilate in Ray's film is a memorable moment in Jesus-film tradition. Ray's Pilate, however, is a cold-hearted, ambitious bureaucrat who sacrifices Jesus to further his own career. Stevens's Pilate is imperially callous but not well developed. While comically portrayed, Jones's Pilate is just as imperially brutal. Scorsese's Pilate handles Jesus informally and with relatively little interest. Jesus is a banal matter; thus Pilate quickly and callously dispenses with him. The Pilate in Arcand's passion play is quite similar to Scorsese's although far more concerned about theology.

Sykes and Krisch try, initially, to make Pilate the motivator of Jesus' passion, blaming Pilate for thousands of crucifixions. But they eventually return to their Lukan source, depicting a Pilate who simply wishes to release Jesus. The Pilates of Jewison and Gibson also wish to release Jesus, but the religious leaders and Jesus subvert their attempts.

Young's Pilate and Livio reduce the entire trial to a farcical game whose primary victim is Caiaphas, not Jesus. Jesus is merely a pawn for Pilate to manipulate in order to make Caiaphas look like a fool.

### The Crucifixion

Early Jesus films offer Jesus' passion as a pageant or as artwork. Ray's crucifixion is particularly antiseptic, thanks in part to Hays Code restrictions. By contrast, Zeffirelli, Sykes and Krisch, and Gibson depict violent, bloody crucifixions. Gibson's is particularly violent, aiming at a visceral experience of that suffering on humanity's behalf.

Arcand finds a midpoint between sanitized and brutal treatments of the crucifixion by offering the "horrors" primarily through characters' voice-over descriptions. Similarly, Young has Satan describe the "horrors" of crucifixion as part of Jesus' last test in Gethsemane. His subsequent cross scenes are relatively brief—in part because his was a made-for-television miniseries.

Crucifixion film oddities include Greene's chain-link, communal crucifixion; Jones's song-and-dance crucifixion; the accidental death of Arcand's Daniel; and Scorsese's nude, bloody Jesus, whose "guardian angel" helps him down from the cross.

### The Resurrection

Zecca and DeMille offer drama and light, with DeMille apparently snagging every available dove in Southern California to symbolize the holiness of Easter morning. Pasolini shows the stone "blown" away from the tomb. Zecca, DeMille, Sykes and Krisch, and Young have dramatic ascensions. Stevens resurrects a gigantic Christ into the heavens and then into church art. Gibson depicts the resurrected Jesus in bright light, with a hole through the palm of his hand.

By contrast, Ray reduces the resurrection to merely a shadow of the cross. While Zeffirelli is not reluctant to film the resurrected Christ, his final shot is of empty grave clothes, and he turns Peter into a modern Christian who believes without seeing.

Olcott, Griffith, Jewison, Greene, and Scorsese have no resurrection scenes. For Arcand, the resurrection is the late-arriving teaching of Jesus' disciples. But Arcand also presents Daniel's organ-harvested body as a modernized resurrection.

## Other Important Characters

New Testament Gospel characters are flat in their representation, but thanks to later church tradition and directors' imaginations, at least some of them have been turned into more complex, round characters in the Jesus-film tradition. Typically, the followers of Jesus who get the most screen time are Judas, Mary Magdalene, Peter, "Doubting" Thomas, John (the Beloved Disciple), and the three siblings—Mary, Martha, and Lazarus. Mary, mother of Jesus, Joseph his "father," John the Baptist, Pilate, Caiaphas, and Herod (Antipas) fill out the Hollywood list of important extras, along with an odd collection of invented characters.

Although our "Gospels Harmony" lists the most important followers/disciples of Jesus, it is not an exhaustive list of their appearances in any films. A complete analysis of a cinematic character will demand a more-careful viewing of the given film than what we can present in our Gospels Harmony, and we offer here only a brief overview of the three most important supporting characters.

## Judas

Ray explains Judas by following De Quincey's hypothesis (cf. Young). Zeffirelli's Judas wants Jewish independence, but he seeks political, not military, means to get this. Like Caiaphas, Jewison's Judas wishes to maintain a troubled peace with Rome (and to demythologize Jesus).

Zeffirelli's Judas is dazed, confused, and duped, so his motivation is somewhat obscure, as is Stevens's Judas.

Scorsese offers a Judas who, as the Beloved Disciple, participates in Jesus' plans to save the world. Without Judas, there would be no redemption. The Judases of Jewison, Greene, and Zeffirelli also participate with Jesus—to a degree. At least, they think— however briefly—that they are doing what Jesus wants them to do.

Zeffirelli and Gibson highlight Judas's divine punishment. Gibson and Sykes and Krisch show Judas's possession by Satan. Hayes gives the most time to the inner workings of Judas's mind, showing this through animated scenes.

## Mary Magdalene

Mary Magdalene is a prostitute/sinner in DeMille, Zeffirelli, Sykes and Krisch, Scorsese, Arcand, Young, and Saville. For DeMille and Hayes, she is a woman cleansed of demons. Ray, Stevens, Jewison, Scorsese, and Gibson depict her as the woman taken in adultery, with Scorsese also accusing her of working (as a prostitute) on the Sabbath. In Zecca, Stevens, Jewison, Zeffirelli, Sykes and Krisch, and Hayes she is the anointing woman. DeMille, Scorsese, and Young spend the most time developing her character prior to her "conversion."

## Mary, Mother of Jesus

DeMille, Ray, and Gibson present the mother of Jesus in the most traditional Roman Catholic view, as the coredeemer who mediates between Jesus and his disciples (typically, Mary Magdalene and John [the Beloved Disciple]). She is there to support Jesus on the Via Dolorosa in DeMille's and Gibson's films, encouraging him to stand when he falls. Pasolini's Mary is a cosufferer with Jesus during his passion.

Young's Mary always seems to know more than Jesus does and pushes him out into his public ministry; nonetheless, his talk about death seems to catch her by surprise. Stevens's Mary is the most Protestant and has virtually no role in his film. Zeffirelli's Mary is the sexiest—especially during the annunciation and when giving birth to Jesus. Ray's Mary, on the other hand, is the most matronly.

## Teaching Jesus Films as Narrative Wholes

The selective use of Jesus-film clips, where teachers "illustrate" a biblical text with a quick visual, unless carefully done, is not far removed from prooftext reading the Gospels. The first part of our book provides interpretative contexts for the films that help to minimize that proof-texting approach. In our own teaching we have moved toward a more holistic use of Jesus films where students watch at least one film in its entirety and then develop research projects where they can continue to work with one or more Jesus films in their entirety. The questions in chapter 1, "Watching Jesus Films," facilitate a more holistic use of the Jesus films for those so inclined. A teacher might make a selection from among those questions and then direct the class to view one or several Jesus films. Our chronological arrangement of Jesus films also invites teachers and students to consider the cinematic tradition and each film as a particular interpretation of Jesus/the Gospels for a specific culture and time.

For those who wish to construct classes using Jesus films even more holistically and substantively, we offer the following topical suggestions:

### Gospel Sources

One might organize a class around Jesus films' use of and interpretation of the Gospels (see W. Barnes Tatum, *Jesus at the Movies: A Guide to the First Hundred Years*. Revised and Expanded [Santa Rosa: Polebridge, 2004]). For example, do the films rely primarily on one Gospel (Pasolini, Greene, Sykes and Krisch, Saville) or on a harmony constructed from the four Gospels (Zecca, Olcott, DeMille, Ray, Stevens, Zeffirelli, Young, Hayes)? Are they passion plays (Jewison, Arcand, Gibson) or fuller treatments of Jesus' ministry? Do the films openly espouse fictionalized accounts of Jesus (Jones, Scorsese, Arcand)? As to other interpretive questions, one might ask how Griffith's use of the Jesus story as a touchstone to interpret other stories and Saville's "literalized" version illustrate the "fictional" status of most Jesus films.

### Religious Films

One might organize a class around the question of the religious character of Jesus films. Here, one might ask whether Jesus films ever take on myth-ritual functions themselves, or one might ask whether particular theologies (e.g., Roman Catholic, evangelical Protestant) provide the interpretative stance for the film. One might also ask, as Margaret Miles and Paul Schrader do (*Seeing and Believing: Religion and Values in the Movies* [Boston: Beacon, 1996]; *Transcendental Style in Film: Ozu, Bresson, Dreyer* [Berkeley: University of California Press, 1972]), whether one can portray the sacred in film. Biblical epics and Jesus films seem to have developed certain "techniques" for that purpose (see Richard Walsh, *Reading the Gospels in the Dark: Portrayals of Jesus in Film* [Harrisburg, PA: Trinity Press International, 2003], 187–89):

- The use of talismans or objects with sacred power: for example, the touch/gaze of Jesus (Zecca, Olcott); his blue eyes (Ray, Stevens, Zeffirelli); Judas and stones (Ray); white cloths, whips, blood (Gibson); doves (DeMille)
- Portrayals of an alternative reality: The use of exotic locales to produce an alternative reality: Olcott, Jewison, Sykes and Krisch, Greene, and Stevens. The use of spectacle to produce an alternative reality: DeMille, Ray, Stevens, and Gibson (see Michael Wood, *America in the Movies* [New York: Columbia University Press, 1989]). The use of music to produce an alternative reality: Jewison, Greene, and Scorsese. The shots of earth from outer space at the beginning and end of Sykes and Krisch's film evoke an overriding sense of divine providence. Scorsese, Young, and Hayes manage to invite the audience into Jesus' visionary world as an alternative reality, although Scorsese leaves significant questions about the value and source of these visions. Arcand goes farther than Scorsese here with his demythologizing of the Jesus tradition, offering through that history a Jesus who is different (an exotic human), but not a sacred reality.
- The use of special effects to create hierophanies: for example, Zecca's hand-colored angels; Zecca's and Young's deus ex machina scenes; DeMille's exorcism/conversion of Mary Magdalene; Pasolini's resurrection; the on-screen miracles (transformations) of Zeffirelli and Sykes and Krisch; Gibson's cross-cuts/flashbacks to the Last Supper when Jesus is on the cross.
- The use of awed faces or transformed lives in the presence of Jesus: for example, Olcott's focus on those whom angels visit or on the faces of those who see miracles; Zeffirelli's transformed apostles; Saville's people in the presence of Jesus; and Sykes and Krisch's little orgasmic gasps.
- The technique of filming Jesus in soft focus (DeMille) or from below (almost everyone but Scorsese). Ray uses close-ups of Jesus' mesmerizing blue eyes in a similar manner. Saville often shoots Jesus in or after flashing sunlight. Saville's visual interpretation of John's prologue also asserts that Jesus is the incarnate Word.
- Stevens's innovative, church location of his Jesus film (see the opening and closing shots of church [Jesus] icons). Zeffirelli does not locate the Jesus story visually in a church, but his relentless focus on the apostles does indicate, in its own way, the institutional locale of the Jesus story (as does his emphasis on the heart, rather than the head). Arcand raises significant questions about the institutional location of the Jesus story.

## Contemporizing Jesus

One might organize a class around Jesus films as modern and/or American interpretations of Jesus. The questions here, of course, are not only of anachronisms but also of deliberate appropriations of the Jesus story for new cultural situations.

## Miracles and Modern Science

Ray reduces Jesus' miracles to shadows and reports. His invented character, Lucius, an incredulous witness, provides a counterpart in the film for those in the audience who have difficulty accepting the miracles. There is also a general tendency in Jesus films to privilege miracles susceptible of psychosomatic interpretations (see Stevens's interpretation of the healing of the lame man). In comparison to the Gospels, the so-called nature miracles are relatively rarer in Jesus-film tradition. There is also a tendency in Jesus films after 1960 to move away from the social and physical religious experiences toward private, subjective experiences. The movement modernizes Christian faith while minimizing potential conflicts between science and faith. Stevens's tendency to turn angelic voices (with Joseph) and demonic voices (some say the Dark Hermit is a visualization of Jesus' and others' internal struggles) into "internal voices" rather than visible characters fits this trend.

Although Zeffirelli's Jesus performs dramatic miracles, his Jesus speaks only of matters of the heart, not of the head or of politics. In fact, Zeffirelli's Judas and Zerah are villainous precisely because of their intellectual and political approaches to life. The Jesus of Sykes and Krisch also performs dramatic miracles, but again he is primarily a preacher of matters of the heart, focusing on individual conversion. Their renderings of Jesus' miracles become lessons in evangelical transformation. While not struggling overtly with the problem of Jesus' miracles, Saville also offers a cinematic Jesus who is primarily concerned with individual, evangelical transformation.

Jesus' miracles are strikingly absent from Greene's film. His eerily empty city and his decision to film in a park (garden) may also suggest the great distance between the Jesus story and modernity. Both Greene and Jones offer a "miracle" that is the result of the naïve misunderstanding of disciples. Arcand stands farthest from the Gospel miracle tradition, having characters openly proclaim the huge gap between scientific modernity and magical antiquity.

Young's film offers viewers the most unabashed perspective on Jesus' miracles in the entire Jesus-film tradition—for him they actually *produce* faith. His film only accepts the distance between the present and the ancient tradition by stating that faith *without* sight (i.e., not seeing miracles = modernity?) is better than faith *because* of sight (seeing miracles = tradition?). For Hayes, Jesus is the healing savior of children. Hayes likewise admits no gap between the ancient world's view of miracles and the modern world's scientific view.

## Peasant Faith and Capitalism

DeMille simply avoids Jesus' challenging sayings on wealth. Stevens's Jesus focuses on the question of one's attitude toward wealth rather than on one's possession of wealth. If one seeks first the kingdom, then one's attitude in other matters (wealth?) will change. Stevens also uses the character Lazarus, created from the Gospels' various wealthy characters, to provide a liaison between Jesus' radical views on wealth and a middle-class American audience. Interestingly, however, Stevens's Lazarus never becomes a disciple.

Generally, Jesus films avoid the tension between "the haves and the have-nots" by anachronistically reducing Jesus' focus of attention to the arena of "religion" (often understood even more anachronistically as apolitical and as a private, subjective matter of the heart).

Pasolini's Marxist ideology rescues Jesus from the religious ghetto and makes him a critic of the bourgeois or institutional powers that oppress the peasants. Nevertheless, Pasolini's Jesus is clearly not of the same social class as those to whom he preaches. His Jesus has clear skin, good teeth, nice hair, and soft, feminine hands. Arcand's film critiques consumer society by focusing on Daniel's—not Jesus'—lonely, artistic integrity and his subsequent destruction. Surprisingly, however, the teaching of Arcand's Jesus on economic matters resembles that of Stevens's Jesus.

## Ancient Colonials and Empire

Ray critiques empire with an opening shot of a forest of crosses and through his characterization of the cold-blooded Pilate. The noble Lucius, however, somewhat defuses this critique, for he suggests to Ray's modern, imperial audience that there might be good rulers in the world. According to Bruce Babbington and Peter William Evans (*Biblical Epics: Sacred Narrative in the Hollywood Cinema* [New York: Manchester University Press, 1993]), this ploy is the typical pattern found in the biblical epic genre: that is, the conversion of Romans to Christianity creates the notion of a Christian Empire (not the end of empire). Greene's association of the Statue of Liberty with Jesus' "light of the world teaching"; Zeffirelli's red-white-and-blue-clothed magi; and DeMille's, Stevens's, Young's, and Gibson's temptation scenes also evoke the world of Christian (U.S.) Empire.

Arcand's rejection of consumerism and of Hollywood film is, of course, an important, alternative voice that critiques the equation of the United States and Christianity. Setting his story in the province of Quebec and using the French language are important elements in his rejection of U.S.-style consumerism. Jones also critiques empires with a forest of crosses, but his parody of the "benefits" of empire (shown by way of a conversation among the members of the People's Front of Judea) somewhat undercuts this criticism, as does the comic genre of the film. Pasolini's critique of empire is perhaps the most thoroughgoing. Tellingly, his is also not an American film. Jewison's tanks and Temple bazaar may also critique empire, but surprisingly, Saville provides one of the most interesting critiques of empire when he focuses on symbols of Roman authority after Jesus' question to Pilate "What is truth?"

Consciously or unconsciously, the films that focus on the Jews' culpability in Jesus' death (Zecca, Olcott); that emphasize Jesus' solitary, heroic suffering (Gibson); or that reduce Jesus anachronistically to the religious sphere (Stevens, Zeffirelli, Sykes and Krisch) all minimize the conflict between colonial artisan / peasant victims and empire. Young's flashforward anticipations of violence done in Jesus' name and his exaltation of individual freedom might be used to critique empire, although Young does not do so.

## Feminist Concerns

The changing role of Mary Magdalene in Jesus films is the most obvious topic of choice here, but one would do well also to analyze the changing roles over the decades of Salome, Herodias, Claudia (Pilate's wife), and Mary, the mother of Jesus.

Jesus' interactions with women, the number and placement of women in various Gospel scenes, and the function of women's voices (Are they merely seen, or do they actually speak? If they speak, to whom and when do they speak?) are all important issues that could be explored with respect to particular Jesus films, or within the context of the entire history of Jesus films. Are women more prominent or less prominent in Jesus films than they are in the Gospels themselves? Do women's roles in Jesus films become more traditional or more radical during different eras? What women-focused Gospel stories are largely missing in the Jesus-film tradition, and why? What is the role of the female body in the Jesus-film tradition?

### Queer Concerns

The portrayals of the highly eroticized Beloved Disciple in Pasolini's *The Gospel According to St. Matthew*, young John in Ray's *King of Kings*, and "Little James" in Stevens's *The Greatest Story Ever Told* would seem to hold fruitful possibilities for queer theory. Perhaps the most interesting and tantalizingly undeveloped relationship is the Judas, Mary Magdalene, and Jesus love triangle that opens DeMille's *The King of Kings*. At the opposite extreme is the long-term, intimate relationship between Judas and Jesus in Scorsese's *The Last Temptation of Christ*. How does Jesus relate to men in the Jesus-film tradition? Whom does he touch, hug, or kiss, and why? What is the role of the male body in the Jesus-film tradition? Does the portrayal of the male body change from decade to decade, and if so, in what ways?

### Anti-Semitism

Over the years, directors of Jesus films have attempted to be sensitive to the charges of anti-Semitism in the Christian tradition. DeMille responded in two ways that have become the model for other directors. First, DeMille added a preface that placed the Jesus story within the broader political and social context of the Roman Empire; and second, he placed the blame for Jesus' death solely on one Jew. For DeMille, that one person was the high priest Caiaphas. Later directors would expand on the sociopolitical context of Roman-occupied Judea and Galilee and would invent characters to bear the brunt of Jewish complicity in Jesus' death (Zerah, Sorak, Livio, the Dark Hermit, and Satan).

The role of Jewish Scripture (Hebrew Bible/Old Testament) in Jesus films is a topic well worth exploring, but our DVD parallels do not list these references. Richard Stern, Clayton Jefford, and Guerric DeBona's *Savior on the Silver Screen* (New York: Paulist, 1999) gives a helpful list of Hebrew Bible references in the nine films they discuss, but their book uses as guides VHS cassettes of the Jesus films. The issue of supersessionism is also worth exploring in relationship to Judaism as portrayed in Jesus films. Here we especially recommend Adele Reinhartz's *Jesus of Hollywood* (New York: Oxford University Press, 2007).

### Cinematic Patterns

Jesus films "sell" themselves by offering their viewers heroes, romance, and something new or exotic.[5] The Magdalenes of DeMille and Scorsese—as well as Ray's Salome—offer exotic, forbidden sexuality. Ray's battle scenes and Gibson's heroic suffering transform the Jesus story into a spectacle. Some films advertise "on location" settings (Olcott) to offer something new and exotic to audiences.

Generally, Jesus films transform Jesus from a first-century subsistence artisan ("carpenter") into a cinematic (middle-class) hero. Accordingly, like the modern heroes of novels and films, cinematic Jesuses typically stand alone against some corrupt group or institution. Furthermore, Jesus—increasingly after the 1960s—develops an inward subjectivity more in keeping with characters in modern novels or films than with characters found in ancient epics or Gospels. Scorsese and Hayes go farthest in visualizing Jesus' internal states or visions, but the inward, religious turn is also evident in Stevens, Greene(?), Zeffirelli, and Sykes and Krisch. Jones's bemused everyman and Young's icon of modern maturity also "modernize" and psychologize Jesus. Cinematic Jesuses also often have love or sex interests; or, at least, some films imagine characters who are sexually attracted to Jesus. Scorsese goes farthest here, imagining a Jesus who is attracted to women and who fantasizes about "normal" family life.

Jesus films also contemporize the Jesus story by reducing Jesus anachronistically to a (mere) religious figure whose interests are only religious matters (Ray, Stevens, Greene?, Zeffirelli, Sykes and Krisch). Here, Pasolini and Arcand are the refreshing exceptions. Perhaps Jewison raises the question of modernization most dramatically with his exploration of Jesus' celebrity status (cf. Greene's Superman-Jesus, Scorsese's exploration of Jesus' sanity, and Arcand's exploration of Jesus as a model for modern artistic integrity).

## The Interpretative Tradition of Jesus Films

The story of the Jesus-film tradition usually pivots on the decade of the 1960s. In this decade, the spectacular Jesus epic ceased to be economically feasible (see Stern, Jefford, and DeBona, *Savior on the Silver Screen*, or Walsh, *Reading the Gospels in the Dark: Portrayals of Jesus in Film* [Harrisburg, PA: Trinity Press International, 2003], 1–19). Thereafter, directors turned to less expensive venues and genres for filming the Jesus story. Jewison and Greene filmed the Jesus story through music; Zeffirelli and Young made TV movies; Sykes and Krisch and Saville made independent films; Jones offered a parody for the limited audience of the Python troupe. Scorsese filmed an epic Jesus film, but on a limited budget. Arcand offered a film about a passion play. Gibson invested his own finances and reputation to bring back the spectacular Jesus-film tradition. Despite criticism and predictions of failure, his film was hugely successful. Perhaps that was the case in part because Gibson was able to tap into the post-9/11 American angst with his bloodied Jesus who victoriously bore the weight of the world.

One might also organize a class around the Jesus films' interpretation of one another. After viewing multiple Jesus films, it becomes clear that directors often draw their inspiration and ideas from earlier Jesus films as much as from the Gospels. Here, DeMille is perhaps most important. He certainly created the Hollywood pattern for future Jesus stories, with Jesus as the center around which swirled stories of conversion (the Magdalene) and degradation (Judas, Caiaphas). He also created the triangle of Jesus, Judas, and the Magdalene, from which Jewison and Scorsese, in particular, borrowed.

Ray changed the tradition significantly by inserting the rather noncinematic Jesus story into the very cinematic tradition of biblical spectacles. Leaving DeMille's sexual suggestions largely aside, Ray offered instead violence—that of the Herods, Pilate, Lucius, Barabbas, and Judas—as well as the nonviolent Jesus. He also innovated by recognizing and filming the difference between the ancient Jesus tradition and modernity through his invented character Lucius.

Pasolini's innovation is seen largely in his rejection of the Hollywood spectacle. He chose instead a documentary style of presentation based on one Gospel. Nevertheless, he did not avoid certain harmonizing tendencies evident in earlier films (see, for example, his subtle use of the Gospel of John).

The music-themed Jesus films of Jewison and Greene are emphatically generic innovations. Yet Jewison clearly depends on DeMille's film for his characters and plot. Greene depends more heavily on the style and atmosphere of the earlier silent films to create a new, comic approach to the Jesus story (cf. Jones's parody). Jewison's other innovation is to focus as much attention on the antihero Judas as on Jesus.

Stevens, Zeffirelli, Sykes and Krisch, and Young innovate with strikingly modern Jesuses—Jesuses who speak only to subjective individuals—not to social issues. Young's film fits best here, and it is most innovative with its portrayal of a smiling, dancing, carefree Jesus. Scorsese also works with a subjective Jesus, but more audaciously by transforming the Jesus epic into a Jesus biopic, thereby allowing audiences to share Jesus' anguished religious experiences (cf. Hayes's approach, although it lacks the anguish). Yet, like Jewison, Scorsese returns to DeMille's romantic triangle for his story. Instead of contemporizing Jesus, Arcand recognizes the chasm between the ancient Jesus story and modernity by telling two stories: that of a traditional, then revised, passion play and that of a modern Christ-figure Daniel. Despite Arcand's innovation, his approach is not unlike Griffith's use of the Jesus story, in which the ancient story becomes an interpretative touchstone for understanding a modern story.

Perhaps Hayes and Saville make the interpretative influence of the film tradition most apparent by borrowing scene after scene from previous filmmakers. This tendency is particularly obvious in Saville, who had the mandate of filming "just one" Gospel, yet borrowed various scenes not from John but from the Jesus-film tradition (as did Sykes and Krisch before him).

Gibson's importance is twofold: he resurrects the spectacle genre, and he introduces a brutal, horrific violence into the Jesus-film tradition. But again, for all his claims to historical accuracy, Gibson's film is heavily dependent on precursors: on Jewison for his depiction of the scourging of Jesus (the counting out of each whiplash); on DeMille for the demonic child who bites Judas; on Pasolini and Jewison for his depiction of Judas's suicide; on Jewison for his portrayal of Herod Antipas; on DeMille for a Mary who wills Jesus back to his feet when he is beaten or stumbles, and for the crow on the cross; on Stevens for the devil-incited crowd and the city gate opening to Calvary; on Scorsese for the kissing of Jesus' bloody, nail-pierced feet.

## Christ-Figure Films

Jesus films place a recognizable Jesus in an "authentic representation" of first-century Palestine or transfigure Jesus into a new, modern setting (for example, Jewison, Arcand). But Jesus films often have less appeal to audiences than do "disguised" portrayals of Jesus—those films that use the Jesus story as a pattern for telling a much different story, or films where only certain viewers sense that Jesus or his story is "behind" a character or film. Peter Malone's *Movie Christs and Antichrists* (New York: Crossroad, 1990) provides an exhaustive list of film possibilities here; and Lloyd Baugh's *Imaging the Divine: Jesus and Christ Figures in Film* (Kansas City: Sheed & Ward, 1997) provides detailed discussions of several of these Christ-figure films and a theological defense of his preference for "Christ-figure" films over Jesus films. Viewers, if they choose, may see almost any unlikely hero, unjust sufferer, or liberator as a Christ figure. For teachers or students wishing to use this type of film in a Jesus and Gospels class as a supplement to Jesus films or instead of Jesus films, we offer the following films as suggestions:

Jesus' temptation or trials: *The Last Temptation of Christ*

Jesus' teaching: *Being There* (1979), *Life of Brian*

Jesus' miracles: *The Magician* (1958), *Leap of Faith* (1992)

Jesus' self-sacrificial healing: *The Butterfly Effect* (2004), *The Green Mile* (1999), *Patch Adams* (1998)

Jesus' apocalyptic teaching: *Apocalypse Now* (1979), *Field of Dreams* (1989)

Jesus' wisdom teaching: *Forrest Gump* (1994), *The Truman Show* (1998)

Jesus' parabolic style: *Parable* (1964), *Strictly Ballroom* (1992)

Jesus' sacrificial death: *Cool-Hand Luke* (1967), *One Flew Over the Cuckoo's Nest* (1975), *End of Days* (1999), *Spitfire Grill* (1996)

Jesus' heroic triumph: *Shane* (1953), *Star Wars* (1977), *Shawshank Redemption* (1994)

Jesus' community: *Bronco Billy* (1980), *Tender Mercies* (1983), *Witness* (1985)

With Christ-figure films one does not need to restrict one's thinking to the life of Jesus. One can imagine the Christ figure simply as a pattern that continues to influence Western culture.

# A Gospels Harmony
# of Jesus Films on DVD

The following eighteen films are listed in the parallels below alphabetically by director. If there are two directors, only the first director is named. DVD chapters are in parentheses; hours / minutes / seconds follow DVD chapter numbers. Since Saville's film follows the exact order of the text of John's Gospel, its scenes are easily accessible and only referenced when other films visually portray the Johannine scene. If a director has combined multiple Gospel stories into one, the film scene is referenced more than once. This Gospel parallels list is not intended to be exhaustive. For example, not every visual reference to Mary Magdalene is listed here. However, we have listed those that we believe are most useful for comparative study with the Gospels.

Arcand, *Jesus of Montreal*, 1989
DeMille, *The King of Kings*, 1927
Gibson, *The Passion of the Christ*, 2004
Greene, *Godspell*, 1973
Griffith, *Intolerance*, 1916
Hayes, *The Miracle Maker: The Story of Jesus*, 1999
Jewison, *Jesus Christ Superstar*, 1973
Jones, *Monty Python's Life of Brian*, 1979
Olcott, *From the Manger to the Cross*, 1912
Pasolini, *The Gospel According to St. Matthew*, 1965 (no DVD chapter divisions)
Ray, *King of Kings*, 1961
Saville, *The Gospel of John*, 2003
Scorsese, *The Last Temptation of Christ*, 1988
Stevens, *The Greatest Story Ever Told*, 1965
Sykes and Krisch, *The Jesus Film*, 1979 (The DVD chapter numbers are always listed first, followed by the "Event Index" number [DVD box insert] in brackets.)
Young, *Jesus*, 1999
Zecca and Nonquet, *The Life and Passion of Jesus Christ*, 1905
Zeffirelli, *Jesus of Nazareth*, 1977

**Preface:** Matt. 1:1–17; Mark 1:1; Luke 1:1–4; John 1:1–18
John 1:1–18
    Saville (1) 0:50
    Stevens (2) 4:48
Luke 1:1–4

Arcand (8) 28:22
Sykes (1) 0:00
Other
    Arcand (1) 0:03
    DeMille (1) 0:27; (2) 1:15
    Gibson (1) 0:21
    Greene (1) 0:15; (2) 1:16
    Griffith (1) 0:10; (3) 8:38
    Jewison (1) 0:20
    Olcott (1) 0:22
    Pasolini 2:57
    Ray (3) 6:14
    Saville (1) 0:00 (John 3:16); (1) 0:04
    Scorsese (2) 0:49
    Sykes (1) 0:01 (This chapter can only be accessed when starting the film from the beginning, after choosing an audio version.)
**John the Baptist**
Birth and Early Life: Luke 1:57–80
    Zeffirelli (8) 19:45
Preaching: Matt. 3:1–12; 14:4–5; Mark 1:2–8; 6:18–19; Luke 3:1–18; John 1:19–28
    Arcand (1) 2:50
    Greene (3) 7:32
    Hayes (4) 8:18
    Pasolini 22:47
    Ray (8) 26:55; (13) 44:32, 46:38
    Scorsese (10) 48:12, 51:41
    Stevens (6) 26:26; (7) 36:36, 38:31
    Sykes (2 [7]) 6:13

Preaching (cont'd)
    Young (7) 28:02; (13) 56:38
    Zeffirelli (27) 1.22:38; (29) 1.32:43; (69)
        1.26:22
Baptizing: John 3:23–36 (see also baptism of
    Jesus)
    Arcand (13) 48:05; (15) 56:03
    Saville (4) 23:24
    Zeffirelli (31) 1.42:10
Arrest: Matt. 4:12–16; Mark 1:14; Luke 3:19–20
    Ray (14) 48:33
    Stevens (13) 1.07:58
    Zeffirelli (29) 1.31:19; (31) 1.42:29
In Prison: Matt. 14:3; Mark 6:17–20; Luke 3:2
    Pasolini 32:03
    Stevens (14) 1.15:12
    Sykes (11 [19]) 33:03
    Young (14) 1.06:55
    Zeffirelli (33) 1.48:44; (40) 2.21:16
Messengers from John to Jesus: Matt. 11:2–19;
    Luke 7:18–35
    Pasolini 55:47
    Ray (18) 1.02:12; (21) 1.10:38; (25) 1.19:50
    Stevens (14) 1.11:48
    Sykes (11 [19]) 33:03
    Zeffirelli (32) 1.49:57
Salome's Dance/John's Death: Matt. 14:6–12;
    Mark 6:21–29; Luke 3:19
    Arcand (1) 2.02; (27) 1.42:13 (death only)
    Hayes (12) 39:57 (death only)
    Pasolini 1.07:55
    Ray (22) 1.12:30; (25) 1.21:19
    Scorsese 1.03:54 (death only)
    Stevens (16) 1.25:27
    Young (16) 1.15:38
    Zeffirelli (29) 1.30:05; (40) 2.25:08; (45)
        2.39:42
Jesus' Question about John's Baptism: Matt.
    21:23–27; Mark 11:27–33; Luke 20:1–8
    (See below, "Controversy," "By whose
    authority?" p. 182)

**Jesus' Birth and Early Life**

Betrothal and Marriage of Joseph and Mary:
    Matt. 1:18; Luke 1:26–27
    Zeffirelli (3) 5:10; (4) 7:13; (8) 18:54; (11)
        27:18
Announcement to Mary: Luke 1:26–38
    Olcott (1) 1:01
    Sykes (1) 0:19
    Young (6) 23:02
    Zecca (1) 0:20
    Zeffirelli (5) 9:06

Announcement to Joseph: Matt. 1:18–25
    Olcott (1) 3:00
    Pasolini 3:04
    Young (6) 23:58
    Zeffirelli (9) 21:50
Mary Visits Elizabeth: Luke 1:39–56
    Stevens (4) 11:31
    Sykes (1 [2]) 1:11
    Zeffirelli (7) 15:37; (8) 18:40
Journey to Bethlehem: Luke 2:1–6
    Olcott (1) 4:30
    Ray (5) 12:57
    Sykes (1 [3]) 1:53
    Zecca (1) 1:29
    Zeffirelli (12) 20:35; (14) 36:23, 37:05,
        37:44, 38:24; (16) 42:54
Birth of Jesus: Luke 2:7
    Arcand (8) 24:07; (10) 35:25; (16) 58:05
    Jones (5) 16:39; (9) 39:41; (15) 1.07:59
    Ray (5) 13:44, 14:40
    Stevens (2) 5:45
    Sykes (1 [4]) 3:12
    Zecca (2) 4:47 (miraculous appearance)
    Zeffirelli (17) 47:04
Shepherds' Announcement and Visit: Luke
    2:8–20
    Hayes (3) 7:36
    Ray (5) 14:52
    Stevens (3) 10:51
    Sykes (1 [4]) 2:46, 3:18
    Zecca (2) 2:39, 4:05
    Zeffirelli (17) 46:37; (18) 49:57
Wise Men's Journey and Visit: Matt. 2:1–12
    Hayes (3) 7:43
    Jones (1) 0:30
    Olcott (1) 7:36
    Pasolini 6:40
    Ray (5) 14:25
    Stevens (2) 6:37; (4) 12:01, 13:51
    Young (11) 51:04
    Zecca (2) 4:05, 4:41
    Zeffirelli (14) 36:38, 37:19, 37:56; (15)
        38:34; (19) 52:27
Circumcision and Presentation in the Temple:
    Luke 2:21–40
    Sykes (1 [5]) 3:36
    Zeffirelli (20) 54:11
Flight into Egypt and Return: Matt. 2:13–15,
    19–22
    Arcand (11) 37:10
    Olcott (1) 13:17
    Pasolini 14:55; 21:21

Ray (6) 17:24, 18:39
Stevens (4) 13:45; (5) 17:40, 22:31
Young (11) 48:50
Zecca (2) 7:30
Zeffirelli (21) 1.02:05; (22) 1.06:54; (23) 1.08:29

Slaughter of Innocents: Matt. 2:16–18
Pasolini 17:20
Ray (6) 16:50, 18:09
Stevens (4) 15:05
Zecca (2) 6:52
Zeffirelli (21) 1.03:12

Death of Herod: Matt. 2:19
Pasolini 20:20
Ray (6) 18:38
Stevens (4) 16:56; (5) 18:40
Zeffirelli (23) 1.07:27

Childhood in Nazareth: Matt. 2:23; Luke 2:51–52
Gibson (20) 1.17:20–1.18:31
Olcott (2) 15:29
Ray (7) 20:51
Scorsese (5) 22:20 (Mary Magdalene)
Stevens (5) 22:31
Zeffirelli (23) 1.09:35

Miracles
Baby Jesus' miraculous appearance in the manger
Zecca (2) 4:47
Baby Jesus sleeping through the Slaughter of Innocents
Zecca (2) 7:37
Holy family hidden from Herod's soldiers
Zecca (2) 9:47
Holy family given water from a rock on journey to Egypt
Zecca (2) 10:25
Life to a dead bird (cf. *Infancy Gospel of Thomas* 2:1)
Young (11) 49:00

Jesus at Twelve in the Temple: Luke 2:41–50
Hayes (3) 6:14; (15) 53:53
Olcott (2) 16:44
Sykes (1 [5]) 4:33
Young (7) 21:14
Zecca (3) 13:55
Zeffirelli (26) 1.17:44

Carpentry Work: Matt. 13:55; Mark 6:3
Arcand (10) 34:35
DeMille (9) 35:21, 35:50; 36:18; 41:35
Gibson (7) 19:55
Hayes (2) 2:30; (3) 5:19

Jewison (1) 8:02
Olcott (2) 21:25
Ray (34) 1.51:56
Saville (10) 57:43
Scorsese (2) 3:55
Young (1) 0:55; (2) 4:28; (4) 11:47, 15:28; (6) 22:22
Zecca (2) 12:03
Zeffirelli (24) 1.10:29

Death of Joseph
Young (4) 19:22
Zeffirelli (30) 1.34:57

**Jesus' Baptism:** Matt. 3:13–17; Mark 1:9–11; Luke 3:21–22; John 1:29–34
Greene (3) 10:20
Hayes (4) 8:43, 9:24
Olcott (3) 21:35
Pasolini 26:25
Ray (10) 33:30
Scorsese (10) 50:42
Stevens (6) 28:40
Sykes (1 [6]) 8:47
Young (7) 29:32; (9) 37:47
Zecca (3) 14:41
Zeffirelli (31) 1.39:12

**Temptations:** Matt. 4:1–11; Mark 1:12–13; Luke 4:1–13
Arcand (21) 1.18:21
DeMille (15) 1.08:48
Gibson (3) 5:53
Greene (14) 1.29:09
Hayes (5) 10:45; (18) 1.03:24; (23) 1.15:05
Jones (10) 43:13 (Matt. 4:5–6; Luke 4:9–11)
Pasolini 28:35
Ray (11) 36:55; (27) 1.32:28
Scorsese (11) 53:06; (24) 2.07:08
Stevens (6) 31:00; (18) 1.40:10
Sykes (2 [7]) 9:53
Young (9) 38:52; (29) 2.16:11
Zeffirelli (31) 1.42:05 (allusion)

**Call of the Disciples** (alphabetical order)
Galilean Fishermen: Matt. 4:18–22; Mark 1:16–20
Olcott (2) 23:23
Pasolini 33:55
Ray (11) 42:05
Saville (2) 8:57
Scorsese (9) 42:08
Stevens (8) 40:35
Zeffirelli (35) 1.54:57

James (little): Matt. 10:3; Mark 3:18; Luke 6:15
Stevens (8) 47:24 (Matthew/Levi's brother)

James (little) (cont'd)
  Zeffirelli (38) 2.13:56 (Matthew/Levi's brother)
John's Disciples: John 1:35–42
  Greene (3) 8:37
  Hayes (4) 9:12 (Peter)
  Pasolini 23:41 (James, John)
  Ray (10) 35:14; (11) 41:26 (John, Andrew)
  Saville (2) 7:59 (Beloved Disciple [John], Andrew)
  Stevens (8) 39:55 (Judas); (14) 1.11:43 (Simon the Zealot)
  Young (7) 28:16 (John, Andrew); (11) 46:40
  Zeffirelli (28) 1.28:47; (31) 1.41:33; (33) 1.47:34, 1.48:15 (Andrew, Philip)
Judas: Matt. 10:4; Mark 3:19; Luke 6:16 (see also below, "Judas," p. 184)
  Hayes (6) 18:22
  Ray (19) 1.04:12
  Saville (9) 57:18
  Scorsese (7) 30:13 (the first disciple); (12) 1.08:58
  Stevens (8) 40:24 (the first disciple)
  Young (15) 1.12:12, 1.13:05
  Zeffirelli (50) 3.03:53
Mary Magdalene (not the "Woman caught in adultery" or "Anointing woman," see also below under "Controversy," pp. 182–83)
  Saville (8) 49:25, 51:39, 54:50, 55:34, 56:46; (23) 1.59:10; (26) 2.12:19; (30) 2.33:27
  Young (17) 1.24:52 (see also [2] 6:34; [16] 1.19:33); (21) 1.34:56; (23) 1.46:57, 1.49:58
Matthew/Levi, the Tax Collector: Matt. 9:9–13; Mark 2:13–17; Luke 5:27–32
  DeMille (9) 40:41
  Hayes (7) 19:09; (9) 30:50
  Stevens (11) 57:55
  Sykes (8 [14]) 21:40
  Young (15) 1.07:48, 1.12:35
  Zeffirelli (36) 2.02:21; (37) 2.05:15; (41) 2.28:42
Others
  Arcand (3) 7:25
  Ray (19) 1.04:01
  Saville (2) 10:18
  Stevens (14) 1.12:50, 1.18:25
Peter: Luke 5:1–11; John 1:41–42
  Arcand (3) 8:12
  Hayes (7) 19:44

Ray (11) 42:05
Saville (2) 9:32
Sykes (6 [12]) 17:11
Young (13) 58:25
Zeffirelli (35) 1.56:46; (38) 2.09:56; (39) 2.14:02, 2.20:05; (41) 2.28:49; (44) 2.37:22
Sons of Zebedee (James and John)
  Scorsese (8) 41:12 (See above, "John's disciples")
Simon the Zealot: Matt. 10:4; Mark 3:18; Luke 6:15
  Jewison (6) 29:40
  Stevens (14) 1.11:43
  Zeffirelli (52) 8:34
Thomas: Matt. 10:3; Mark 3:18; Luke 6:15; John 11:16; 14:5; 20:24–29
  Arcand (6) 17:59; (8) 25:39
  Stevens (14) 1:12:51; (17) 1.34:34
  Young (14) 1.06:35
  Zeffirelli (42) 2.32:31; (43) 2.35:43
**Choosing the Twelve:** Matt. 10:1–4; Mark 3:13–19; Luke 6:12–16; John 6:66–71
  Greene (4) 15:33
  Hayes (9) 29:38
  Pasolini 36:00
  Ray (30) 1.39:16
  Saville (9) 56:15
  Stevens (17) 1.31:32
  Sykes (8 [15]) 22:53
  Young (21) 1.36:12
**Sending out the Twelve:** Matt. 10:1–11; Mark 6:7–13, 30; Luke 9:1–6, 10
  Ray (30) 1.41:13
  Zeffirelli (54) 16:34; (56) 23:20 (return)
**Peter's Confession/First Prophecy of Death:** Matt. 16:13–23; Mark 8:27–33; Luke 9:18–22; John 6:68–71
  Arcand (12) 41:55, 42:35; (29) 1.51:52
  Jones (14) 1.01:20
  Pasolini 1.14:50
  Saville (9) 56:55
  Scorsese (12) 1.06:20; (17) 1.31:00
  Stevens (17)1.33:56 (Mary Magdalene is in the scene)
  Sykes (14 [26]) 44:33
  Young (26) 2.00:32 (Judas); (26) 2.02:03
  Zeffirelli (56) 23:35; (58) 33:06
**Miracles of Jesus**
General
  Arcand (11) 36:29
  Jewison (9) 40:39

Olcott (3) 25:23; (4) 34:34; (5) 48:24

Scorsese (13) 1.09:26 (exorcisms)

Stevens (16) 1.25:57

Reports

Ray (20) 1.08:05

Stevens (17) 1.33:08

Young (22) 1.43:56

*Not in the New Testament*

Blind Girl

DeMille (5) 15:20 (quoting Mark 3:2)

Childhood Miracles (see above, under "Jesus'
Birth and Early Life," p. 177)

Exorcism of violent man

Ray (19) 1.04:36

On the Via Dolorosa

DeMille (23) 2.02:22, 2.04:25

Sacred Heart of Jesus

Scorsese (12) 1.07:59

*In alphabetical order*

Bent Woman: Luke 13:10–17

Sykes (17 [35]) 56:25 (Sabbath)

Blind Bartimaeus: Matt. 20:29–34; Mark
10:46–52; Luke 18:35–43

Olcott (4) 42:16

Sykes (19 [40]) 1.02:32

Blind from Birth: John 9:1–41

Jones (14) 1.01:00

Saville (13) 1.16:06

Stevens (18) 1.36:51, 1.39:27; (19)
1.43:25; (27) 2.39:29

Zeffirelli (68) 1.18:00; (69) 1.22:06

Blind Man and Spittle: Mark 8:22–26

Arcand (11) 38:17

Scorsese (13) 1.10:30

Blind Men: Matt. 9:27–31

Olcott (3) 28:42

Ray (15) 53:51

Boy Possessed by a Spirit: Matt. 17:14–21;
Mark 9:14–29; Luke 9:37–43

DeMille (8) 30:32

Sykes (16 [30]) 49:17

Zeffirelli (34) 1.52:00 (see also "Capernaum Synagogue" under "Teaching of
Jesus," below, p. 180)

Canaanite Woman's Daughter: Matt.
14:21–29; Mark 7:24–29

Young (22) 1.44:45

Catch of Fish: Luke 5:1–11

Hayes (7) 21:53

Sykes (6 [12]) 17:11

Young (13) 58:25

Zecca (3) 21:01

Zeffirelli (35) 1.57:56

Centurion's Servant/Son Healed: Matt.
8:5–13; Luke 7:1–10; John 4:46–54

Saville (6) 31:35

Zeffirelli (67) 1.13:40; (85) 2.48:59

Coin in Fish's Mouth: Matt. 17:27

DeMille (9) 35:53, 41:10

Ear of the Slave (see below, "Betrayal and
Arrest," p. 185)

Feeding the Five Thousand: Matt. 14:13–21;
Mark 6:30–44; Luke 9:10–17; John
6:1–15

Arcand (12) 39:49

Jones (13) 1.00:10

Pasolini 52:07

Saville (8) 43:05

Sykes (14 [25]) 42:02

Zeffirelli (51) 2:27

Fig Tree Cursed: Matt. 21:18–22; Mark
11:12–14, 20–24

Greene (5) 24:02 (see also below, "Teaching
of Jesus," "Parables," "Mustard Seed,"
p. 181)

Pasolini 1.26:14; 1.42:50

Gerasene demoniac: Matt. 8:28–34; Mark
5:1–20; Luke 8:26–39

Sykes (13 [24]) 39:52

Hemorrhaging Woman: Matt. 9:20–22; Mark
5:25–34; Luke 8:42–48

Hayes (11) 37:02

Stevens (16) 1.24.07

Jairus's Daughter: Matt. 9:18–26; Mark
5:21–43; Luke 8:40–56

Arcand (11) 38:59

Hayes (11) 34:40

Ray (20) 1.07:52

Sykes (7 [13]) 16:18

Zecca (3) 18:58

Zeffirelli (42) 2.31:47

Lame Man: John 5:1–18

Pasolini 50:02 (on the Sabbath; see also
"Withered Hand," below)

Saville (6) 34:14

Lazarus Raised: John 11:1–46

DeMille (11) 45:37

Hayes (5) 13:06; (14) 48:09

Olcott (4) 37:57

Saville (17) 1.30:31

Scorsese (12) 1.01:40; (15) 1.19:22; (17)
1.29:05 (killed by the future apostle
Paul); (26) 2.18:19 (Jesus marries his
sisters, Mary and Martha)

Lazarus Raised (cont'd)
   Stevens (8) 49:22, 50:30; (9) 51:55; (18)
      1.41:25; (20) 1.45:14; (21) 1.47:41
   Young (4) 11:24; (6) 25:21; (23) 1.48:56;
      (24) 1.51.24
   Zecca (3) 22:16
   Zeffirelli (59) 38:10
Leper Cleansed: Matt. 8:1–4; Mark 1:40–45;
      Luke 5:12–16
   Jones (4) 14:38
   Olcott (3) 28:24
   Pasolini 38:44
Mary Magdalene's Demons Cast Out: Luke 8:2
   DeMille (3) 1:52; (6) 21:30, 22:15
   Hayes (2) 2:53, 3:45; (7) 18:52; (9) 28:07
   Sykes (11 [18]) 32:27
Mute Man Cured: Matt. 9:32–33; Mark
      7:31–37
   Jones (13) 58:26
Paralytic Healed: Matt. 9:1–8; Mark 2:1–12;
      Luke 5:17–26
   DeMille (4) 10:26
   Hayes (8) 24:41
   Olcott (3) 29:08
   Ray (15) 52:03
   Stevens (11) 1.00:55 (Sabbath)
   Young (14) 1.03:16
   Zeffirelli (36) 2.01:20; (37) 2.06:54
Paralyzed Man by Pool: (see above "Lame
      Man")
Raising of Lazarus (see above "Lazarus Raised")
Stilling the Storm: Matt. 8:23–27; Mark
      4:35–41; Luke 8:22–25
   Ray (20) 1.07:52
   Sykes (13 [23]) 37:45
Syro-Phoenician Woman's Daughter (see above
      "Canaanite Woman's Daughter")
Transfiguration: Matt. 17:1–8; Mark 9:2–8;
      Luke 9:28–36
   Sykes (15 [29]) 47:38
   Zecca (3) 23:38
Walking on Water: Matt. 14:22–33; Mark
      6:45–52; John 6:16–21
   Arcand (11) 37:21
   Olcott (4) 34:21
   Pasolini 54:20
   Saville (8) 47:21
   Young (22) 1.40:09
   Zecca (3) 20:23, 21:03
Water into Wine: John 2:1–11
   Griffith (11) 1.01:56
   Olcott (3) 26:25

Saville (3) 12:51
Scorcese (13) 1.11:30
Young (11) 52:05
Zecca (3) 15:26
Widow's Son Raised: Luke 7:1–10
   Olcott (3) 31:31
   Sykes (11 [19]) 33:03
Withered Hand (Sabbath): Matt. 12:9–10;
      Mark 3:1–3; Luke 6:6–8
   Pasolini 50:02 (see also "Lame Man,"
      above; and "Controversy," "Sabbath [no
      miracle]," below, p. 182)
**Teaching of Jesus** (alphabetical order)
Apocalyptic Discourse: Matt. 24:1–51; Mark
      13:1–37; Luke 21:5–36
   Arcand (26) 1.41:38
   Jones (10) 44:52; (12) 52:39
   Pasolini 1.41:50
   Scorsese (22) 1.55:35
   Zeffirelli (69) 1.26:00
Capernaum Synagogue: Mark 1:21–28; Luke
      4:31–37; John 6:25–59
   Saville (9) 52:40
   Stevens (11) 1.00:55
   Zeffirelli (34) 1.50:25
Conditions of Discipleship (after Peter's Con-
      fession): Matt. 16:24–28; Mark 8:34–9:1;
      Luke 9:23–27
   Greene (12) 1.13:53 (see also [5] 22:30)
   Hayes (15) 56:37
   Jones (15) 1.06:38
   Pasolini 1.16:50
   Ray (16) 56:33
   Stevens (9) 53:21
   Sykes (14 [28]) 45:50
   Young (26) 2.01:14
Greatest Commandment: Matt. 22:34–40;
      Mark 12:28–31; Luke 10:25–29, 37
   Greene (10) 1.09:34
   Hayes (13) 45:51
   Pasolini 1.34:54
   Ray (27) 1.27:57
   Stevens (9) 51:55
   Sykes (18 [38]) 1.00:08
   Zeffirelli (53) 12:24
Lord's Prayer: Matt. 6:9–15; Luke 11:2–4
   DeMille (16) 1.12:55
   Hayes (6) 14:39
   Ray (28) 1.35:05
   Stevens (17) 1.32:51; (20) 1.46:39
   Sykes (16 [31]) 51:27
   Zeffirelli (57) 30:40

Mary at the Feet of Jesus: Luke 10:38–42
 Greene (5) 22:30
 Hayes (6) 13:36
 Jewison (2) 12:21 (Mary Magdalene; see below, "Controversy," "Anointing Woman," p. 182)
 Olcott (4) 35:15
 Scorsese (12) 1.03:40
 Zecca (3) 16:49 (Magdalene)
Mission Discourse: Matt. 10:5–42; Luke 10:1–24
 Griffith (11) 1.02:35
 Pasolini 36:00
 Zeffirelli (42) 2.30:00, 2.31:16; (54) 16:34; (62) 56:25
Nicodemus: John 3:1–21 (see also John 7:50–52; 19:39–42)
 Saville (4) 19:37
 Zeffirelli (70) 1.29:34
Parables (alphabetical order)
 Good Samaritan: Luke 10:29–37
  Greene (6) 35:11
  Hayes (13) 45:51
  Ray (27) 1.28:24
  Sykes (18 [39]) 1.00:49
 Good Shepherd: John 10:1–18
  Gibson (25) 1.31:00
  Ray (27) 1.28:24
  Saville (15) 1.24:18
 Lamp: Mark 4:21–25; Luke 8:16–18
  Sykes (15 [21]) 37:11
 Lost Sheep: Matt. 18:10–14; Luke 15:1–17
  Pasolini 1.18:45
  Ray (19) 1.05:35
 Mustard Seed: Matt. 13:31–32; Mark 4:30–32; Luke 13:18–19
  Greene (5) 24:02
  Hayes (7) 20:53
  Sykes (17 [34]) 55:22
 Pharisee and Tax Collector: Luke 18:9–14 (cf. Matt. 6:5–6)
  DeMille (see below, "Controversy," "Woman Caught in Adultery," p. 183)
  Greene (4) 19:58
  Griffith (7) 10:04
  Sykes (5 [11]) 16:18
 Prodigal Son: Luke 15:11–32
  Greene (9) 58:44
  Scorsese (29) 2.37:18
  Zeffirelli (39) 2.14:54
 Rich Man and Lazarus: Luke 16:19–31
  Greene (6) 38:53

Sheep and Goats: Matt. 25:31–46
 Greene (5) 26:50
 Zeffirelli (62) 58:06
Sower: Matt. 13:1–23; Mark 4:1–20; Luke 8:4–15
 Greene (8) 52:48
 Jones (12) 55:15 (secrets)
 Olcott (4) 33:45
 Pasolini 2.09:57
 Scorsese (7) 37:33
 Stevens (18) 1.40:28
 Sykes (12 [20]) 34:51
Talents: Matt. 25:14–30; Luke 19:12–27
 Jones (12) 54.00
Treasure, Pearl, Net: Matt. 13:44–50
 Young (17) 1.22:03
 Zeffirelli (36) 2.03:09
Two Sons: Matt. 21:28–32
 Arcand (12) 41:38
 Pasolini 1.29:55
 Zeffirelli (64) 1.05:52, 1.07:13
Wedding Banquet: Matt. 22:1–14; Luke 14:16–24
 Pasolini 1.32:15
Weeds: Matt. 13:24–30, 36–43
 Ray (16) 56:41
Wicked Tenants: Matt. 21:33–41; Mark 12:1–12; Luke 20:9–19
 Pasolini 1.30:44
 Sykes (22 [48]) 1.12:50
Repent, for the Kingdom of God Is at Hand: Matt. 4:12–17; Mark 1:14–15; Luke 4:14–15
 Pasolini 33:37
 Zeffirelli (32) 1.45:59; (36) 2.04:25; (36) 2.05:05; (52) 6:10
Rich Young Man: Matt. 19:16–30; Mark 10:17–31; Luke 18:18–30
 Pasolini 1.05:20
 Scorsese (12) 1.08:44
 Stevens (9) 51:55
 Sykes (18 [36]) 57:56
 Zeffirelli (42) 2.30:45, 2.31:26; (49) 3.02:05
Samaritan Woman: John 4:1–42
 Saville (5) 25:35
 Zecca (3) 17:56
Sermon on the Mount/Plain: Matt. 5:1–7:28; Luke 6:12–49; 11:9–13; 12:22–34
 Arcand (11) 38:51; (12) 40:00, 41:48; (19) 1.10:32
 Gibson (25) 1.29:31

Sermon on the Mount/Plain (*cont'd*)

    Greene (4) 15:35, 19:34; (5) 25:55, 29:21;
        (6) 37:45; (7) 44:32; (8) 48:54; 51:55;
        (9) 56:24, 1.04:59

    Hayes (6) 14:47

    Jones (3) 7:00; (12) 52:50

    Pasolini 41:35

    Ray (26) 1.21:51; (27) 1.25:09

    Scorsese (8) 39:45; (9) 44:24

    Stevens (8) 41:17; (17) 1.31:20

    Sykes (9 [16]) 24:51; (16 [32]) 52:18; (16
        [33]) 53:44; (17 [34]) 56:08

    Young (15) 1.10:00; (20) 1.31.44

    Zeffirelli (42) 2.30:35; (49) 2:58:48; (50)
        3.06:23; (53) 11:54; (57) 28:23; (63)
        1.01:51; (65) 1.07:50

Woes against the Pharisees and Scribes: Matt.
    23:1–39; Luke 11:37–52

    Arcand (19) 1.10:47, 1.11:44

    Greene (10) 1.10:02

    Pasolini 1.35:26

    Stevens (23) 2.11:15

    Zeffirelli (69) 1.25:12

**Controversy** (alphabetical order)

Anointing Woman: Luke 7:36–50

    Arcand (17) 1.02:36 ("Mary Magdalene")

    Hayes (9) 32:26 (Mary Magdalene)

    Jewison (2) 12:21; (9) 43:14; (19) 1.19:44
        (Mary Magdalene; see also above, "Teach-
        ing of Jesus," "Mary at the Feet of Jesus,"
        and below, "Anointing in Bethany,"
        p. 183)

    Olcott (3) 32:30

    Stevens (22) 2.03:35 (Mary Magdalene)

    Sykes (10 [17]) 29:35 (Mary Magdalene)

    Zeffirelli (48) 2.53:43; (51) 5:19; (53)
        13:00 (Mary Magdalene)

By Whose Authority? (John's Baptism): Matt.
    21:23–27; Mark 11:27–33; Luke 20:1–8

    Arcand (12) 42:23

    Greene (10) 1.08:00

    Zeffirelli (64) 1.05:08

Coin in Temple Treasury (see "Widow's Mite"
    below, p. 183)

Little Children: Matt. 18:1–5; 19:13–15; Mark
    9:33–37; 10:13–16; Luke 9:46–48;
    18:15–17

    Arcand (8) 26:36; (19) 1.11:23

    DeMille (10) 42:46

    Griffith (16) 1.36:58

    Hayes (13) 44:46

    Pasolini 1.07:13; 1.17:24

Stevens (14) 1.18:03

Sykes (18 [39]) 1.01:55

Prince of Demons: Matt. 12:22–24; Mark
    3:19–22; Luke 11:14–16

    Gibson (8) 25:10

    Hayes (10) 34:31

    Scorsese (4) 12:31; (14) 1.17:13

Rejection in Nazareth: Matt. 13:54–58; Mark
    6:1–6; Luke 4:16–30; John 4:43–45

    Pasolini 1.02:34

    Saville (5) 31:10

    Scorsese (14) 1.14:56

    Stevens (18) 1.36:51

    Sykes (5 [10]) 15:11

    Zeffirelli (32) 1.43:00

Rejection of Family: Matt. 12:46–50; Mark
    3:31–35; Luke 8:19–25

    Jones (15) 1.04:00

    Pasolini 1.00:46

    Scorsese (14) 1.18:10

    Sykes (12 [22]) 37:45

    Young (20) 1.34:33

    Zeffirelli (54) 18:35

Render unto Caesar: Matt. 22:15–22; Mark
    12:13–17; Luke 20:20–26

    DeMille (9) 35:53

    Greene (10) 1.08:50

    Hayes (15) 55:07

    Jones (7) 28:24

    Pasolini 1.32:50

    Sykes (22 [49]) 1.14:33

    Young (18) 1.26:24 (see also [5] 16:25; [15]
        1.07:59); (19) 1.27:35

Sabbath (No Miracle): Matt. 12:1–8, 11–12;
    Mark 2:23–28, 3:4; Luke 6:1–5; 14:5

    Pasolini 48:00

    Scorsese (7) 33:46 (see "Woman Caught in
        Adultery," below, p. 183)

    Zeffirelli (53) 10:54

Tax Collectors and Sinners: Matt. 9:10–13,
    11:19; Mark 2:15–17; Luke 5:29–32; 7:34

    Arcand (8) 25:31

    Griffith (13) 1.13:28

    Hayes (10) 32:55

    Jones (7) 28:24

    Ray (27) 1.29:37

    Sykes (17 [34]) 55:42

    Young (16) 1.13:58 (see also [5] 16:25; [15]
        1.07:59)

    Zeffirelli (38) 2.09:56, 2.12:04; (48) 2.57:06;
        (53) 10:22

Temple Taxes: Matt. 17:24–26

DeMille (9) 35:53

**Temple Teaching:** John 8:20–59; 10:30–33
  Jones (3) 10:40 (a stoning for blasphemy)
  Olcott (4) 36:56
  Saville (11) 1.09:39
  Zeffirelli (69) 1.26:45

**Widow's Mite:** Mark 12:41–43; Luke 21:1–4
  Stevens (9) 54:18
  Sykes (22 [46]) 1.11:13

**Woman Caught in Adultery:** John 7:53–8:11
  Arcand (5) 14:37
  DeMille (12) 52:06; (13) 55:45
  Gibson (18) 1.06:11 (Mary Magdalene)
  Griffith (13) 1.13:28
  Jones (14) 1.02:50
  Ray (16) 57:03 (Mary Magdalene)
  Saville (11) 1.05:17; (25) 2.08:22
  Scorsese (7) 33:46 (Mary Magdalene; see also
    [3] 9:06; [4] 14:59)
  Stevens (15) 1.19:30 (Mary Magdalene)
  Young (17) 1.21:00 (Mary Magdalene
    watches)
  Zeffirelli (66) 1.10:18

**Zacchaeus:** Luke 19:1–10
  Sykes (20 [41]) 1.04:08

**Journey to Jerusalem:** Matt 20:20–28; Mark
    10:32–45; Luke 9:51–53; 22:24–27
  DeMille (10) 42:46
  Hayes (12) 41:45
  Ray (34) 1.52:04, 1.53:00
  Scorsese (18) 1.33:53
  Stevens (18) 1.41:25
  Sykes (18 [36]) 57:55
  Young (23) 1.48:48
  Zeffirelli (58) 33:04, 35:19

**Lament over Jerusalem:** Matt. 23:37–39; Luke
    13:34–35
  Greene (11) 1.12:16
  Jewison (6) 34:42
  Pasolini 1.40:50
  Stevens (8) 49:36
  Sykes (21 [43]) 1.08:15
  Zeffirelli (69) 1.26:35

**Anointing in Bethany:** Matt. 26:6–13; Mark
    14:3–9; John 12:1–11
  Jewison (4) 18:10 (Mary Magdalene); for
    Judas's response, see also (1) 6:35; (9)
    43:14; (19) 1.19:44 (see also above, "Con-
    troversy," "Anointing Woman," p. 182)
  Olcott (4) 42:55
  Pasolini 1.43:00
  Saville (20) 1.40:51

Stevens (22) 2.03:35 (Mary Magdalene)
Zeffirelli (53) 15:50 (Mary Magdalene; see
    above "Controversy," "Anointing Woman,"
    p. 182)

**Triumphal Entry into Jerusalem:** Matt. 21:1–9;
    Mark 11:1–10; Luke 19:28–40; John
    12:12–19
  DeMille (15) 1.06:12; (16) 1.12:02, 1.12:27
  Gibson (20) 1.14:09
  Hayes (15) 51:31
  Jewison (4) 23:24, 23:57; (5) 26:07
  Olcott (5) 45:18
  Pasolini 1.20:50
  Ray (35) 1.53:28
  Saville (21) 1.43:15
  Scorsese (18) 1.35:50
  Stevens (15) 1.20:24 (Capernaum); (22)
    2.07:45
  Sykes (21 [42]) 1.06:59
  Young (25) 1.57:55
  Zecca (3) 24:33
  Zeffirelli (61) 48:35

**Cleansing the Temple:** Matt. 21:12–16; Mark
    11:15–19; Luke 19:45–48; John 2:12–22
  Arcand (17) 1.03:40
  DeMille (14) 1.01:10
  Hayes (15) 53:36
  Jewison (8) 37:21
  Olcott (5) 46:27
  Pasolini 1.24:19
  Saville (3) 16:26
  Scorsese (16) 1.24:42; (18) 1.37:12
  Stevens (23) 2.10:30
  Sykes (21 [44]) 1.08:56
  Young (18) 1.25:40; (19) 1.28:28
  Zecca (3) 25:16
  Zeffirelli (61) 51:16; (64) 1.04:39

**Plots against Jesus:** Matt. 12:14; 26:1–5; Mark
    3:6; 14:1–2; Luke 6:11; 13:31–33; 22:1–2
  Arcand (16) 59:11
  DeMille (12) 52:06
  Griffith (7) 26:47
  Hayes (8) 23:41; (12) 40:49; (15) 57:06
  Jewison (3) 15:54
  Olcott (5) 47:24
  Pasolini 51:50; 1.42:00
  Ray (29) 1.38:46
  Stevens (14) 1.13:20; (16) 1.31:12; (17)
    1.35:35; (23) 2.13:25
  Sykes (21 [45]) 1.10:40
  Young (17) 1.21:30; (22) 1.43:56; (26)
    1.59:12

**Plots against Jesus** (*cont'd*)
Zeffirelli (60) 46:10; (61) 55:18; (68) 1.17:18
**Sanhedrin Meeting:** John 7:50–52; 11:46–53
Arcand (9) 31:52; (23) 1.26:08
Hayes (15) 52:56
Jewison (4) 22:21, 23:58
Saville (11) 1.04:42; (19) 1.38:50
Young (25) 1.55.20; (27) 2.04:26
Zeffirelli (71) 1.31:52
**Judas:** Matt. 10:4; Mark 3:19; Luke 6:16
Prior to Meeting Jesus
Hayes (6) 17:25
Ray (8) 23:33; (9) 28:56; (16) 54:58
Young (15) 1.07:57, 1.11:43
Zeffirelli (47) 2.50:17; (49) 2.58:20
Becomes a Disciple (see "Call of the Disciples,"
above, p. 178)
Questions and Concerns
Jewison (1) 6:05
Scorsese (3) 4:21; (12) 1.06:20
Young (22) 1.46:08; (23) 1.44:45; (26)
2.00:27
Zeffirelli (52) 6:32; (55) 22:12; (56) 27:10;
(63) 1.02:27; (69) 1.28:26
Plans the Betrayal: Matt. 26:14–16; Mark
14:10–11; 22:3–6; John 6:70–71
DeMille (16) 1.13:42
Gibson (2) 3:23
Greene (12) 1.16:58
Hayes (16) 57:16
Jewison (10) 48:14
Olcott (5) 49:34
Pasolini 1.45:45
Ray (37) 2.01:02; (38) 2.08:42
Saville (9) 57:18; (23) 1.56:00; (24) 2.04:35
Scorsese (9) 43:41; (19) 1.40:36; (28)
2.34:04
Stevens (24) 2.18:45; (25) 2.32:58, 2.33:36;
(26) 2.35:46
Sykes (23 [52]) 1.20:31
Young (26) 2.02:36; (28) 2.12:01
Zeffirelli (60) 46:10; (72) 1.41:49; (73)
1.50:04
Betrayal (see "Betrayal and Arrest" below)
Repentance: Matt. 27:3-5
DeMille (22) 1.59:30, 2.00:30
Gibson (10) 31:51
Hayes (22) 1.11:00
Jewison (20) 1.23:20
Ray (44) 2.27:01
Pasolini 2.00:36

Stevens (29) 3.00:00
Young (33) 2.39:40
Death: Matt. 27:3-10; Acts 1:15-20
DeMille (22) 2.00.34, 2.01:10; (24) 2.09:18;
(25) 2.17:37, 2.20:07
Gibson (11) 35:50
Jewison (20) 1.27:12
Olcott (7) 58:59
Pasolini 2.01:50
Ray (49) 2.41:35
Stevens (30) 3.02:55, 3.03:55, 3.04:19
Zeffirelli (78) 2.12:28
Resurrection
Jewison (22) 1.35:40
**Washing the Disciples' Feet:** John 13:1–17
Gibson (16) 1.02:10
Greene (13) 1.21:24 (faces)
Olcott (6) 51:28
Saville (22) 1.51:12
**Last Supper:** Matt. 26:20–35; Mark 14:17–31;
Luke 22:14–38; John 13:18–16:33
Arcand (24) 1.31:14
DeMille (17) 1.15:28
Gibson (9) 30:01; (19) 1.11:11; (26)
1.34:09; (27) 1.35:06, 1.36:15, 1.37:00,
1.40:48, 1.42:34
Greene (13) 1.21:08
Hayes (17) 58:17
Jewison (12) 53:33
Jones (12) 55:35 (gourd and sandal)
Olcott (6) 52:29
Pasolini 1.46:20
Ray (38) 2.02:49
Saville (22) 1.51:37
Scorsese (20) 1.44:50
Sykes (23 [50]) 1.15:21
Young (28) 2.07:59
Zecca (4) 26:19
Zeffirelli (73) 1.45:15
**Prayer in the Garden:** Matt. 26:36–44; Mark
14:32–40; Luke 22:39–46; John 17:1–26
DeMille (18) 1.25:50
Gibson (1) 0:32; (2) 4:39
Greene (14) 1.27:14
Hayes (18) 1.01:19
Jewison (12) 1.00:17
Olcott (7) 56:01
Pasolini 1.49:50
Ray (39) 2.09:25
Saville (26) 2.14:30
Scorsese (21) 1.52:39

Stevens (27) 2.33:22
Sykes (23 [53]) 1.20:48
Young (29) 2.13:19
Zecca (4) 27:22
Zeffirelli (74) 1.55:45; (75) 1.56:53

**Betrayal and Arrest:** Matt. 26:45–56; Mark 14:41–52; Luke 22:47–53; John 18:1–12

Arcand (12) 42:45; (19) 1.11:55; (24) 1.33:35
DeMille (18) 1.26:55, 1.30:54
Gibson (4) 9:15
Greene (14) 1.30:12
Hayes (19) 1.04:08
Jewison (13) 1.06:30
Jones (15) 1.09:56
Olcott (7) 57:55
Pasolini 1.53:38
Ray (40) 2.13:00
Saville (26) 2.13:04, 2.13:45; (27) 2.18:48
Scorsese (21) 1.52:37
Stevens (26) 2.37:43
Sykes (23 [54]) 1.23:04
Young (29) 2.15:26; (30) 2.20:16, 2.21:33
Zecca (4) 27:02, 28:27
Zeffirelli (75) 1.58:39

**Jesus before the High Priest/Sanhedrin and Peter's Denials:** Matt. 26:57–27:2; Mark 14:53–15:1; Luke 22:54–23:1; John 18:13–38

DeMille (19) 1.35:12
Gibson (5) 16:23; (8) 23:13
Hayes (19) 1.06:10
Jewison (15) 1.10:12
Jones (3) 10:40 (a stoning for blasphemy)
Pasolini 1.56:25, 1.59:50
Ray (40) 2.14:04
Saville (28) 2.21:36
Scorsese (23) 1.58:48 (denials only)
Sykes (24 [55]) 1.27:54
Young (30) 2.22:00
Zecca (4) 29:13
Zeffirelli (77) 2.04:37

**Trial before Pilate:** Matt. 27:11–31; Mark 15:2–20; Luke 23:2–6, 13–25; John 18:28–19:16

First Meeting with Pilate
Arcand (8) 29:20; (19) 1.14:07; (20) 1.17:45
DeMille (20) 1.40:00
Gibson (12) 38:57; (15) 48:17; (19) 1.08:09; (30) 1.53:01
Hayes (21) 1.08:51; (22) 1.11:22

Jewison (17) 1.14:03; (21) 1.28:10
Jones (15) 1.10:08 (see also [9] 38:20)
Olcott (7) 1.00:01
Pasolini 2.02:33
Ray (41) 2.26:37
Saville (29) 2.24:31
Scorsese (22) 1.53:49
Stevens (27) 2.45:22; (29) 2.52:39
Sykes (24 [56]) 1.29:45, 1.32:57
Young (31) 2.25:38; (32) 2.32:51
Zecca (4) 30:30
Zeffirelli (79) 2.14:14; (80) 2.17:49; (81) 2.25:27

Scourging/Crown of Thorns: Matt. 27:26–31; Mark 15:15–20; Luke 22:16, 22; John 19:1–3

Arcand (13) 43:08
DeMille (20) 1.45:49; (21) 1.47:38
Gibson (16) 52:04 (scourging); (17) 1.05:06 (crown of thorns)
Hayes (21) 1.10:41
Jewison (21) 1.31:20
Olcott (7) 1.02:10
Pasolini 2.04:15
Ray (44) 2.25:41
Saville (29) 2.27:54
Scorsese (22) 1.57:36
Stevens (28) 2.53:53 (stated but not carried out)
Sykes (24 [56]) 1.34:07
Young (32) 2.35:14, 2.35:56
Zecca (4) 31:35
Zeffirelli (81) 2.23:31

Pilate's Wife's Dream ("Claudia"): Matt. 27:19
DeMille (20) 1.45:12
Gibson (12) 38:04; (14) 44:10; (15) 51:34; (16) 59:54; (19) 1.08:46, 1.09:23, 1.10:24, 1.12:12
Jewison (7) 35:37
Ray (44) 2.25:57
Stevens (22) 2.09:43; (25) 2.32:25

Release of Barabbas: Matt. 27:15–21, 26; Mark 15:6–15; Luke 23:18–25
Arcand (20) 1.15:45
DeMille (20) 1.47:10; (22) 1.54:11
Gibson (15) 49:17
Hayes (22) 1.12:12 (stated, but not shown)
Jones (17) 1.14:29, 1.20:45; (19) 1.26:51
Pasolini 2:03:27
Ray (45) 2.28:27
Saville (29) 2.27:18 (stated but not shown)

Release of Barabbas (*cont'd*)
  Stevens (28) 2.54:15
  Sykes (24 [56]) 1.33:37
  Young (32) 2.33:54; (33) 2.36:16, 2.36:31
  Zeffirelli (79) 2.12:56; (81) 2.28:23; (82) 2:31:10
Pilate Washes His Hands: Matt. 27:24–25
  DeMille (22) 1.58:52
  Gibson (19) 1.10:59, 1.11:45
  Hayes (22) 1.12:38
  Jewison (21) 1.34:40
  Olcott (7) 1.03:35
  Stevens (28) 2.57:14
  Young (33) 2.37:11
  Zecca (4) 33:20
  Zeffirelli (79) 2.15:32
Jesus and Herod: Luke 22:7–12
  Arcand (20) 1.15:54
  Gibson (13) 44:10
  Hayes (21) 1.10:09
  Jewison (18) 1.16:14
  Olcott (7) 1.01:12
  Ray (43) 2.22:30
  Stevens (28) 2.48:23
  Sykes (24 [56]) 1.31:11
  Young (32) 2.29:30
Via Dolorosa: Matt. 27:31–32; Mark 15:20–22;
    Luke 23:26–32; John 19:16–17
On the Way
  Arcand (13) 44:25
  DeMille (23) 2.01:26
  Gibson (20) 1.12:29
  Griffith (24) 2.34:13; (27) 2.56:37
  Hayes (23) 1.12:59
  Jewison (22) 1.38:04
  Jones (17) 1.19:32, 1.21:34; (18) 1.22:41, 1.23:02
  Olcott (7) 1.04:45
  Pasolini 2.05:00
  Ray (46) 2.32:05
  Saville (30) 2.33:19
  Scorsese (23) 1.59:15
  Stevens (29) 2.57:28
  Sykes (25 [57]) 1.35:27
  Young (33) 2.37:50
  Zecca (4) 33:32
  Zeffirelli (83) 2.35:51
Veronica
  Gibson (20) 1.20:03; (22) 1.23:42; (23) 1.26:59, 1.27:10
  Ray (46) 2.24:25
  Stevens (29) 2.58:50

Zecca (5) 34:15
Zeffirelli (83) 2.38:24
Simon of Cyrene: Matt. 27:32; Mark 15:21;
    Luke 23:26
  DeMille (23) 2.05:05
  Gibson (21) 1.21:25
  Jones (17) 1.20:25; (18) 1.23:58
  Olcott (7) 1.05:51
  Pasolini 2.05:23
  Ray (46) 2.34:13
  Stevens (28) 2.55:53; (29) 3.00:35; (30) 3.07:10
  Sykes (25 [57]) 1.36:10
Crucifixion: Matt. 27:31–32; Mark 15:20–22;
    Luke 23:26–32; John 19:18–22
Crucifixions—Not Jesus
  Arcand (4) 12:05; (13) 43:10, 46:42; (25) 1.34:39
  Jones (4) 14:31; (11) 50:25; (15) 1.10:20; (16) 1.13:20; (17) 1.16:54; (18) 1.22:48, 1.23:04
  Pasolini 2.07:05
  Ray (4) 12:14; (48) 2.39:38
  Scorsese (3) 7:46; (18) 1.34:43; (22) 1.57:02
  Stevens (5) 22:52
  Sykes (18 [37]) 59:32
  Young (8) 37:02
Jesus Nailed to the Cross: Matt. 27:35–38; Mark
    15:25–27; Luke 23:32–34; John 19:18–22
  Arcand (13) 44:58
  DeMille (24) 2.09:29
  Gibson (27) 1.35:46
  Greene (15) 1.32:30
  Hayes (23) 1.14:16
  Jewison (22) 1.39:08
  Jones (18) 1.24:23 (Brian)
  Olcott (7) 1.06:57
  Pasolini 2.08:30
  Ray (47) 2.37:05
  Saville (30) 2.34:00
  Scorsese (23) 2.02:48
  Stevens (30) 3.04:09
  Sykes (25 [57]) 1.38:55
  Young (34) 2.40:34
  Zecca (5) 36:43
  Zeffirelli (83) 2.39:15
Chief Priests and Others Mock: Matt. 27:39–44;
    Mark 15:29–32; Luke 23:35–38
  Arcand (25) 1.34:53
  DeMille (24) 2.10:40
  Gibson 1.43:58
  Hayes (23) 1.14:57

Jewison (23) 1.40:07
Jones (19) 1.25:21 (see also "Centurion's Witness," below)
Scorsese (23) 2.04:34; (24) 2.06:41
Stevens (30) 3.05:32
Sykes (25 [57]) 1.41:07
Young (34) 2.41:22
Zecca (5) 38:21
Zeffirelli (83) 2.40:04; (85) 2.46:20
Dividing Jesus' Garments: Matt. 27:35; Mark 15:24; Luke 23:34; John 19:23–27
Gibson (29) 1.47:01
Olcott (7) 1.07:22
Saville (30) 2.35:40
Sykes (25 [57]) 1.41:59
Young (34) 2.42:27
Zecca (5) 38:31
Penitent Thief: Luke 23:39–44
DeMille (24) 2.12:19–2.15:18
Gibson (28) 1.43:29, 1.44:49, 1.45:02; (29) 1.50:33
Jones (18) 1.24:51
Olcott (7) 1.07:48
Ray (47) 2.37:52
Stevens (30) 3.05:37
Sykes (25 [57]) 1.44:03
Zeffirelli (84) 2.41:19
Darkness: Matt. 27:45, 51–53; Mark 15:33; Luke 23:44
Arcand (26) 1.40:34
DeMille (25) 2.15:17
Gibson (29) 1.46:34
Griffith (29) 3.11:21
Hayes (23) 1.14:10, 1.15:24
Olcott (7) 1.09:07
Pasolini 2.11:23
Ray (48) 2.40:51
Scorsese (24) 2.05:24
Stevens (30) 3.06:46
Sykes (25 [58]) 1.44:57
Young (34) 2.42:16
Zecca (5) 38:53
Zeffirelli (86) 3.50:49
Wine Mixed with Myrrh: Matt. 27:34; Mark 15:23
Arcand (13) 44:45
DeMille (24) 2.08:55
Pasolini 2.06:21
Sour Wine on a Stick: Matt. 27:49; Mark 15:38; Luke 23:36; John 19:28–29
Arcand (13) 46:16
Gibson (29) 1.49:14

Olcott (7) 1.08:11
Pasolini 2.10:30
Saville (30) 2.37:09
Stevens (31) 3.07:40
Sykes (25 [57]) 1.42:55
Death: Matt. 27:50, 55–56; Mark 15:37, 40–41; Luke 23:46, 48–49; John 19:30
Arcand (13) 46:42
DeMille (25) 2.17:00
Gibson (29) 1.52:18
Greene (15) 1.35:00
Griffith (29) 3.11:21
Hayes (23) 1.16:04
Jewison (23) 1.41:58
Olcott (7) 1.09:41
Pasolini 2.10:52
Ray (48) 2.40:44
Saville (30) 2.37:54
Scorsese (29) 2.39:26
Stevens (31) 3.08:58
Sykes (25 [58]) 1.46:10
Young (34) 2.43:08
Zecca (5) 38:51
Zeffirelli (85) 2:50:25
Spear Thrust / Breaking Legs: John 19:31–37
Arcand (13) 47:20
DeMille (25) 2.20:26
Gibson (30) 1.53:40
Saville (30) 2.38:02
Zecca (5) 39:02
Centurion's Witness: Matt. 27:54; Mark 15:39; Luke 23:47
DeMille (25) 2.20:35
Gibson (30) 1.54:24, 1.54:44, 1.55:05
Hayes (23) 1.16:26
Jones (19) 1.25:21
Ray (49) 2.41:16
Stevens (31) 3.09:14
Sykes (25 [58]) 1.46:20
Zecca (5) 39:09
Zeffirelli (85) 2.48:59 (see also "Miracles" "Centurion's Servant/Son Healed" above, p. 179)
Veil of Temple Torn: Matt. 27:51; Mark 15:38; Luke 23:45
DeMille (25) 2.20:53
Gibson (30) 1.53:21, 1.54:33, 1.54:52
Hayes (23) 1.16:04
Stevens (31) 3.09:29
Sykes (25 [58]) 1.58:27
Earthquake: Matt. 27:51–52; 28:2
DeMille (25) 2.19:06

Earthquake (*cont'd*)
Gibson (30) 1.52:40
Olcott (7) 1.09:24
Pasolini 2.10:53
Young (34) 2.43:25
Zecca (5) 38:53
Deposition: Matt. 27:57–59; Mark 15:42–46;
Luke 23:50–53; John 19:38–40
Arcand (27) 1.44:49
Gibson (30) 1.55:40
Greene (15) 1.35:30
Hayes (24) 1.16:38
Pasolini 2.11:57
Ray (49) 2.41:52
Saville (31) 2.39:41
Sykes (25 [58]) 1.46:29
Young (34) 2.43:48
Zecca (5) 39:14
Zeffirelli (86) 2.51:49
Burial: Matt. 27:60–61; Mark 15:46–47; Luke
23:53–56; John 19:41–42
Hayes (24) 1.17:14
Pasolini 2.13:42
Ray (49) 2.43:14
Saville (31) 2.40:27
Stevens (31) 3.10:18
Sykes (25 [59]) 1.46:54
Young (34) 2.44:17
Zecca (5) 40:32
**Resurrection Appearances**
Roman Guards: Matt. 27:62–66; 27:4, 11–15
DeMille (26) 2.23:32
Pasolini 2.14:37
Stevens (31) 3.10:27; (32) 3.14:17
Zecca (6) 41:31
Zeffirelli (87) 2.53:46; (88) 2.58:49; (90)
3.07:30
Descent into Hell: 1 Peter 3:19
Arcand (26) 1.41:52
Easter (No Resurrection)
Arcand (14) 48:20
Greene (15) 1.35:52
Jewison (23) 1.43:40
Jones (20) 1.29:33
Easter Morning: Matt. 28:1–10; Mark 16:1–8;
Luke 24:1–12; John 20:1–18
Arcand (14) 50:42; (29) 1.51:35, 1.52:39;
(26) 1.40:09; (29) 1.51:35, 1.52:39

DeMille (26) 2.22:42
Gibson (31) 1.57:24
Hayes (24) 1.17:52
Pasolini 2.14:59
Ray (50) 2.44:31
Saville (31) 2.40:46
Stevens (32) 3.11:57, 3.13:22
Sykes (26 [60]) 1.48:29
Young (35) 2.45:22
Zecca (6) 41:13
Zeffirelli (87) 2.56:04
Emmaus Road: Luke 24:13–32
Arcand (14) 51:16
Hayes (25) 1.21:06
Sykes (26 [61]) 1.51:11
Behind Closed Doors: Luke 24:33–49; John
20:19–29
DeMille (26) 2.29:22
Hayes (24) 1.20:43; (25) 1.24:19
Saville (32) 2.44:09
Stevens (32) 3.12:48, 3.14:05
Sykes (26 [61]) 1.51:12
Young (35) 2.48:37
Zeffirelli (43) 2.35:42; (88) 2.59:05; (90)
3.08:41
Great Catch of Fish: John 21:1–23
Ray (51) 2.46:33
Saville (33) 2.47:33
Great Commission: Matt. 28:16–20
Arcand (29) 1.51:54, 1.53:50
Hayes (26) 1.25:30
Pasolini 2.16:04
Stevens (32) 3.14:57
Sykes (27 [63]) 1.53:20
Young (35) 2.51:36
Zeffirelli (90) 3.09:32
Ascension: Luke 24:50–52; Acts 1:6–11
DeMille (26) 2.36:25
Hayes (27) 1.26:09
Jewison (22) 1.35:23
Stevens (32) 3.14:47
Sykes (27 [63]) 1.53:30
Young (35) 2.52:13
Zecca (6) 42:06
Apostle Paul Preaches the Death and Resurrec-
tion of Jesus: Acts 9:1–22; 1 Cor. 15:3–9
Scorsese (27) 2.22:15

# Notes

## Preface

1. *The Nativity Story* was released on DVD in March 2007, too late to be included in our handbook.
2. Adele Reinhartz's *Jesus of Hollywood* (New York: Oxford University Press, 2007) discusses some of the harder-to-find Jesus films, particularly older, foreign ones.

## Chapter 2

1. The halo looks suspiciously like a film reel.
2. The Pathé Company colorized some scenes by hand-stenciling color on objects in each frame of film.
3. The Samaritan woman is a rare character in later Jesus films; however, women in general are quite prominent in this film.
4. Should the audience be impressed with the technological power of cinema or with Jesus' power? The miracle at Cana functions similarly, with the audience at "center stage" for the event. In the actual miracle story (John 2:1–11), it is unclear as to when the miracle occurs or who actually knows of it.
5. The transfiguration is relatively rare in film. It also appears in Sykes and Krisch's *The Jesus Film*.
6. The actual resurrection of Jesus is rare in film. Pasolini (*The Gospel According to St. Matthew*) shows the stone blown away from the tomb, but most directors are content with the empty tomb and subsequent appearances.
7. One can also imagine a narrator providing a running commentary for the film.
8. In a series of blog entries (February and March, 2006), Matt Page discusses a DVD that he had recently won on eBay titled *Early Religious Films*. Two of these, *Life of Christ* and *Death of Christ*, seem to be early segments of what eventually became Zecca's 1905 film (http://biblefilms.blogspot.com/2006_02_01_biblefilms_archive.html).

## Chapter 3

1. Actually, Olcott uses two types of intertitles: (1) Scripture references for individual scenes and (2) "chapter" intertitles. The chapter intertitles use artwork as well as summary phrases. As a result, the film is a pastiche of Scripture, art, and moving pictures. Interestingly, many of the Scripture intertitles are incorrect and sometimes do not match their scenes. For example, the intertitles pair the healing of a blind man at Jericho with Matthew, even though that Gospel has two men healed; and it pairs Judas's complaint regarding the anointing woman (although Judas has not yet been identified) with Matthew's Gospel even though it is only John's Gospel that identifies Judas as the complainer.

189

2. John 18:6. Olcott includes many more scenes of Jesus' teaching than do Zecca or DeMille. However, for Olcott, Jesus' teaching centers on two revelatory "I am" statements (John 8:58; 18:6).
3. Jesus' suffering on the "cold stone" is a commonplace in Christian art.
4. The scene was filmed on the traditional Via Dolorosa in the Old City of Jerusalem, with the *Ecce Homo* arch in the background.
5. One-reel passion plays had already been made, but Olcott's film was the first five-reeler of his day. He made his place in film history prior to *From the Manger to the Cross* with a spate of one-reelers, including *Ben Hur* (1907), which focused on the chariot race.

## Chapter 4

1. An intertitle also describes the film as "A Drama of Comparisons." The second act includes an additional intertitle: "A Sun-Play of the Ages."
2. Adele Reinhartz states that the film originally had about thirty cuts to the Judean story (*Jesus of Hollywood* [New York: Oxford University Press, 2007], 206). Reportedly, Griffith cut large segments of Jesus material from his film because of prerelease complaints about anti-Semitism.
3. The woman is unnamed.
4. This repeated intertitle is the name of a poem appearing in Walt Whitman's *Leaves of Grass*.
5. Griffith was making this modern romance, titled *The Woman and the Law*, when criticism of *The Birth of a Nation* led him to *Intolerance*'s epic form. The modern story and the Babylonian story, which cost the most money, are the longest segments. When *Intolerance* failed at the box office, those two pieces were rereleased as separate films in 1919. The Jesus segment is by far the shortest piece.
6. It may be significant that there are three reformers/uplifters and also three fates.
7. Griffith makes this distinction only here and subsequently loses sight of it.
8. From here on the plot summary focuses only on the modern story and the Jesus segments. While including the other two tragic stories of young love undone by religious intolerance would not significantly change the plot summary, our summary does not reflect the film's pacing. After a leisurely opening, the film gradually builds to a climax that cuts frantically back and forth between the four stories of doomed innocents. Griffith's *The Birth of a Nation* has similar pacing.
9. The segment's intertitle is bitingly ironic, for Christian orphan homes often had this Scripture text (Mark 10:14) hanging on their walls. Does Griffith purposely misquote the Markan text? The King James Bible reads, "Suffer the little children. . . ." By deleting the word "the" from his intertitle, Griffith turns the saying of Jesus from a command to allow the children to come to him to an abusive exclamation: "Suffer, [you] little children!"
10. The only time the modern couple is seen praying, the Dear One addresses a Madonna and Child statue in her apartment. Is she praying to Mary or to Jesus? Is she thankful for her salvation, or is she confessing her sins? Griffith does not make this clear.
11. Lillian Gish plays this woman. Gish also starred as Elsie Stoneman in Griffith's *The Birth of a Nation*.
12. The Director's Guild of America's National Board gives a lifetime directorial achievement award in his name. However, Griffith should share credit with his cameraman, G. W. Bitzer, for inventing many film techniques.
13. The film was first released as *The Clansman*, and only later was the title changed to *The Birth of a Nation*.
14. Another intertitle claims that the film "is not meant to reflect on any race or people of today," but those words fail to counter the images that follow.
15. Adding insult to injury, Griffith used white characters in blackface for most of the

prominent black and mulatto roles. The NAACP challenged the film's racist ideology and historical mistakes even at the time of the film's debut.

16. The KKK riders look like something from a Sir Walter Scott romance, a genre beloved by those who bemoaned the South's fate. Griffith's father was a Confederate officer and hero who regaled the young Griffith with romantic tales of the South.

17. A troubling, fantastic scene intercedes between the two, with a supernatural rider wielding a sword and lording it over worshipers to his right and over a field of the slain to his left. Is this the single most concise visual of the American Jesus ever offered the viewing public?

18. Griffith's crosscutting of four stories imperially submerges their differences and renders them "one story." The New Testament canon similarly casts four different Gospels as one.

## Chapter 5

1. This synopsis describes the full-length, road-show version of the film. The Criterion Collection DVD also includes the 1928 version that was edited for general release (112 minutes). For some of the significant materials edited out of the shorter 1928 version, see notes 10, 11, 15–17 below.

2. It is not clear how much of the integrated plotline should be credited to the screenwriter Jeannie MacPherson, a woman who wrote many screenplays for DeMille and who had a long-lasting affair with him. She was on set with DeMille often during the filming of *The King of Kings* and seems to have drawn her opening scene with the love triangle between Jesus, Judas, and Mary from Paul Heyse's play *Mary of Magdala*. Heyse's theatrical production ran on Broadway from November 1902 through February 1903 ("New Plays Come to Broadway: Mary Fiske as Mary of Magdala," *New York Times* [16 November 1902], 27), with Tyrone Power playing the role of Judas. Paul Heyse would go on to win the 1910 Nobel Prize for literature.

3. The homoerotic undertones in the conversation are quite obvious.

4. While nearly two-thirds of the remaining film focuses on the last days of Jesus' life, the first third centers on Jesus' miracles.

5. This seems to be DeMille's visual interpretation of Jesus' statement "'Truly I tell you, whoever does not receive the kingdom of God as a little child will never enter it'" (Mark 10:15), which is reinforced later on when Jesus gathers children around him and "heals" a child's broken doll (DVD ch. 10).

6. DeMille opens the film with light breaking in on a dark horizon. The scene reappears repeatedly as the backdrop for intertitles.

7. DeMille takes only four miracles clearly from the Gospels: the exorcising of the demons from Mary Magdalene (Luke 8:2), the exorcism of the "lunatic" boy (Mark 9:14–29), the coin in the fish's mouth (Matt. 17:24–27), and the raising of Lazarus (John 11). DeMille attaches quotes from the Gospels to other miracles, but they are not actually from the Gospels (e.g., the healing of the blind girl, the healing of the boy Mark).

8. Because of prerelease complaints about anti-Semitism, DeMille distinguishes Caiaphas from other Jews in the story in two notable ways: (1) an opening intertitle states that he was appointed by the Romans; (2) in the Temple, after the veil is torn, Caiaphas confesses that he alone is guilty for Jesus' death (and not the Jewish people as a whole).

9. In the future, whenever Matthew appears in a scene he will be writing—presumably taking notes for his future Gospel.

10. The 112-minute film version omits this entire 12 ½-minute sequence.

11. For DeMille, the woman caught in adultery is clearly not Mary Magdalene. In the 112-minute version of the film, DeMille puts this scene *before* the raising of Lazarus.

12. Borrowing freely from the Gospels, DeMille repeatedly departs from their order and

also freely excises material. For example, he moves the wilderness temptation narrative from the beginning of the Gospels to the last days in Jerusalem, and he reduces the temptations from three to one.

13. The high priest's servant asks for a sign from Judas to make sure they will seize the right man, so Judas betrays Jesus with a kiss. DeMille seems to have forgotten that he had placed the same servant of the high priest in the presence of Jesus on numerous earlier occasions in the film—most notably at the raising of Lazarus from the dead.

14. Reversing the Gospels' pattern, DeMille places the onus for Jesus' death on the Romans and tries to minimize corporate Jewish guilt. He only hints at the Jewish Sanhedrin trial and places a Roman eagle prominently in the background throughout Jesus' trial.

15. The 112-minute version of the film omits Pilate's wife.

16. One notable man in the crowd refuses to be bribed, saying, "You cannot bribe me, a Jew, to cry for the blood of an innocent brother!" However, the 112-minute version of the film omits this sequence.

17. The 112-minute version of the film omits this character.

18. The opening and closing scenes in color nicely visualize DeMille's sin-to-salvation pattern.

19. A cross on the door turns to light, and then Jesus appears through the door. Jesus thus "literally" becomes the door (John 10:9) through its embedded cruciform.

20. Corresponding to an opening intertitle, this end presents the film as faithful obedience to Jesus' command to witness.

21. DeMille leaves out the eschatological conclusion "even unto the end of the age."

22. The revelation's sum total—as Rudolf Bultmann also said of the Gospel of John's revelation—is that Jesus is the revealer. Likewise, DeMille gives his viewers virtually no clue as to the *content* of that revelation. Is Jesus' revelation about who God is? The kingdom of God? Who he himself is in relation to God? What will happen in the future? How people ought to treat others? DeMille's Jesus gives viewers little to work with.

23. Like Griffith's *Intolerance*, DeMille's *The Ten Commandments* paired a biblical story with a modern story—the biblical story providing the interpretative frame for the modern story. But unlike Griffith, DeMille did not crosscut. After a biblical preface that climaxes with the Sinai orgy (Exodus 32), he moves to the modern tale of a moral and immoral son and their respective (moralistic) fates. The good son, of course, ultimately gets the girl.

24. DeMille comes on-screen himself—as he did in many of his films—to introduce the film and to moralize about its contemporary significance. Like *The Sign of the Cross*, *The Ten Commandments* also features a struggle for political power, here between Moses—representing freedom—and Ramses (Yul Brynner)—representing tyranny.

### Chapter 6

1. Ray apparently learned from DeMille and earlier biblical epics to present Jesus' story as the story of the converted (Lucius?) and the degraded (Judas). Ray also significantly expands the roles of John the Baptist and Pilate.

2. Judas has not yet been identified.

3. Cf. the function of the Gethsemane scene in Gibson's *The Passion of the Christ*. Both Gibson's and Ray's scenes are ineffectively brief. Both are also brief compared to the pattern of the standard Hollywood biopic. Not surprisingly, the Jesus figures of these biopics remain quite undeveloped.

4. However, a voice-over provides Jesus' answer to John, while John folds his hands and weeps just before his murder.

5. Two decades later, the German New Testament scholar Gerd Theissen wrote a first-century spy novel titled *The Shadow of the Galilean* (Philadelphia: Fortress Press,

1987), in which a Jew is blackmailed into spying for Pilate. The conceit introduces historical Jesus research to unsuspecting college students.

6. In part 1 of the film, Ray juxtaposes Barabbas's raid on the arriving Romans with Jesus' spectacular sermon. In part 2, he contrasts the slaughter in the Temple with Jesus' crucifixion. Ray clearly intends the sermon to be spectacular, using over 7,000 extras in the scene. But there is little drama in Jesus' presentation, and his message of peace fails to excite the crowd's (or viewing audience's) imagination.

7. Ray's film is one of the very few that does not show Jesus cleansing the Temple, which would perhaps be a bit too violent for Ray's "man of peace."

8. Lucius's defense may be Ray's attempt to link a pacifist icon (Jesus) with the U.S. military empire that is his audience. If so, it works by rendering Jesus politically irrelevant; a religious teacher with a message about a personal or possibly family ethic. One might wonder, however, if Lucius (and Ray) or Pilate is right about the political significance of Jesus' teaching.

9. Ray's ambitious, cold-blooded Pilate is one of the vilest in film. He differs markedly from the Gospels' weak, evasive Pilate.

10. Violence—John's beheading, Jesus' scourging, and the nailing to the cross—occurs offscreen, in keeping with the Hays Code. Contrast this approach with Gibson's concentration on violence in *The Passion of the Christ*.

11. Since Lucius does not reappear in the film after the crucifixion, it is difficult to know what he believes. *The Robe* (1953) offers a clearer story of the conversion of the centurion at the cross. The conversion of Romans to Christianity is a standard pattern in the biblical epics. Such epics feature the birth of Christian (read U.S.) Empire.

12. A DVD extra titled "The Camera's Window to the World" emphasizes the complex planning that went into the scene, which made use of over 7,000 extras.

13. Reportedly, Ray did not want the dominating voice-overs, and they were added after he lost direct control of the film.

14. In the finale the knife fight takes place at the planetarium. There, the kids listen to a lecture on humanity's dismal fate in a dying solar system.

15. Scorsese's Jesus in *The Last Temptation of Christ* is more like Ray's alienated protagonists.

## Chapter 7

1. He visited Israel and considering shooting on location. However, he rejected the idea, disappointed in the appearance of the country.

2. This is the first visibly pregnant Mary shown in film (cf. for example, Ray's fleeting view of the pregnant Mary in *King of Kings*).

3. Matthew 2:19 merely states that Herod died. The scene of Herod's death in the film lasts 1 ¼ minutes.

4. By choosing to film one particular Gospel, Pasolini has already removed Matthew from the canon, since the canon includes four. But he also departs from Matthew as text by interpreting that text with visuals and music. Pasolini uses an original percussive "Gloria" by the Argentinean Luis Bacalov for the peasant scenes, black spirituals for suffering scenes, and classical music for ominous scenes and scenes featuring Jesus' antagonists.

5. Jesus' opening words in Pasolini's film are by far the most challenging ever shown in the Jesus-film tradition.

6. Pasolini often films the healings with three shots: (1) the problem, (2) a shot of Jesus, (3) the problem fixed. The miracles are, thus, on-screen, yet offscreen. The walking on the water and the stone removed from Jesus' tomb are more spectacular miracles.

7. Pasolini places this confrontational section of his film after the missionary discourse (Matt. 10) and immediately before Peter's confession at Caesarea Philippi (Matt. 16); however, in doing this, he omits the parable discourse (Matt. 13).

8. Pasolini omits the apocalyptic discourse (Matt. 24–25).

9. Pasolini departs from Matthew's Gospel to follow John's Gospel.

10. No other Jesus film places more responsibility on the Jewish leaders for Jesus' death than does Pasolini's film. However, the bizarre, medieval *Christian* headgear of the Jewish leaders (see below) mitigates charges of anti-Semitism for attuned viewers.

11. Pasolini cast his own mother as the elderly Mary, mother of Jesus.

12. The visuals and order emphasize Jesus' liberating message for the audience.

13. See below, "Cultural Location."

14. "'*UDISTE CHE FU DETTO.* . . , *MA IO DICO CHE* . . .' Pasolini as Interpreter of the Gospel of Matthew" (Dissertation, Graduate Theological Union, 2004), 55–73.

15. Reportedly, Pasolini chose Matthew for its "national-political" mythical quality, over Mark's crudeness, Luke's bourgeois nature, and John's mysticism. His faithfulness to Matthew's Gospel has something to do with the fact that Pasolini was himself a poet. He also felt that Matthew's "rough" style nicely illustrated Jesus' violence.

16. Pasolini decided to make the film after being "trapped" in a hotel room in Assisi by the pope's motorcade. With nothing to do, he read the Gospel and was enthralled by Jesus' potential for violent rebellion.

17. Pasolini's films subsequent to *The Gospel According to St. Matthew* moved away from the documentary style toward a stylized treatment of the bourgeoisie (in *Teorema*) and to explorations of dark, erotic, violent mythologies. He claimed that he was trying to portray the diseased bourgeoisie and to create art that bourgeois society could not easily consume. *Teorema* (1968) has a mystical or spiritual tone. Pasolini depicts a mysterious stranger, who visits and undoes a bourgeois family, as divine love. That stranger resembles the stranger-Christ of John. The combination of religion and sex in this film—the stranger has sex with every member of the family— did disturb many.

## Chapter 8

1. John the Baptist later will quote Isa. 60:1, "Arise, shine, for your light has come. . . .'"

2. Thus, Stevens has both imagined Jesus as light for a dark world and also used the church as a vehicle for the modern audience to enter—or at least to view—the Jesus story.

3. The Dark Hermit is Stevens's invention. He represents the Satan of the Gospels and appears sporadically throughout the film to agitate for evil. This Satan figure has more screen time than any of his precursors in film. However, some think that the Dark Hermit is simply the dark voice within everyone and not a supernatural evil being.

4. This teaching scene is taken largely from the Sermon on the Mount. The setting is clearly symbolic, for as Jesus gets ready to talk to his new followers about worldly anxieties, a band of Roman soldiers literally marches above them. The traditional Sermon on the Mount will be spoken later in Galilee. Stevens also has Jesus recite the Lord's Prayer twice, once in Judea and once in Galilee, and there are two triumphal processions—one in Galilee and one in Judea.

5. Perhaps Jesus' message is pointed at the film's producer, who was quite concerned that the film cost over twenty million dollars.

6. Lazarus is an important character for Stevens. That Jesus does not reject this "friend" (Lazarus is never called a "disciple") helps reconcile Jesus' social ethic with Stevens's American audience. Lazarus provides a way into the film for materialistic Americans, for he demonstrates that what matters is one's attitude towards wealth rather than one's actual wealth.

7. Contrast this with Jesus who later forgives Mary Magdalene, a woman caught in the act of adultery.

8. Stevens greatly expands the character of John the Baptist over his precursors. Only Ray's John the Baptist has similar importance.

9. The oil contrasts with the Gospels' "ointment of pure nard" (Mark 14:3; John 12:3).

10. Significantly, Stevens's Judas is not part of this crowd.

11. In a moment of cinematic humor, Peter and "Little James" get into a tiff over Little James's response to Peter's guarded question "Who is it?"

12. Judas's motive for betrayal is ambiguous. Is he motivated by the Dark Hermit? Is he trying to protect Jesus? Is he a disenchanted insurgent? In plot terms, Judas's betrayal is absolutely necessary for Stevens's film. Stevens needs the betrayal to bring the authorities' story and the Jesus story together because the political and religious authorities have been unable to arrest Jesus for some time. However, Stevens does not explore Judas's possible motives as do DeMille and Ray.

13. Stevens offers one of the most developed Jewish trials in film up to this time.

14. In fact, these are Jesus' last words to Pilate.

15. Stevens uses a voice-over to quote part of the Apostles' Creed at this point.

16. Stevens often places Jesus in gates or doorways. It is as if Jesus is always the Johannine stranger arriving or leaving: the "door" to the Father (John 10:7). Most of the crucifixion scene focuses on the three crosses on the hill or offers close-ups of Jesus' anguished followers. Stevens brings the camera closer for the nails, although the nailing is offscreen, and offers close-ups of Jesus during the "I thirst" and "Into thy hands" sayings.

17. "Master, are men like circles in the water? Do they just float away and are lost?"

18. Does Stevens intend these words as a hopeful message to Americans in the midst of the Cold War and an escalating war in Vietnam?

19. He recites the Shema before Pilate and fingers his tzitzit in prayer in the Capernaum synagogue.

20. When Jesus' opponents in Nazareth accuse him of blasphemy, he responds to them by saying, "You have ears but do not hear." Is Stevens implying that Jesus' "God language" is metaphorical and not to be taken literally?

21. Mary's voice is only heard two times: (1) in a voice-over echoing the angel Gabriel's annunciation (Luke 1:32–33); and (2) at the appearance of the magi when she asks, "Who are you?" and tells them that her child's name will be Jesus.

22. More than any previous director, Stevens foregrounds competing interpretations of Scripture—particularly in the discussion in Herod's court about the birth of a messiah and in the religious leaders' discussion about the resurrection. Does this reflect the growing pluralism of American culture in Stevens's day? It certainly anticipates later academic discussions about ideology, for the interpretations clearly reflect the perspective and interests of the speakers. Stevens also abandons the scriptural patterns of previous filmmakers in another sense. The silent films connected Gospel scenes with Scripture intertitles. Ray connected scenes with an omniscient narrator. Stevens often moves from one scene to another with a slow dissolve that allows a character from the last or upcoming scene to speak as a voice-over for the visuals. For example, at the Roman trial the Dark Hermit (who is shown on-screen), reads John 3:16 as a voice-over.

23. This is a particularly Johannine motif that first appears in John 2:4 and culminates at the crucifixion (John 13:1; 19:27).

24. John 1:29. The latter is both Scorsese's and Gibson's emphasis.

25. Given at Rice University, September 12, 1962. Like Stevens's Jesus, Kennedy quotes the Hebrew prophets in both his nomination speech and his inauguration speech.

26. Ironically, the primary speakers in the film (John the Baptist and Jesus) reject religious ritual in favor of attitudes of the heart, repeatedly citing Hos. 6:6.

### Chapter 9

1. A more recent version of the musical was produced for PBS television in 2000 and released on DVD the same year by MCA Home Video. Directed by Gale Edwards and Nick Morris, it starred Rik Mayall, Jerome Pradon, and Glenn Carter (112 minutes; English, with English and French subtitles).

2. In contrast to the musical genre, everything in the film is sung. For the soundtrack listing, see IMDb.com. Tim Rice was the lyricist; Andrew Lloyd Webber was the composer.

3. Jewison frequently cuts from a crowd scene to a lone character in the wilderness singing a solo. This device heightens the audience's sense that it knows that character's true self/feelings.

4. A rumor, denied by the cast, claims the film was tentatively titled *The Gospel According to Judas.*

5. The Romans march above the cavern while Jesus and his disciples sing. Is this the director's way of implying that Jesus is an "underground" revolutionary? Interestingly, during the last part of his trial before Pilate, Jesus is again underground in a dungeon-like cavern.

6. Films have a tendency to offer audiences an effeminate Jesus, drawn from comfortable Sunday-school images. Jewison's Jesus—with his shrill voice and victim-like demeanor—is chief among these.

7. Judas remains somewhat of an isolated figure throughout the film. He repeatedly says that he just wants to understand what it is that motivates Jesus.

8. The Palestinian shepherd was not part of the script. He accidentally walked across the scene as the camera was rolling. However, Jewison liked the effect and its symbolism and kept the shot.

9. The later films of Jones and Arcand also deal with the disjunction between reality and interpretation.

10. Note the numerous times he goes off into the desert by himself to reflect on who Jesus is and what his relationship to him is. Judas is played by the African American actor Carl Anderson, and some critics viewed this as a racist choice when the film first appeared (i.e., black skin as a sign of God's curse). However, no one seems to have objected to the racially mixed Yvonne Elliman (she is half Japanese) playing the role of Jesus' seductress. Is she then the stereotypical "Oriental Dragon Lady"?

11. The black, vulture-like appearance of the Jewish priests also reinscribes the Christian stereotype of Jewish villainy. Jewison's choice of the priests' headgear seems to be modeled on that of Pasolini's priests in *The Gospel According to St. Matthew.*

## Chapter 10

1. "Godspell" is a play on the Old English word *godspel,* from which we get the modern word *Gospel: Gōd* = good, *spel* = tidings. Here, *gōd* becomes "God," while "spell" takes on a magical connotation, as in "casting a spell." The soundtrack listing is available at IMDb.com.

2. The only "miracle" in the film is when a blonde-haired girl plants a little sumac in a pot in the junkyard (DVD chap. 5). Unbeknownst to her, "John the Baptist" comes along and puts a much-larger sumac shrub in the pot, tossing away the one she planted. When she comes back, she is amazed at the miraculous growth. The sequence evokes the parable of the Mustard Seed (Matt. 13:31–32) and pokes fun at directors from the silent-film era with their film cuts that "produced" Jesus' miracles for awed audiences.

3. The opening shot of New York City with the not-yet-completed Twin Towers in the background is a jarring juxtaposition for our post-9/11 world, especially in the context of the God voice-over. As John the Baptist begins to hum "Prepare the Way of the Lord," the Twin Towers come into view again, and the audience hears the loud engine roar of a jet plane overhead. Then, suddenly, the city streets teem with people.

4. The fountain gets its name from a healing story in the Gospel of John (John 5:2, KJV). Interestingly, at the conclusion of Tony Kushner's 1993 award-winning play *Angels in America,* the central character, Prior, who suffers from AIDS, is seated at the same fountain.

5. The troupe's creative reworking of junkyard material seems to echo the "new wineskins" saying of Jesus (Matt. 9:15–17). But is the director saying that Jesus' teachings do not belong to the modern city since the troupe leaves the crowded streets to act out his teachings? Does this change of scene represent a religious retreat, or is it a condemnation of modernity?

6. *Godspell* is the first Jesus movie to treat Jesus and his teaching comically. The contrast between Pasolini's angry Matthean Jesus and Greene's whimsical Matthean Jesus could not be greater. Presumably, Greene's comedy is the (sacred) carnival that will remake society (see Mikhail Bakhtin, *Rabelais and His World*, trans. Hélène Iswolsky [Bloomington: Indiana University Press, 1984]). Unlike its precursors, *Godspell* treats the teaching of Jesus as a community's performance, not a master's soliloquy. For example, in one effective sequence the disciples begin the Beatitudes and Jesus completes each line.

7. The teaching of Jesus dominates this Jesus film as no other. *Godspell* visualizes these teachings by treating them as performance scripts.

8. This is the film's most explicit tribute to the silent-film era. But the entire film can be viewed as a return to the style of early-twentieth-century Jesus films.

9. Do these juxtapositions imply that the United States has now taken on the role of "messiah" for the world?

10. The choice of a robot as Jesus' primary adversary is unusual, and it reminds one of the tanks chasing Judas across the desert in *Jesus Christ Superstar*. Does the robot-as-opponent reflect a critique of modern, industrial society? Or does it perhaps reflect a 1960s rejection of "the System"?

11. At this point the song "By My Side" evokes the discipleship language of Matt. 16:24–26; 24:9–13. But in Greene's film the cross of Jesus is replaced by "a pebble in my shoe" called "Dare."

12. There is a delightful ambiguity in these words. Does the disciples' exclamation mean that God is dead, or is their "Oh God!" simply an expletive like "Oh shit"?

13. Is this an existential, Bultmannian ending to the story? Has Jesus been "raised up" into his disciples' songs (their faith and teaching)? Or is the ending simply a rhetorical move to focus on the disciples' responsibilities to tend God's garden?

14. The film *Parable* is perhaps consciously evoked in the film's opening scene, where John the Baptist calls his and Jesus' future disciples. One girl in particular stares at a toy-store window display depicting a circus ringmaster surrounded by animals, when suddenly John the Baptist replaces the ringmaster and winks at her.

15. In fact, one might see the movie as a followers' film rather than a Jesus film. If so, the followers attempt to discover the meaning of Jesus' teaching as they perform it. Stephen Schwartz, lyricist, claimed that the musical was about the formation of community.

16. Some scenes, like the face washing at the Last Supper, seem to allude to the Gospel of John. However, in John's Gospel Jesus washes his disciples' feet, not their faces (John 13:1–11).

## Chapter 11

1. Most Jesus films depict Judaism as either messianic or legalistic and certainly as part of the opposition to Jesus. Despite the care with which Zeffirelli dramatizes first-century Judaism, his film ultimately exacerbates the problem of anti-Semitism, because for him the church clearly supersedes Judaism.

2. Anna is named as the mother of Jesus in the second-century apocryphal *Protevangelium of James*.

3. Like Ray and Stevens, Zeffirelli cuts back and forth between Jesus and his opponents. In the first half of the film he uses conversations in Herod's court to explain Jewish customs.

4. Joseph and Anna see this as a fulfillment of messianic prophecy, as Mary is about ready to give birth.

5. Zeffirelli's film is the first to "show" the birth of the Christ child on-screen. However, Mary's groans and gasps, coupled with Zeffirelli's camera shots, seem more evocative of sexual orgasm than childbearing. Are Jesus' gasps and groans on the Via Dolorosa intended, like those of Mary, to symbolize pain—or perhaps the spiritual ecstasy of being "born again"?

6. The two raised fingers on Jesus' right hand represent his dual nature—fully human and fully divine. So is Zeffirelli's Jesus a Jew or the first Christian? Later on in the film, when Jesus talks with Joseph of Arimathea about Torah, Joseph asks Jesus, "Are you willing to accept *our* laws?" Tellingly, Jesus does not respond, "They're my laws too." At the film's midpoint, Zeffirelli includes Jesus' statement to Peter "Upon this rock I will build what I must call my church"; later on, in Jerusalem, when the woman caught in adultery is brought to him, Jesus kneels down and draws the Christian fish symbol in the dust. Finally, toward the end of the film, when Pilate says to the Sanhedrin representatives, "I'll talk to him—*your* Jesus," they reply, "Not our Jesus." Pilate then shouts back, "If not yours, whose? Whose?" Whose indeed.

7. Perhaps an allusion to John 1:51, the scene shows Jesus' spiritual proclivities. Not coincidentally, as Jesus looks down from the heights, he sees a shepherd pass by, herding sheep.

8. Zeffirelli does not make much of the imagery of Jesus as God's sacrificial lamb (cf. Scorsese's *The Last Temptation of Christ*); however, this scene and others are clearly intended to be symbolic, because Zeffirelli shows other Jewish pilgrims carrying lambs on their shoulders when Jesus enters Jerusalem at the end of his life.

9. Perhaps Zeffirelli's Jesus is too iconic a figure to face such difficulties as the wilderness temptations.

10. Zeffirelli renders Jesus' miracles more dramatically than his precursors in film tradition. Instead of cutting to Jesus in the midst of the healings, as Pasolini often does, Zeffirelli lingers long over the miraculous transformations of those being cured.

11. Zeffirelli cuts away from Jesus and the apostles to show the fate of John the Baptist and the resulting Zealot activities. The former ominously suggests Jesus' fate. The latter provide a foil for Jesus' mission.

12. Significantly, Zeffirelli adds the words "in Galilee" to Mark 8:27.

13. The final section of the film completes Peter's character development as Peter becomes the spokesperson replacing Jesus.

14. When first shown on television, the film was divided in two segments, with this scene ending the first half.

15. This scene (DVD 2, ch. 71) is purely a Zeffirelli invention.

16. Unlike Stevens, Zeffirelli does not show Jesus in Judea after his baptism, and thus he has not hinted at any long-term friendship between Lazarus, his sisters, and Jesus.

17. This replaces the question of paying taxes to the emperor, which most Jesus films portray but which is left out of Zeffirelli's film.

18. Like Judas, Nicodemus says, "My heart is troubled and my mind, confused." Jesus then quotes John 3:16–17.

19. Like Stevens, Zeffirelli takes great pains to show that part of the Sanhedrin supports Jesus.

20. The invented character Zerah allows Zeffirelli to rehabilitate Judas's image somewhat. So, too, does the sequence linking Peter's anguish over his denial with Judas's anguish over his betrayal. However, the hanging, with the money beneath his feet, returns Judas to his traditional status.

21. Zeffirelli does not include the hearing before Herod Antipas.

22. There is no Simon of Cyrene to take Jesus' cross, and Jesus never falls on the Via Dolorosa. However, Veronica does appear out of the crowd to wipe Jesus' face.

23. Of course, Zeffirelli's violence pales in comparison to Gibson's in *The Passion of the*

*Christ*. At the scourging, the audience never sees the whips strike Jesus' back. They know the violence from the size and exertions of the tormentors, from Jesus' writhing hands, and from the starting of horses at the noise. At the cross, Zeffirelli briefly shows the nails being hammered. Jesus' heavy breathing should perhaps be contrasted with Mary's heavy breathing in Zeffirelli's nativity scene.

24. For Zeffirelli, messianic Judaism has now been born again as (spiritual) Christianity.

25. Only Peter believes without seeing. As befits the rock of the church, he is shown leaning up against a large rock when he says he believes "because he [Jesus] said so," and because he "knows in his heart" that Jesus would not abandon them.

26. While Zerah has no supernatural qualities, he is more reminiscent of the Dark Hermit than Sorak.

27. Like Stevens, Zeffirelli populates his movie with a cast of stars, many of them taking the roles of apostles.

28. "George Stevens by Paul Cronin." This essay first appeared in the book *George Stevens: Interviews* (http://www.pbs.org/wnet/americanmasters/database/stevens_g.html).

29. Ibid.

30. Ibid.

31. Made famous in fundamentalist Christianity for its advertising symbols, which were thought to symbolize Satanic power.

32. Sykes and Krisch's *The Jesus Film*, used widely in evangelism, has perhaps now been seen by more people. And Gibson's film may now be supplanting Zeffirelli's for American audiences.

33. And television will tell you that you can have him with a soft drink and fries.

34. This allows for adding more details to the story, if not depth of character.

35. For example, surely one of the more bizarre juxtapositions of marketing the Jesus story occurred during the Good Friday, March 28, 1997, showing of the 1995 film *Mary of Nazareth* on the Lifetime channel. The first commercial break occurred just after Joseph discovered that Mary, his betrothed, was pregnant. Knowing that he is not the father, Joseph goes immediately outside the house to announce to Mary's worried parents that he has resolved to go through with the betrothal and marriage to their daughter. Cutting to the first commercial, the sponsors announced that the film was being brought to viewers by E.P.T., the early pregnancy test—"for those who just want to be sure. It is the name women trust."

36. *The Andy Griffith Show* was one of television's most popular shows from 1960 to 1968.

37. Traditionally, Melchior represents Asia, Caspar represents Europe, and Balthazar represents Africa.

38. It gets worse. The African king is the least knowledgeable of the three; the Asian king has the greatest religious knowledge; and the European king is the most rational and scientific of the three.

39. We will resist the urge to comment on the significance of President Jimmy Carter's initials and their incidental connection to the Jesus story.

## Chapter 12

1. John Krisch's last name is incorrectly spelled "Kirsch" on the DVD credits and "Krish" on the *Internet Movie Database* (IMDb) Web site. The IMDb Web site also incorrectly lists him as the first director.

2. Except for this opening quote, the film's narrator is Alexander Scourby, known for his 1966 award-winning reading of the King James Bible.

3. The Good News Bible is the film's translation of choice, with occasional borrowings from the KJV. "Absolute" does not appear in either version of Luke's preface.

4. This "lavish" setting, however, is not unknown in paintings of the annunciation.

5. Cf. Mary's home in Pasolini's *The Gospel According to St. Matthew* and in Zeffirelli's *Jesus of Nazareth*.

6. Not surprisingly, Jesus' woes against the Pharisees (Luke 11:37–54) and John's advice to soldiers and tax collectors (Luke 3:10–14) are missing from the film.

7. Perhaps Elizabeth's unborn child's recognition of the Messiah in Mary's womb is intended to be a pro-life critique of the 1973 U.S. Supreme Court decision granting women the right to abortion.

8. Curiously, the twelve-year-old Jesus is briefly shown talking with John the Baptist just before his parents arrive.

9. In some media software formats, the film's title will appear only if the subtitles option is turned on. Thus the film is "anonymous" or nearly so.

10. This text is missing from the oldest Greek manuscripts of Luke.

11. Jesus' quote is a confused rendering of Isa. 48:14–15, which speaks of God's coming judgment on Babylon and the Chaldeans. The text is quoted nowhere in the New Testament, and Sykes and Krisch's reason for adding it to their film is not at all clear.

12. Sykes and Krisch film Jesus' miracles much as Zeffirelli did. They leave the healed on-screen for viewers to see their physical transformations.

13. Sykes and Krisch present most of the "Sermon on the Plain" (6:20–41) but end it with Luke 11:27–28 and a question from a bystander: "Do you think he might be the Messiah?" Like Ray (*King of Kings*), they present the sermon with Jesus walking about, interacting with different groups in the crowd.

14. There is no evidence in Luke's Gospel that the anointing woman of Luke 7:36–50 is Mary Magdalene, but Sykes and Krisch present her as such.

15. First three crosses, then four, come into view. One is empty—and then two are shown to be empty. Is one Jesus' cross? Is the other empty one for Peter, who is walking beside Jesus (or for the audience)?

16. The location is not named, but the geography is easily recognizable to those who have seen photographs of the area near the Dead Sea.

17. Sykes and Krisch's triumphal entry is strangely muted. The crowds do not "recite the deeds of power that they had seen" (19:37) nor do they shout, "Blessed is the king who comes in the name of the Lord" (19:38).

18. Although the Lukan Jesus does, Sykes and Krisch's Jesus does not drive anyone out of the Temple (cf. Luke 19:45). Moreover, even though the Lukan Jesus does not overturn tables and release animals, their Jesus does. Although the film's disciples do not participate in the mayhem, they do seem to protect Jesus' exit from the Temple.

19. Sykes and Krisch seem to have constructed this scene from the history of Hollywood Jesus movies, since it does not appear in Luke and no one in their film has said anything about Jesus being a king. In fact, except for a few remarks from the narrator, Sykes and Krisch have carefully avoided connecting Jesus to anything that a modern viewer might construe as political.

20. The caveat is an attempt to diminish the anti-Semitism of Luke's Gospel (cf. 19:47–20:1). Griffith (*Intolerance*) and Saville (*The Gospel of John*) have similar introductory qualifications.

21. Sykes and Krisch do not include the esoteric questions about resurrection and David's son (Luke 20:27–47) nor the apocalyptic discourse (21:5–38), but they do include Jesus' dire predictions about Jerusalem's destruction (19:43–44; 23:28–31).

22. Here, Sykes and Krisch provide the cinematic precursor to Gibson's Satan figure.

23. Not everyone in the crowd wants Jesus dead. Some voices shout, "Set him free," and some shout, "He is the Messiah."

24. Luke's Pilate mentions scourging as a threat. But there is no evidence in Luke that Pilate carried it out. Sykes and Krisch also add a beating before Herod Antipas that is not mentioned in Luke 23:11.

25. In contrast to Luke's Pilate, who three times states Jesus is innocent, Sykes and Krisch's Pilate only says this twice. However, Sykes and Krisch's Pilate had earlier

expressed concern over the claim that Jesus was king, and he seemed to have been the one who called the meeting with the priests. So why has Pilate now so quickly reversed his opinion? Is it simply that the crowd clamors for crucifixion? If Sykes and Krisch's earlier description of a vicious Pilate was an attempt to diminish Luke's anti-Semitism, the contrast now simply heightens "the Gospel's" anti-Semitism.

26. In the history of Jesus films, Zeffirelli, Sykes and Krisch, and Scorsese are Gibson's closest precursors in filmed violence.

27. Luke does not specifically mention the disciples' presence, but see 23:49.

28. Only Young's Jesus smiles as often as Sykes and Krisch's. This portrayal thus dramatically differs from the cinematic norm.

29. The setting is purely a Sykes and Krisch invention but may be modeled on the night-time confessional scene in Zeffirelli's *Jesus of Nazareth*.

30. The question of whether Christians can "lose their salvation" is an important one for many evangelicals. The doctrine of "eternal security" argues that Christians cannot "lose" their salvation if their conversions have been sincere.

31. In the VHS version of the film, the title *The Public Life of Jesus* appears just before Jesus' baptism. But in some DVD software formats, the title *Jesus* will appear only if the subtitles option is turned on. The words "a documentary taken entirely from the Gospel of Luke" follow the word *Jesus*—but again, only in some DVD software formats.

32. The documentary claim of the film appears to be somewhat problematical even to the producers of the film, in that only the portion of the film that deals with Luke 3–24 is called a documentary. Presumably, the producers put this claim *after* the infancy narratives because Luke 1–2 is not quite as public as the ministry and passion of Jesus. But, if the infancy of Jesus is not public documentary, are the resurrection appearances? The Gospel itself does not make any such distinctions. Perhaps the filmmakers place the word "documentary" after the infancy narratives because they intend the film to be the cinematic equivalent of the transfiguration of Jesus. The filmmakers, that is, intend their film to make a personal encounter with the supernatural (cinematic) Jesus a "documentable" reality. Such an epiphany would certainly collapse distinctions between private and public, literal and true, text and reality, film (or film-maker) and the divine.

## Chapter 13

1. In the PFJ's endless debates about oppression and resistance, they offer an amusing riff on the "benefits" of Roman oppression: aqueducts; sanitation; safety; etc. Imprisoned shortly thereafter, Brian shares a cell with an old man who claims that crucifixion is the best thing the Romans have done for the Jews. The second scene nicely undercuts the first.

2. Modern film, like the modern novel and modernity itself, typically feeds the contemporary myth of individualism. *Life of Brian* is a rare cinematic critique of this myth.

3. Like Ray's *King of Kings* and Pasolini's *The Gospel According to St. Matthew*, Jones calls attention to the fact that Jesus' crucifixion was only one among many in the course of the Roman colonization of Judea. Such attention profanes the cross of Jesus. Only Pasolini's *La ricotta* does this as effectively as *Life of Brian*.

4. The crucified victims all claim to be Brian—perhaps a mocking allusion to the "I'm Spartacus" finale of *Spartacus* (1960).

5. This is a mockery of the rock 'n' roll Jesus films (*Jesus Christ Superstar* and *Godspell*).

6. The movie was rereleased in theaters for its twenty-fifth anniversary. The timing also coincided with the huge success of Gibson's epic *The Passion of the Christ*. Apparently, the troupe did not need to adjust the parody to take on a new victim.

7. In fact, much of the film is given to reconfiguring the cross: those who die on crosses are the lucky bastards. It can't be so bad, since it gets you out in the open air, etc. The song-and-dance finale is, of course, the ultimate transfiguring of the cross.

8. "Story alongside" might be a decent description of parable (literally "cast alongside"). In his book *The Dark Interval: Towards a Theology of Story* (Sonoma, CA: Polebridge Press, 1988), John Dominic Crossan defines parable as "the dark night of story," or something that raises questions about a culture's myth (myth being a story defending a culture's institutions and its common sense). According to the Gospels and historians, Jesus taught using parables. Is it possible, then, that the historical Jesus is closer to the Monty Python troupe than to the canon?

9. There are nineteen chapters listed on the DVD title menu and in the title sheet insert. However, there are twenty chapter stops on the DVD. The DVD chapter stop that is missing from the Commentary chapter menu and the title sheet insert is our no. 13. We have added this DVD Commentary chapter stop and given it the title "Hermit in a Hole." All Commentary chapters after no. 12 are one number greater than those on the title menu and title sheet insert.

10. See n. 9. The DVD chapter stop that is missing from Commentary 2 is our no. 14. We have added this Commentary chapter stop and given it the title "How Shall We Fuck Off?" All chapters after no. 14 are one number greater than those on the Commentary chapter menu and title sheet insert.

11. See nn. 9–10. The DVD chapter stop that is missing from the title menu and the title sheet insert is our no. 13. We have added this DVD chapter stop and given it the title "Give Us a Sign." All chapters after no. 12 are one number greater than those on the title menu and title sheet insert. If the viewer goes to chapter 13 on the DVD (using the title menu) and double-clicks on it, the viewer is not taken to "Hail Messiah." And when the viewer double-clicks on the DVD title menu chapter 14 ("A Very Naughty Boy"), the viewer is taken to the correct plot sequence, but it is marked as chapter stop 15.

## Chapter 14

1. Both Young (*Jesus*) and Gibson (*The Passion of the Christ*) mimic Scorsese's camera shot in the opening scenes of their films.

2. This camera shot differs from the Jesus-film tradition in several ways. First, the camera sees Jesus from above while the standard Jesus camera shot looks up at Jesus. Perhaps not coincidentally, the same camera shot was first used in Jewison's *Jesus Christ Superstar* as Jesus died on the cross; and the same camera shot reappears in *The Last Temptation of Christ* when Jesus dies on the cross (Gibson uses the same camera shot in his crucifixion scene [*The Passion of the Christ*]). Second, for the first time in Jesus-film tradition, the audience is unequivocally in the mind of Jesus. By this device— and by treating Jesus' visions as reality—Scorsese presents Jesus as a visionary. But these visions—this sense of God—are torture, not a blessing.

3. Olcott (*From the Manger to the Cross*) was the first to use the cross early in Jesus' life as foreshadowing. In that film, Jesus' boyhood shadow casts a cruciform pattern on the ground that his mother, Mary, notices. DeMille (*The King of Kings*) also uses the cross as foreshadowing. In his film, Jesus planes a piece of wood that he suddenly realizes is an unfinished cross. Not coincidentally, Judas stands by, watching him. Thereafter cross foreshadowing became one of the common tropes of Jesus films.

4. In an allusion to Jesus' future Via Dolorosa, both Mary, his mother, and Mary Magdalene appear as Jesus carries Lazarus's cross. Interestingly, neither woman is there during Jesus' own Via Dolorosa.

5. Scorsese lets the audience see an encounter between Jesus and a monk and only later lets the audience know that the monk was already dead when Jesus "met" him. Jesus' visionary reality has thus become the audience's visual reality.

6. Jesus' public ministry is relatively unimportant in Scorsese's film compared to Jesus' visions, temptations, and conflicts with the leaders in the Temple.

7. For the first time, Jesus replaces Judas as the director of events.

8. Scorsese often mutes external sound to highlight certain moments that the audience shares with Jesus: e.g., the baptism, the Temple cleansing, the Via Dolorosa, and the cross. One should also note that the crucifixion sequence parallels the opening crucifixion sequence. Now, however, Jesus carries the cross in submission to God's will, not to make God angry.

9. Apart from the fantasy sequence, no supernatural events attend the crucifixion except for a mighty wind that only Jesus and the audience hear.

10. While this Jesus dies entirely for himself, to accomplish his own spiritual triumph, presumably this death also validates the message of a rather slimy Saul (Paul) of Tarsus. We may also have here the glimmer of an idea, sometimes occurring in scholarship and in the popular media, that Paul is the true creator of Christianity.

11. Admittedly, even the earlier biblical epics (with the notable exception of DeMille's *The Ten Commandments*) understood religion primarily as a matter of family values or personal ethics that had little to do with social and political issues. See our discussion of drop-out religion and capitalism in Jones's *Life of Brian*.

12. The real humanity of this Jesus is the basis for critics' claims that Scorsese's film challenges Gnosticism.

13. This means that Scorsese has created Jesus according to the modern heroic conventions of novel and film, rather than the ancient conventions of epic and Gospel.

14. Compare our discussion of Ray's film's (*King of Kings*) failure as a Jesus biopic.

15. Such triangles remain important even in Scorsese's more recent *Gangs of New York* (2002).

## Chapter 15

1. Following Arcand's perception of the social location of Jesus' own disciples, Daniel's troupe comes from the bottom of the acting profession.

2. A woman shelving books asks Daniel if he is looking for Jesus. When he nods yes, she tells him that it is Jesus who will find him. The woman reappears later in the film with a "new age" companion (probably a Raelian), who asks the actors if they have been "contacted." As the film progresses and Daniel becomes more and more Jesus-like, the woman's words are eerily prophetic. So, too, are the words of René, who twice tells the group that it is bad luck to do a tragedy.

3. Although the term "Deep Throat" is not used in *Jesus of Montreal*, the fact that Daniel meets the theology professor in a parking garage appears to be an ironic allusion to Bob Woodward's secret source in the 1976 film *All The President's Men*.

4. Both the whipping and crucifixion scenes feature a naked Jesus. The crucified Jesus declares his thirst and his forsakenness. In the subway, Daniel also describes himself as forsaken by his father. Is this true of Daniel or has he delusionally *become* Jesus?

5. In fact, actors often provide voice-over narration in scenes where other players are acting. This device resembles the Scripture intertitles and voice-overs of older epic Jesus films.

6. The play within the movie format resembles Jewison's *Jesus Christ Superstar*, but Arcand gives more time to the actors' "real" lives than Jewison does.

7. Critics often describe Daniel as a Christ figure. Some critics distinguish between Jesus movies, which stage the Jesus story in a set or location replicating the first century, and Christ-figure movies, which tell a story about a character who adopts a role like Jesus or takes on characteristics of Jesus in another cultural setting, such as twentieth-century Montreal.

8. The reference is probably to the Magdalen Islands in the Gulf of St. Lawrence. The name of the restaurant *Chez Charon*, with emblematic ship, evokes Greek mythology, where Charon is the ferryman of the dead who carries souls across the river Acheron into Hades.

9. No providence directs this demythologized passion. Neither is there any obvious

reason—other than method acting or the story's inherent power—for Daniel to take on the role of Jesus in his "real" life.

10. Pascal was Daniel's "John the Baptist" forerunner at the beginning of the film. He has now betrayed authentic art (acting) by stooping to commercials. Accordingly, like Greene's John the Baptist in *Godspell*, he is both Baptist and Judas. Although he does not actually betray Daniel, he does betray himself.

11. The language recalls that of the Eucharist. The doctor also describes Daniel's body as a "Godsend."

12. Perhaps the move from the church to the subway indicates that the story of Jesus no longer belongs exclusively to the church. Or perhaps it is simply another instance where something originally religious becomes a commodity for sale.

13. Interestingly, when epic Hollywood Jesus films ceased to be financially successful, Jesus made a comeback in smaller-budgeted cinematic passion plays like *Jesus Christ Superstar* and *Godspell*.

14. The play includes some of Jesus' teaching, most of which is drawn from the Sermon on the Mount, especially those parts advocating a relaxed lifestyle with regard to finances.

15. Arcand brought back most of the cast of *The Decline of the American Empire* for his 2003 film titled *The Barbarian Invasions*, a film about the death by cancer of the protagonist, the member of the troupe who has led the most self-absorbed, narcissistic life. Despite the film's title and the protagonist's characterization, he achieves a reunion with his family and friends before his death. And while the film ends with his death, the tone is more hopeful than Arcand's earlier films *The Decline of the American Empire* and *Jesus of Montreal*.

## Chapter 16

1. Young invents this character, a figure comparable to Ray's Lucius in *King of Kings*.

2. Other filmmakers use voice-over narration in this capacity. Zeffirelli also uses palace discussions to explain customs.

3. Although Joseph's house does not appear to be a wealthy man's house, Mary is always dressed in the rich red-and-blue-dyed clothes of the elite, in keeping with her portraits in later Christian art. Moreover, when Jesus returns from the desert, he sleeps in a separate room, on a bed with sheets and a pillow.

4. Young handles Jesus' infancy and childhood through visual flashbacks that are characters' memories of the past. Interestingly, there is no explicit reference to the virginal conception, only to the angel's visits.

5. Young's Jesus somewhat resembles Scorsese's soul-searching, flesh-denying Jesus, but Young portrays Jesus with a lighter touch that most Americans would find more palatable.

6. John's recollection is told retrospectively. In the flashback (recalling the "forest of crosses" that the infant Jesus sees in Stevens's *The Greatest Story Ever Told*), Jesus seems to see the hanging victims—but he is also squinting, and Mary quickly shields him from the view. Does the sunlight blind him from the awful scene?

7. Significantly breaking with Jesus-film tradition, Young consistently calls this experience a "test" and not a temptation.

8. Cf. Philippians 2:6–8. This introduction to the testing scene is described as a "challenge," one that Satan believes he can win.

9. In an unfortunate, unintentional echo of the future *Matrix* (1999, 2003) film trilogy, Mary and Jesus' disciples call Jesus "The One" on a number of occasions.

10. As in Scorsese's *The Last Temptation of Christ*, Jesus also dances at the wedding, but Andrew, one of his new disciples, disapproves. This is one of only two instances in film of Jesus dancing, and it shows that Young's Jesus visibly enjoys life (cf. Griffith's Jesus in *Intolerance*).

11. Jesus' miracles are perhaps more important in this movie than in any other. They

induce belief in Jesus as "The One," the Messiah. However, Jesus does quote John 20:29 at the end of the film ("Blessed are those who have not seen"), and both Joseph (Jesus' other father) and John (the Beloved Disciple) believe without seeing. Thomas is the opposite; he sees much but does not quite believe.

12. Jesus tells Judas, "I am the way" (John 14:6) and that he will teach him to be free. He then tells Judas, "Come with me. Your fate is with me."

13. Caiaphas first calls Jesus "Joseph of Nazareth," and Jared, Caiaphas's assistant (a secret sympathizer with Jesus), has to correct him.

14. He begins to tell the parable of the Hidden Treasure (Matt. 13:44). Although Jesus has been called a "rabbi" on a number of earlier occasions, this first teaching scene occurs nearly halfway through the film.

15. Notably, Jesus does not touch the sacrificial animals. Those will be handled by the Zealots later in the film. Livio raises the question of paying taxes to Caesar, and after Jesus' "Give to God what is God's," Peter and Judas help him finish clearing the Temple.

16. Jesus' Sermon on the Plain (Mount) is extremely short. It privileges the Beatitudes, emphasizing that riches cannot buy life or a good heart, incorporating antiritual material like that found in Mark 7, and ending with the declaration that those who do God's will—and not Jesus' family—are blessed (cf. Sykes and Krisch's ending to the Lukan Sermon on the Plain in *The Jesus Film*).

17. The story of the Syro-Phoenician woman (called a "Canaanite" in this film and in Matt. 15:21–28) is found nowhere else in the Jesus-film tradition.

18. The contrast between the failed resurrection of Joseph and the successful resurrection of Lazarus indicates that Jesus has found his mission.

19. Like Ray's De Quincey Judas (*King of Kings*), Young's Judas tries to force Jesus to bring in a Jewish kingdom.

20. Seth, Young's invention, depends on precursors like Stevens's Sorak (*The Greatest Story Ever Told*) and Zeffirelli's Zerah (*Jesus of Nazareth*). Young makes little use of him, however, because he uses Livio much more often to manipulate actions.

21. Young's notion that Jesus dies to show God's love is relatively rare in film (even though many filmmakers quote John 3:16). Most directors prefer to emphasize the perversion of justice that leads to Jesus' death, to show his death as a sacrifice for sins, or to show his death as a conflict with Satan.

22. Young's Jesus prophesies Peter's "betrayal" rather than using the traditional term "denial," thus putting Judas and Peter on the same level.

23. Young's Pilate plays the entire trial scene as if it were a game for his and Livio's amusement. The motif of games and play is an important one throughout the film.

24. The crucifixion sequence is extremely short compared to the rest of the movie.

25. After Jesus says these words, Livio responds, "We do, in fact, know what we are doing."

26. There is no penitential thief, no spear thrust, and no centurion saying, "Truly this man was the Son of God."

27. For example, the May 2000 broadcast version of the movie managed to sandwich commercials about noodles in a cup, cosmetics, Gas-X, IAMS cat food, US West ("I've got the power!"), and Kentucky Fried Chicken, all between Jesus' baptism and his desert testings. Later on the movie segued, without irony, from Jesus' ascension and the disciples' final prayer to a commercial advertising a phone number where viewers could place orders for VHS tapes of the movie for $29.98. One thinks, with irony, of the parody ending of *Life of Brian*.

28. Young's Jesus character is almost the religious equivalent of the male characters in the 1990s television hit comedies *Seinfeld* and *Friends,* which focused on thirty-somethings who could not quite make commitments or decide who they were.

29. Tellingly, Young begins the test to "Throw yourself down from the Temple" with a ground-shaking explosion.

30. Compare also the different ways that Stevens (*The Greatest Story Ever Told*) and Young deal with the "forest of crosses" near the beginnings of their respective films.

31. The only religious film touting freedom as much as Young's *Jesus* is DeMille's *The Ten Commandments*. Of course, DeMille's film glorified the freedom made possible by American nationalism. That is, the freedom was a political, social entity. Young's freedom is more individual and subjective. One wonders, however, if DeMille's *The Ten Commandments*, which in the last decade or so has appeared more regularly on TV than Zeffirelli's *Jesus of Nazareth*, might not have influenced Young's freedom motif.

## Chapter 17

1. It is not clear at this point who has sent Asher, but from his headgear he apparently is a priest; and he is deeply concerned about keeping the priesthood in some semblance of control in Judea.
2. Curiously, the disciples hear "from *Jerusalem*" that Herod has killed John.
3. The director nicely contrasts three different approaches to power: Herod's, Jesus', and Caesar's.
4. The centurion does not really need to be educated in crowd control, having just put down a rebellion in Galilee, led by Barabbas, where 117 Galilean Jews were crucified.
5. The raising of Lazarus is depicted through animation and is retrospective.
6. This is the first of a number of animated cuts that take viewers into the mental and emotional states of Judas.
7. Jesus' cleansing of the Temple is juxtaposed to a flashback of him in the Temple at twelve years of age.
8. Jesus and his twelve disciples sit at the traditional long, rectangular table while the others sit and look on from a short distance away.
9. Jesus almost has to force Judas to leave, as Judas seems to be having second thoughts about his planned betrayal.
10. Jesus says this in response to his disciples' desire to fight back.
11. Jairus is the unnamed disciple of Luke 24:13–18.
12. The word "Pharisee" does not occur in the film, but Jesus does mention a "rich and powerful Sadducee" in the parable of the Good Samaritan.
13. *"Making of"* Documentary (DVD Extra).
14. Ibid.
15. Ibid.
16. A Special Edition DVD with commentary by the director and producer was released in March 2007, too late to be included in our analysis.

## Chapter 18

1. At the same time, the allusions to Gen. 1:1–3 are obvious: there is water; there is light; and birds circle in the morning sky.
2. Christopher Plummer has top billing in the credits. Of course, the credits are in order of appearance; nonetheless, Plummer's voice dominates the movie.
3. Translators are not sure where to end the quotation marks in these two monologues, and different translations put them in different places. There were no quotation marks in the ancient Greek text, so it is not clear in these places whether Jesus or John the Baptist is still speaking, or whether the narrator has taken over the speaking role. Today's English Version puts closing quotes at John 3:15 and John 3:30.
4. The narrator also occasionally speaks Jesus' and other characters' words (e.g., 11:3–7, 37).

5. The narrator's effect far surpasses the narration of Ray's *King of Kings* and even the Scripture intertitles of the silent films. Notably, the film never states that the narrator expresses the retrospective witness of the Beloved Disciple (cf. 21:24); moreover, the voice of the narrator is not that of the character the Beloved Disciple (cf. 1:38; 19:35).

6. On occasion, Saville renders the Johannine "Jews" as "the Jewish authorities" (e.g., 7:13, 15). Some scholars would agree with his interpretation. This device does more to minimize the potential anti-Semitism in the Gospel than do the rather ineffective caveat-intertitles that open the film.

7. The Beloved Disciple wears a distinctive, tight-fitting skullcap, but he is not actually identified as the Beloved Disciple until John 13:23. The screenwriter believes him to be John, the disciple and son of Zebedee, but this is not stated in the film itself ("Production Design: The Making of *The Gospel of John*—Screenwriter: John Goldsmith" [DVD Extra]). See n. 5.

8. This is an allusion to Mark 1:16. There is no hint in the Gospel of John that any of Jesus' disciples are fishermen, except at the end of the book (John 21:1–3). Visually this seaside scene recalls the opening sunrise in the film, where the sun rose out of the sea, and the closing scene in the film (21:1–23).

9. The religious leaders do contend with the Baptist and argue with Jesus' disturbance in the Temple, but they are questioning reactions rather than accusatory.

10. Mary Magdalene's clothing suggests the traditional image of her as a prostitute—something not present in the Gospel of John. The costume designer confirms this sexually scandalized view of Mary Magdalene ("Production Design: The Making of *The Gospel of John*— Costume Designer: Debra Hanson" [DVD Extra]).

11. These visuals rely either on the Jesus-film tradition or the other Gospels, because Judas is absent from John from 13:30 until 18:2.

12. The screenwriter, John Goldsmith, calls the farewell discourse a "summation" of Jesus' ministry, thus legitimizing his use of visual flashbacks ("Production Design, Screenwriter: John Goldsmith" [DVD Extra]). The first flashbacks are in color: the audience sees Jesus' self-baptism during the Baptist's speech in 1:32–33 and Nathaniel's religious vision during Jesus' speech in 1:48.

13. DVD Extra, "Production Design: Director."

14. DVD Extra, "Production Design: Costume Designer."

15. DVD Extra, "Production Design: The Making of *The Gospel of John*— Screenwriter: John Goldsmith." See n. 5.

16. DVD Extra, "Production Design: John Goldsmith."

17. DVD Extra, "Production: Director of Photography."

## Chapter 19

1. The camera shot is reminiscent of Scorcese's opening shot of Jesus in *The Last Temptation of Christ*. Throughout the film Gibson shows his awareness of the Jesus-film tradition by mimicking plot elements and camera shots from earlier films. He borrows most heavily from DeMille's *The King of Kings*, Stevens's *The Greatest Story Ever Told*, Jewison's *Jesus Christ Superstar*, and Scorsese's *The Last Temptation of Christ*.

2. Gibson deliberately pairs Satan and Caiaphas in subsequent scenes at the beginning and end of the film. While Satan appears in the crowd at various points and has an opening speech dissuading Jesus from his redemptive mission, Caiaphas is the prime villain. He is the one who thwarts Pilate's judicial efforts and who leads the mob to ask for crucifixion.

3. Gibson barely hints of Joseph of Arimathea's and Nicodemus's objections during the Sanhedrin trial. Unless viewers are familiar with Stevens's *The Greatest Story Ever Told* or Zeffirelli's *Jesus of Nazareth*, they would have no clue that Gibson's Sanhedrin was not unanimously supportive of Caiaphas's call for crucifixion.

4. Simon seems remarkably like John Bunyan's Pilgrim in *A Pilgrim's Progress*. He bears Jesus' cross and then goes "free," as a Roman soldier remarks at Calvary.

5. Gibson's original languages are Aramaic and Latin rather than Greek and Aramaic.

6. Gibson is quite fond of ground-level camera shots: Mary's ear pressed to the pavement, listening to Jesus who is in a dungeon below her; Jesus being dragged after his horrific beating; Mary and Mary Magdalene wiping up Jesus' blood after his beating; Mary Magdalene the adulteress, saved by Jesus; Mary running to rescue the child Jesus after he falls; and more.

7. Gibson is, of course, Australian, and the film was made in Italy. Nonetheless, we speak of the film's American cultural location here. Other discussions might relate the film to Gibson's reactionary Catholicism.

8. For example, compare this with Jesus' temptations fifteen years earlier in Scorsese's *The Last Temptation of Christ*. There the satanic voice (represented by the very human voices of Mary Magdalene and Judas) asks, "Why are you trying to save the world? Aren't your own sins enough for you? What *arrogance* to think you can save the world! The world doesn't have to be saved" (56:26). The satanic voice then adds that Jesus can have "Any *country* [he] want[s]" (58:40).

9. In fact, we have located Gibson's film in the genre of religious horror. In the nonepic era of religious film, horror was a fruitful genre for religious themes and desires.

10. If this comparison is apt, Gibson's film is irredeemably anti-Semitic.

11. Gibson, who plays Wallace, provides the final voice-over summary of this "miracle." Thus he lives on beyond his death. Not coincidentally, Gibson plays a different role in *The Passion of the Christ*. There, it is Gibson's own hand that helps nail Jesus to his cross.

12. A two-DVD, *Definitive Edition* of *The Passion of the Christ* was released in March 2007, too late to be summarized in our book. But it includes a commentary by Mel Gibson, and one by the producer, Stephen McEveety, as well a thirteen-minute "Below the Line Panel Discussion" (where the special effects team descibes the cross as "its own character, just as Christ is"). Numerous other special features make this new edition a worthwhile addition to the classroom.

## Chapter 20

1. The suggested film clips are by no means exhaustive. For other occurrences of the various Gospel episodes described here, see "A Gospels Harmony," below.

2. Cf. the self-baptism of the Apostle E.F. in the film *The Apostle* (1997).

3. A shocking contrast is Stevens's depiction of John the Baptist's forcibly baptizing Herod's men who come out to arrest him.

4. Although Gibson is not American, his film is completely a part of the Hollywood Jesus-film tradition.

5. See Walsh, *Reading the Gospels in the Dark*, 21–43, 173–85.